GARDENING
WITH
TORTOISES

Dedicated to tortoises and parrots
around the world

GARDENING
WITH
TORTOISES

NATURE, NATURISM AND
NATURALISM IN EUROPE

P. D. Aspy

Bluemoose

Copyright © P.D. Aspy 2007

First published in 2007 by
Bluemoose Books Ltd
25 Sackville Street
Hebden Bridge
West Yorkshire
HX7 7DJ

www.bluemoosebooks.com

British Library Cataloguing-in-Publication data
A catalogue record for this book is available from the-British-Library

ISBN 978-0-9553367-2-0

Printed and bound in the UK by Cromwell Press, Trowbridge

Foreword

'I'd never have dreamed of taking tortoises and parrots on holiday' ... a not uncommon remark when swapping holiday experiences. Hearing this on numerous occasions made me stop and think – maybe it *was* a bit odd but I never thought it *that* peculiar a thing to do. It seemed logical – lots of animals – no one to animal-sit – want a holiday – buy house somewhere warm and take animals with you – simple! I suppose it seemed a little odd that we took our plants with us too. As it was, I began to think that not everyone looked upon our travelling menagerie as being the norm when we were returning from Floriers in 1993. Andy had come out to us in early summer for a couple of weeks and rather than return by train, she elected to travel back with us (an excellent plan as she entertained the 2 parrots though complained bitterly later that one of them had eaten her jacket!).

It just so happened that we were travelling in late June – not a good choice as all the tortoises were very active. Having several different species and sexes, dividing everyone up in order to avoid fights and displays of a Hugh Grant nature was a bit difficult and the 24-hour journey necessitated several roadside breaks. As the day wore on, the breaks became more frequent and lasted longer until we finally decided to stop and let everyone (except the parrots) out for a bit of exercise. We had chosen what, at first glance, appeared to be a secluded, empty lay-by and the road was fairly quiet. Great, we thought and began to decant the tortoises so that we could clean out their travel boxes and let them have a bit of a wander. Bearing in mind that we had 22 tortoises, we began with the smallest and Andy herded them to a little patch of greenery and stood guard. We'd just got that sorted and a car turned in. Despite the lay-by being several hundred yards long, the driver pulled up within feet of us (must be the sheep syndrome – everyone bunches together no matter the amount of free space) and proceeded to pour himself a cup of coffee from a flask. At this point, he was still sitting in his car and idly glanced over at Andy and her little retinue without much interest.

As Ed and I began to unload the medium sized tortoises the guy in the car climbed out to stretch his legs. Still holding his cup of coffee, he began to take little sideways glances at us which became more obvious the more tortoises we unloaded from the car. Apart from an initial 'Bon soir' we had no further conversation with him – we were all hot and fraught and not in the mood for small talk. I could see his eyes swivelling from the baby tortoises to the medium tortoises (now delighted to be out and arguing amongst themselves) and noticed, with some satisfaction, a rather 'trapped with mad people' expression dawning. He had walked someway along the lay-by but came up against Andy and the baby tortoises and had immediately turned back only to be faced with me shepherding the medium tortoises and at that point, came to a bit of a full stop. By this time, Ed was carefully unloading the Bigs – the Indian Star, at 5 kilos but shy and not into distressing people, just sat and looked around but the African Spurred, at 14 or 15 kilos, was another matter entirely. Having placed her on the ground, she made an immediate beeline towards this poor French guy – just lumbered up to him doing her usual begging for food act. Looking back, it was quite funny actually – I'm not sure which of them moved the fastest – whether it was Sudie trying to get into this guy's car in case he had food in there or was it the guy himself flinging his coffee into the air and climbing into his car and gunning the engine! Whichever, he certainly left a bit of rubber on the road. Maybe he thought we would unload something even more awful than Sudie or maybe he'd just had enough. I can just imagine the conversation he had with his wife/in the bar or whatever. 'Well, on my way back from wherever and pulled in to have a coffee break. Thought it would be ok as there was only one other car parked there. Too late I realised the car had GB plates but anyway, what the hell. They are Europeans now – they'll be normal. You wont *believe* what happened – God knows what they would have produced next. *And* I heard someone say 'Merde' but it wasn't any of the 3 people I saw – do you think they could have had a parrot in the car too? No, I agree, even for English that would be overdoing it!' On the other hand, this guy probably just wrote his experience off as a bad dream – after all, it's not *really* likely to happen is it?

Who's Who

Pippa	Letter-writer, gardener, parrot-keeper, tortoise-breeder, birdwatcher
Ed	Husband, naturist by inclination, engineer by profession
Andrea	Sister, also known as Andy, Pandy and Pand
Morgan	African Grey parrot, easily bored
Curry	Indian Star tortoise
Sudie	African Spurred tortoise, with a passion for passionflowers

Cornwall, 1988

Hi Pand,

Well, here we are at last – Cornwall.

Our first day here has certain overtones – presage of things to come? The guy next door came round in the evening for change to use in his electric meter. Ed of course was dressed as normal – nothing on – but as I was upstairs, he answered the door. I didn't actually see his reaction and you know Ed – well, the guy came to the door, asked for change, I found him some, introduced myself, no problem! Rural Cornwall? We'll see!

Actually, I haven't got much room to talk – met our other neighbour yesterday – Farmer Broad – he and his family farm/own most of the land round us. In fact, Farmer Broad and his wife have the new-built cottage directly opposite but are supposedly retired (apart from a few pedigree sheep – more later) – eldest son Francis now runs the farm (mostly dairy) and youngest son runs a garden centre and fishing lake/camping ground. Anyway, Farmer Broad turned up after we had been here a couple of days and, of course, I wasn't exactly in meet-the-neighbours mode. To be honest, I was running around sweating like a silly beggar because 3 of the tortoises were due to lay eggs and being landed in the midst of what is, virtually, a field, they had nowhere suitable to dig a nest. So, usual thing, I traipsed around after them and every time they sniffed the ground and turned around a couple of times, I plied the trowel and started a hole. You know how fussy they are – Pip, it doesn't face the right way; Pip, there's a big stone in the way; Pip, the soil doesn't feel right; Pip, see that brick wall over there? Why don't you go and smack your head against it?

I'd been farting around like this since about 11 am and so when our new neighbours arrived to welcome us, what they actually saw was a pretty cool nude person building a parrot aviary and a pretty uncool dressed person brandishing a muddy trowel and going 'Oh for Christ's sake – give us a break – do you want this hole or not?' Typical isn't it? Anyway, we had a cup of tea (managed to find enough cups to appear civilised) and a chat and seems like they were interested in the tortoises and parrots and didn't particularly appear to think we were totally mad! Well, I think the breeding aspect probably did the trick – cows, sheep, tortoises – much the same really!!

Much of the garden stuff has survived the move but you should see it here – violets and primroses absolutely everywhere – it really is so pretty and being surrounded by woods and fields, the views are brilliant. The river runs just down the bottom of the road and it's an easy walk into Launceston without going on the road.

Anyway, not long til you see it for yourself.

Cornwall, 1988

Hi Pand,

Great to see you the other week – hope you've recovered from the short cut into Launceston! We must have turned left at the wrong bit I think – there's no way we should have been in that farm yard (tho the farmer was pretty laid back wasn't he? Well, I assume he was pretty laid back – I couldn't actually understand a bloody word and you weren't much help – sniggering into your collar! Anyway, it was a nice walk and at least you saw something of the countryside. And there are all those sloes we can pick for your sloe gin – got to be easier than collecting tons of rosehips and making rosehip syrup or whatever it was we did. Hard to believe that we once spent a holiday collecting rosehips and sieving them and stuff – mind you, that quick hike over half of Devon wasn't exactly holiday material was it? Looking back I can't actually believe we did that – tho was that the summer we lost the M4 (or was it the M5) at Harpenden or somewhere? I must admit I never heard of anyone else, ever, having to go thru gated roads to get on to a (fairly major) motorway? Odd really – that part of England is pretty well built up – you'd think a motorway was fairly obvious. In retrospect, I think our biggest problem was totally ignoring the directions people gave us – God only knows why we thought we knew better but it seemed almost inevitable – Excuse me – can you tell us how to get to Blah Blah? And they'd say – yes – turn right at Blah and carry on for miles and then turn left at Blah blah and before you know it, you'll be in the right Blah and we'd go – Yep, right, ok, foot down, what the hell do they know, (they're only locals after all!), check the map, we're on one of these white roads and if we go this way, that's a short cut which will lead us into ... erm ...! We really need to get this navigation stuff sorted out before you come down again – I can't be doing with going down that god-awful lane in Dartmouth again – even with the wing mirrors bent in, we were scraping the sides of those houses. I mean, people came out just to look at us. We have to have some proper method next time – smaller car, use the bus, don't go out – whatever, we need to deal with this problem!

Hey listen, we have discovered the remnants of an old cockpit in the woods beyond the garden. I went out for a Sunday walk with Farmer Broad and his wife the other day – we did a bit of a circuit and returned along the field at the back of our garden. You remember that bit of a dell directly behind us? Well, turns out that this was the local cockpit in times gone by. Mr. B traced out the actual pit for me – quite exciting really – once it was pointed out, it was quite obvious even 150 years on. Though the trees had taken over, you could see the outline of the pit itself and it didn't take a lot of imagination to visualise the scene. Scores of scruffy bearded men ringing the pit and yelling madly for their particular rooster. A 19th C usherette shimmying around trying to sell slices of roast Hedgehog and the punters yelling 'Out the way, silly cow' ... Oh My God, I just lost the housekeeping'. Something similar anyway – just a little frisson of a different life! I wonder if I went back there and poked around a bit – whether I would find something of interest? Let's face it, some of these archaeology programmes – they prod about to a depth of 6 inches and turn up all sorts of relics. You and I would completely discount this stuff – yeah, yeah, bit of stone – but it's all grist to the mill. Well, it's all grist. Actually, I've no idea exactly what 'grist' means. Do you? I'll look it up and let you know.

Bye for now

Cornwall, 1989

Hi Pand,

How's it going? Am still trying to get over the wild weekend we had dredging your car out of the driveway. That was BAD and did nothing for my reputation. Well, I suppose my reputation is fairly well shot anyway – what's a half buried car? Still, it was lucky Francis was at home and was willing to get the tractor out – otherwise you'd still be here and I'd be having to phone the V and A and tell them you had been struck down with some unidentified disease whilst holidaying in the country. That old water course is a bit of a bugger tho being so close to the drive. Still, at least you know about it now. Best try and avoid it next time!

Did I tell you that Morgan is driving Francis absolutely mad? You know the cows come down past the house every day to go into the field? And you know how narrow the road is? These cows come within inches of Morgan's big window and Francis and his dog always shout 'Come on', 'Up now', and other meaningless phrases (well, Francis does anyway – I must admit I never heard the dog shouting but you know what I mean) and Morgan is beginning to learn the lingo. I don't really know that the cows take any more notice of Morgan than they do (seemingly) of Francis, but they have taken to stopping outside the window and peering in at Morgan. He is, of course, absolutely thrilled – to have such power over 30 or 40 cows has quite gone to his head – he gaily whistles and shouts at the cows and they all bunch up at the window and gaze at him as if he was some Guru or other. It's all very well but there is a hell of a lot of shit to clear up under the window at the end of the day (plus I think Francis is getting fed up too!).

It's not much better with the sheep – you know I said Farmer Broad does pedigree sheep as a hobby? Well, it's actually turning out to be a bit more of a hobby than he thought. He runs these sheep in the field at the back and he's training a couple of young sheepdogs at the moment. Bad move! As the weather warms up, Morgan spends more time in the back garden – within whistling distance of the sheep you might say! This is about Week 3 and the scenario is always the same – sheep come out complete with Farmer Broad and 2 sheep dogs. Into the field and prissy around a bit and then the whistle commands. Up til now, Morgan has watched but kept his beak zipped. However, the first whistle, Morgan cocks his head, (I hide mine in a bucket) and it starts – the whole exercise is pointless. You've got half a dozen posh fluffy sheep rushing hither and thither round the field going 'Did you hear that?' 'Oops, was that Turn Right or Left', 'What?' and then going into a huddle saying 'Bugger this for a game of soldiers'. The 2 dogs have long given up – 'If you can't give clear commands then we aren't playing' – and can be seen hanging over the garden fence of a cottage further down the hill lusting after the very posh weekend dog which is (sensibly) kept under lock and key whenever it comes down here.

Anyway listen, this isn't actually why I wrote – you know I said we were thinking of buying a house in France? It's done Pand … well, practically done anyway … in the south west … get your map out … not far from Cahors (north east of Toulouse). Just think: holidays – stuff the tortoises and parrots in the car and away. Sounds simple doesn't it? Then I have to get all the paperwork for the animals – CITES and veterinary stuff – but looking on the bright side, it has to be easier than getting a house sitter who is also willing (and able) to look after the animals – especially with the new baby torts.

Cornwall, 1990

Dear Pand,

Sorry about the gap – things to do, places to go, you know what its like! No – only joking! Simply that I haven't really told you about the house in France – well, other than having bought it, I still hadn't seen it but after the first trip (somewhat fraught) I can now tell you from personal experience!

I told you vaguely where it was – South West France I think was as far as we got on the last phone call so I think I should try and describe it and the location a little more thoroughly (you will need to know your holiday destination for next year, after all).

So, find Cahors on the map (technically speaking, a bit above and to the right of Toulouse) and go right a bit and down a bit on the little roads and there we are! Really easy, and I happen to know that buses run to Cahors so that is you sorted!

Our house is a part-converted barn (a SMALL part-converted barn) and sits in the Oak forest about a km or so from the village. The forest stretches for miles with endless walkways taking you from forest to heath to pastureland and back again. It is a little paradise and so many birds, flowers, insects and stuff (plus the outside chance of finding a truffle or two!).

Before I get too carried away, the house itself is small – 2 floors of 30 sq m each, which basically means the ground floor consists of (or WILL consist of) Living/Dining /Kitchen and the first floor for Bedroom/Bathroom and a titchy bit for letter writing. We have managed to get a local builder to install a septic tank and a toilet for us, so that's a beginning at least. The chemical loo was a bit of a No-No after the first trip – particularly as we only had one cold water tap on the ground floor at the time – middle of winter, chemical loo, cold water – not EXACTLY what holidays are made of!

Now for the ground: 8000 sq m (2 acres to you and I), part-walled on the north and east (part being the operative word) and roughly fenced to the south and west. Lots of trees as you would expect in the middle of an Oak forest but as well as the Oaks a secondary forest of all sorts of interesting stuff – offhand I can think of the wild Bird Cherry, Juniper, Ash, Maple, Holly, Hawthorn, Blackthorn, Birch, Sycamore and the undergrowth is pretty energetic too – Honeysuckle and Clematis (both the wild type), Arums, Violets, Primrose, wild bulbs such as Jacinthe and a Gladiolus type (will check these out eventually and let you know exactly) and … Orchids too!

Lots of small people about too – mice, voles, crickets, beetles, spiders, frogs, mantis and the birds of course – but more of that later.

Bye for now

Cornwall, May 1990

Dear Pand,

The super note paper (and writing) is due to the fact that I am writing this whilst sitting outside. Yes – not working but just sitting and it's still daylight – smack my wrist!

The greenhouse is doing well. You remember one of the Gardenias had buds on? Well, they've turned into flowers now – no surprise there you may think but in fact, the last time they flowered was 6 or 7 years ago. The Daturas are also flowering away (from a sowing last month) but they are only annuals as opposed to the big shrubby types. However, they are wonderfully scented but tend to close up in the daytime so first thing in the morning is best – open the greenhouse door and the perfume smacks you in the nose! The cacti are really coming along well now – one of the small round green jobs has sprouted 2 babies on one side – it's the only one that has done so – forward little creature.

The Thrush still sits on his perch in the trees at the front singing away but seems to have lost heart recently since you went back. The cock Chaffinch has started banging at the back door at 6 am asking when he can have Morgan's used seed. What with him and the fact that Mr Lory is being bolshy about going to bed much before 10 pm (still quite light at that time), I seem to be putting in a hell of a long day, pandering to everyone's desires.

The tortoises are all fine and with this really nice weather (typically, as I write, a bloody great cloud obscures the sun) they've all been rushing in and out thoroughly enjoying themselves. Hebe has increased her weight and is now 28 grammes – never before reached by her, so things are looking up. If allowed to get her own food though, she still sometimes has difficulty and I've had to clear her mouth out twice but at least it wasn't absolutely full so an improvement. Helen laid 4 eggs the other day but I have been *very* strong minded and dug them up and won't incubate them. It's getting a bit beyond a joke (at least until we move) and I really only want some off Rover (and Beryl if she will ever lay any). Besides, after the blind one and One Eye, I think it wise to leave it. Something wrong somewhere. Bet you didn't think I had that much will power, did you? Ed was surprised too when I told him. It's probably the thought of coping with Sudie for the next 50 years or so actually. Now it's hot, she's being her usual summertime pain in the bum – can't find anywhere to sit – too hot here, too cold there, no room to dig a burrow in the garden, so she has now chosen the hottest place to dig. Her stable isn't 'quite right' any more for the daytime so she has moved a few feet along and is digging at the base of the big Passion Flower. The fact that Rover, Helen and Beryl's stable is now ventilated by a 3 foot gap at the bottom seems to be of no account to Sudie when burrow hunting. Nor does the fact that the passion flower is now baring its roots and beginning to send out distress signals. Sudie really does have the makings of a typical property developer – prime site so bugger the natives! Oddly enough though, she will always go back to her own stable in the early evening so I suppose she shows *some* sense of loyalty ...

Have just spotted Mrs Blackbird digging in the lawn and Mr B is usually about every day – looks a bit harassed and scruffy so presumably the kids are being rather demanding. Have only seen the robin a couple of times this past week – he too looks a bit harassed. I bet if I opened up a little shop selling bird contraceptives there'd be a queue a mile long! One of the wrens has just been down for a bath – I haven't seen both of them together for some time so I suspect they have children too. Swallows are swooping around every afternoon, the buzzards constantly in the field and a pheasant came and sat in the bottom hedge the other day – kept peering at me over the blackberry brambles and making little gobbling noises – whether this is normal or he was just being rude, I'm not sure. Oh God – the thrush has started up again – must know I'm writing to you. Wait a mo – yes – he wants me to take this down – Tweet, ya ya, whistle, ya boo – I *think* that's right – I'll just read it back to him for any correction. What with all that *and* the damn sheep plus Morgan copying everyone (please, not the sheep!), the peace of the countryside is just a myth. By the way, Morg has started saying 'Shall we?'. This I *think* refers to 'Shall we have a drink?' So long as he doesn't start putting 'shall we' and the pouring-from-a-bottle noise together, I think we may just get away with it. As he also says 'Tea, Pip?' in an interrogative sort of manner, I think this should be enough to confuse the enemy – at least for a while.

Well Pand – oops, 2 greenfinches just landed at my feet, probably begging for contraceptives – the garden isn't looking too bad and have at least now got some of the greenhouse plants outside. Mind you, with the new tree seedlings as well, space is still at a premium. Sudie has again scoffed the purple Passion Flower – I'd spread it over Curry's side but with Beryl (wants to dig a nest but won't) as an accomplice – the pot got tipped over, Beryl walked off (Nothing to do with me Pip, honest!) and Sudie ate it within an inch of its life. Basically, I think she and I have the same taste in things – the plants I prize, she does as well! The Forget-me-nots are beginning to bore her now we have loads of them and so today, she ate a whole Alchemilla (for your information, nice plant, big pleated leaves and long sprays of greenish/yellow flowers, much prized both by flower arrangers and African Spurred tortoises). At least she was gracious enough to leave one tiny leaf in the centre. Still, I've got plenty of seedlings from last year so it's not that devastating. Well, I suppose if you are that particular plant, it's pretty devastating isn't it? However, as I'm not, it isn't but if I was, it would be!

Have just spotted the cock chaffinch feeding an offspring on top of what remains of the compost heap. That's the first baby chaffinch I've seen this year. All together now: Aahh!

Better do some work now I suppose.

Cornwall, 1991

You know I mentioned about the paperwork necessary to take this lot on holiday? And how I thought maybe it wouldn't be QUITE that simple? Well, for once, I was right. I have the feeling that this will just be the beginning of endless problems whenever we set foot out of the UK.

This of course could just be due to the fact that we are travelling with 2 cars which are stuffed full of 20 torts (give or take), 2 parrots, plus my favourite tropical plants (ie those which couldn't be entrusted at home on their own for several months) and a supply of Darjeeling tea (unobtainable in France at this time).

On this occasion, we were flagged down as we came off the ferry: 'Park your vehicles over there and come with us.' A bit nerve-racking as we were, for want of a better phrase, actually frog-marched from one end of the dock to the other – and our attendants had Guns (holstered it is true but a sobering experience nevertheless). Even though it was late at night, there were other passengers around and we felt uncomfortably conspicuous on the long walk to the Customs office. When the staring and pointing became too obvious, we shrugged our shoulders and pantomimed 'No idea – not doing drugs, not gun-running, not people-trafficking – just on holiday with our pets!' At the end of the day, however, we were still under guard like criminals and as we got further away from the cars, we could hear both Morgan and Mr Lory shouting – Morgan doing a clear 'Just going to the shops' and Mr Lory just shrieking.

Arrived at the Customs office and asked to explain our cargo. We just said we were going on holiday to our house in S. France and taking our pets with us – here are the relevant papers and vet certificates, etc – did they have a problem with this? Seemingly they did. The Chief Customs officer kept getting out folders of papers and frowning over them and saying 'Vacances?' in a questioning sort of voice. After about half an hour of this we were becoming thoroughly fed up and with about 500 miles to drive to our destination we weren't inclined to continue faffing about wasting time. On the other hand, the smuggling trade in endangered species is a real problem and we were therefore mindful of Customs being careful and doing their job and so we were, despite the hour, very patient. All the paperwork being in order, the real problem seemed to be that this guy couldn't grasp the idea of going on holiday with a small zoo – Why would you do this? – Well, if you have an hour or two, I'll explain – or maybe not. Eventually it was Ed, being fairly well experienced in bureaucratic paperwork, who said 'OK, all you do is take the CITES papers and the vet certificates, bung an official stamp on them, make a note in your records, give us all the papers back and everything will be fine'. To our surprise, this actually worked and with a last disbelieving poke at the tortoises (our guards had already discovered the error of poking the parrots when we were first pulled over), they let us go. It was almost as if it was a weird thing to take your animals on holiday for a few months. I have the horrid feeling that this sort of problem is likely to become a fact of life.

Actually driving a few hundred miles with this lot was something else entirely – a source of amazement, amusement (not often to us though). This last trip, we got a puncture on the trailer. We were in Limoges, right in the city centre in the rush hour of course, and a very nice well-meaning person behind us signalled that we had a flat. Not expecting to have a problem, we had put the spare trailer wheel in the car – gasp, horror – UNDER the animals! We were left with no alternative but to pull over, decant 2 caged parrots and a number of boxed tortoises on to the pavement, jack the trailer up (plants getting excited: Are we there yet? No, you're NOT there yet – just shut up and don't give us any grief). It really was SO embarrassing – loads of people stopped and peered at us as if we were some kind of street theatre – which I suppose we were really. Just needed an organ and a pathetic-looking dog or monkey and we could probably have collected enough to pay for the holiday.

Remind me before the next trip to look up another route which avoids Limoges in case we get that same well-meaning person. Had we had the sense, we should just have ignored him and trundled on with the flat – at least to a dark, uninhabited place where all our wordly parrots and tortoises wouldn't have to be on show.

Will write again soon

Cornwall, Autumn 1991

If you got Beryl's postcard, you will know that we spent quite a long time in France earlier this year – went early March and returned mid June. Sorry I never wrote earlier but have had so much go wrong that I think my brain has a hard time keeping up with things! Firstly, we did sell this cottage in February this year only to find that it fell through just a week before we went to France and believe it or not, exactly the same thing happened just a week ago! It really is getting beyond a joke – even the torts are getting fed up with this 'we're moving, no we aren't'. At the moment, Ed is in Poland his first contract since finishing in China last October (except for a few days lecturing in London in December). We were planning on returning to France next month but Ed's agent rang yesterday with the offer of 2 or 3 months in Canada so will hang on for a while and see if it happens.

Beryl thought France wonderful (as did all the tortoises) – really took to sunbathing in gaps in the walls and ate lots of strange vegetation! In actual fact, the weather was not too brilliant whilst we were there – we did have some really hot days but I think we could have done much better and of course, they were all without their greenhouse. We did take their frames though so it wasn't too bad. However, few of the dandelions which I sowed last year came to anything and I was really scratching around for stuff for them. Luckily there were some good growths of dandelions in the forest around but had to do an expedition on my bike most days to collect enough for all of them. Sudie adapted quite well as did Curry – though Curry did scare us at one point by getting very frothy around the mouth and having blocked nostrils. I was worried at first that she had eaten something which had disagreed with her but in fact I think she just got overheated – unlike her usual self she had been sitting out in the open whilst it was hot and didn't think to shuffle off under cover early enough. Anyway she is fine now but still seems to suffer from one nostril blocking up in this hot dry weather. Did I tell you that whilst she was ill and (supposedly) suffering at the Tortoise Trust last year she was photographed and appeared on an educational poster for Tortoise conservation – she really looked quite splendid and there was I frantically worrying about her! She also appears on the dust jacket of a new book about Tortoises and Turtles of the Asian

Sub-continent – now she's insisting that I buy her a copy (at £40 a time). I'll be negotiating her fee for chat shows next! Actually, it is an excellent book – I wrote a review for it and it does contain quite a lot of up-to-date information on Indian Stars so I'll perhaps submit to Curry's demands.

The tortoises had plenty of wildlife to keep them company – in the first enclosure (now officially for the males, Smalls and babies) there is a huge rockery (well, to be fair it's just a heap of boulders at the moment) and there are loads of lizards in and out of there and, latterly, some snakes. The 2nd enclosure is for the females and then Curry and Sudie have a separate part each. This latter had wire netting for one boundary as we ran out of stones. We were going to leave the netting up for when we came again but a couple of weeks before we left for England, a large snake got stuck in it! It had got about half way through one of the holes and then couldn't go any further. After staring hard at it for some time, we decided that either it had no reverse gear or we were putting it off. Anyway, back to the house to consult our snake book, then back to the snake with the book (must have been a good brain day!) because neither of us could quite remember its pattern. After much consultation, we still couldn't agree whether or not it was a venomous type and so, in the best tradition, we made a forked stick and set about rescuing it. Ed pinned the poor creature's head down with the stick whilst I lay on the ground and snipped away at the wire around its body. As the last strand was cut, Snake slithered over me and ran off into the undergrowth. We were pleased but as his/her tail disappeared under the bushes realised too late that we could have taken a photo – but didn't! Walking round the next day, I could hear a lot of rustling just beyond the boundary wall and, perching rather precariously on top of the wall, I spied a pair of snakes mating (I'd love to say it was a snake shouting 'Yes, Yes, YES' which made me look but that would be completely untrue). Anyway, it was all terribly exciting and one of the pair definitely looked like our snake of the previous day. At least the whole episode made us think, though, and we removed all the wire netting when we left – if it hadn't been for the snake getting caught we would never have thought about it I'm afraid.

Also had some very useful Dung beetles – they really cleared up after the tortoises (couldn't believe their luck when they came across the heaps left by both Curry and Sudie!). I have seen them very occasionally at work in parts of Devon (years ago) but these were extremely industrious and great fun to watch. One lot had youngsters with them and though I know nothing about their family life, the adults did seem to let the small ones have a bit of a practice ('No – how many times have I TOLD you? Roll it NEATLY'!) before rather more professionally rolling their booty off into the sunset.

Left to graze as they would normally be in the garden at home, it was amazing just what the tortoises found to eat – they even took leaves of shrubs (small bilberry type things) and very thin succulent type plants. We have tried to bring small plants and seeds of their favourite food and start them here but the vast army of slugs and snails had the better of us. Every day I would conscientiously water the seedlings in the tortoise enclosures and cover them with polythene to conserve the moisture but the slugs/snails were obviously trained to go for the slightest bit of green and basically decimated everything! At one point, I herded several tortoises at a time along the track from our entrance to the main track some few hundred yards away. There's clover and plantain to a certain degree but it can be time-consuming and panicky with everyone running off in different directions (am going to have to work out a proper shift system here) and once or twice the locals have caught me out. Bit embarrassing but I shall have to persevere! Sudie had already showed burrowing tendencies and at over 3 kilos she made a few inroads in the enclosure – it can prove a bit of a battle to drag her out at times.

Bird life is quite spectacular too – it's the first time for years that I have heard so many cuckoos – they called from 4 in the morning right through until midnight at times and I saw several (or I saw one several times!). Most days there were at least 5 or 6 individuals calling in the immediate vicinity and I wasted hours trailing about trying to spot them. A number of Golden Orioles came into the garden and despite their secretive nature, we did manage to see them on several occasions. Also Chaffinches (seemed bulkier than English ones), Long Tail and Blue Tits, Short-Eared and Barn owls, Buzzards, etc.

Mr Lory's aviary is set between the house and the first tortoise enclosure so that he has something to occupy himself with – once all the trees had leafed up, he was quite happy and spent a lot of time outside his nest box. As a rain forest parrot, he dislikes the full sun and prefers dull days or evenings. Morgan seemed immediately at home – indoors he had a wide window ledge to sit on if the weather wasn't too great and outside he had his table placed under a large oak tree. Oddly enough at one point the local farmer herded his cows along the track past the gate and so it was just like home for Morgan and he was greatly impressed by this. Thank God French cows don't respond to 'Oy' and 'Come on then'. Well, that is to say, French cows don't respond to this yet ... there's always time!

This trip has left a lasting impression – Three went missing some 2 weeks before we left to return to England. We missed him when we fed them at lunchtime and spent the remaining days searching our 2 acres and the adjoining woodland but no luck. I couldn't believe it – we had spent just over 3 months there and all had been well. I can only think it was the old trick of one tortoise levering away at another against the walls and Three found himself level with the top of the wall, toppled over and went off to explore. Unfortunately, we were still in the process of rebuilding several gaps in the boundary walls and one has to assume that he found one still left to be repaired and wandered off into the surrounding forest. Although we searched diligently from dawn to dusk (and stayed for an extra couple of weeks), it was really like looking for a needle in a haystack. There are hundreds of acres of forest surrounding us and once he left the garden, he could literally have been anywhere. We told many people round about in the hopes that someone may stumble across him but to be honest I don't hold out a lot of hope. I had a letter last week From M. and Mme. Berengier (an elderly couple from Toulouse with a weekend house in the village) but despite keeping an eye out when they walked their dog in the forest, they report no sign of a tortoise.

Sad news apart, I should really tell you a little more about Floriers. In many ways, we chose the best time to come this year as the wild flowers in Spring were really quite amazing with both fields and roadside verges ablaze. In our own patch, we have hundreds of Orchids – Early Purple, Pyramid, Green and Burnt winged, Bee, and Butterfly and also Narrow Leafed Helleborines. Field Gladioli and Cowslips abound along with Violets, Sedums and all sorts of stuff. The forest trees are mainly Oak (hence it being an important Truffle area) but there are also Ash, Maple, Wild Cherry, Juniper and Pine along with a variety of shrubby stuff such as Blackthorn and others I have yet to identify. Also many different bees and spiders and lots of insects which I haven't come across before – all of which make for hours of entertainment!

Wonderful find one day – on the track just outside our gateway we discovered several Lizard Orchids and about 3/4 of an hour away is a sort of Heath area where we found a number of Bee and Fly Orchids growing along with 2 Spider Orchids. Several other interesting looking things just rearing their heads – we need to plan our trips so that we eventually cover every season of the year. In a mad spree at a Nursery in Albias, we bought a European Fan Palm and later, 2 Olive trees (Picholine and another variety whose name escapes me at the moment).

Floriers itself has some wonderful buildings – a nice church and a splendid Nunnery as well as some beautiful houses. More noticeable now than when we first visited France in 1968 is that the average French householder is becoming almost as crazy as the English in their penchant for retail nurseries and Garden Centres (as befits a nation which created some of the best gardens in Europe, I have to add). However, many of the gardening books I've seen for sale hereabouts are by English authors (but in French of course – why make things easy?) One garden in Floriers has a stupendous array of Cacti and Lilies – every time we walked past there, I would hang longingly over the garden wall in the hopes of striking up a conversation with the owner but no luck so far.

In complete contrast, our ground is proving very hard work – full of stones and the Junipers which are planted around the young oaks – I gather to make the oaks grow straight and quickly (well, as quickly as one could expect an oak to grow – bit like Parrots really – don't even think about dating until they are into their 30's). Despite our rather naive hopes of finding truffles under every tree in the garden, this has not turned out to be the case (surprise, surprise) even though we are officially in the Black (posh) Truffle area. In fact our nearest town (well, large village really) Lalbenque is one of the major Truffle centres of the Perigord region. One of our neighbours assures us that he once found a Truffle on his patch – about 2 inches across and by the time he shared it out with his family, they each managed virtually just a sniff.

Having mentioned the Convent building in the village, we met Veronique (a nun from said convent) when we were on the track on a dandelion picking expedition. She had apparently come looking for the English couple she'd heard about (slightly worrying!) to see if she could borrow some reading material suitable for her young niece, Jeanne.

Having promised to go through our book stock, V was then intrigued about the dandelions and so we explained to her why we were gathering. A couple of days later she and two other nuns including Sister Marie (a Mother Superior type of figure) came to look and wonder at the tortoises and parrots. Came home from Cahors one day to find 2 large sacks full of dandelions by the gate – V had been busy on the tort's behalf. Unfortunately, rather than just gathering the leaves, V had pulled whole plants so had to induct her into the correct method before the whole forest/ village was stripped of dandelions (not good for us later in the year!).

We were then invited to the house which V appeared to share with Marie and which was attached to the convent at the eastern end. The house itself was large and rambling and after a quick tour, we were settled into a comfortable kitchen/sitting room. To one wall was fixed a large blackboard which we each used in turn to write our names and then it was down to Ed and I. First a rough (very rough!) map of England with a big cross over Cornwall in answer to the 'Where do you live in the UK?' We also managed, after a fashion, to do 'How many sisters/brothers/ mothers/fathers do you have?' What are their names, where do they live, how old are they, what do they do? Then, how many tortoises, how old are they, what are the parrots called, how old are they? and so it went on. It transpired that the blackboard was really for Jeanne's benefit – her mother is a Detective Inspector with the Toulouse police and Jeanne spent a great deal of time at the convent when mama was working. She also suffered from some mystery illness and seemed to be off school for long periods of time. V and M tried to keep up her education as best they could but I think sometimes found it hard as J was in fact a rather precocious child. This was the first occasion we had actually met Jeanne and she was persuaded (didn't take much persuasion, actually) to stand at the blackboard and sing us a couple of songs.

About a week into this holiday, V invited us to the house again and the
evening started off in much the same manner as previously. However, on
this occasion we were invited to taste some of the home made wine. In
true tradition, the nuns used everything growing around them to produce
both food and drink and their alcohol production was truly staggering.
This evening, the big kitchen table was covered with a stunning array of
home made wine and liqueurs – each bottle with a carefully waxed cork
and a beautifully printed label (which often included a small drawing of
whatever the drink was made from). So off we start – the Cowslip first I
think. This was sweet and didn't immediately appear to have a particularly
high alcohol content (how wrong can you be?). As we hadn't noticed a
bucket in amongst the bottles, glasses and other necessary paraphernalia,
we were obliged to swallow everything. This didn't seem too onerous a task
– or at least, not to begin with! Sister Marie poured (and she wasn't exactly
mean with it either) whilst V handed us the glasses and watched intently
for our reactions to each different one. Some time between the carrot and
the blackberry, M rather unsportingly gave up and after rather garbled Bon
Nuit's all round, she gamely staggered off to bed. Ed and I were beginning
to feel a little ragged round the edges but V was in no mood to let us go
before we had got to the last bottle. We tried (admittedly rather feebly) to
say 'Let's just finish this one off'. 'No, no,' V giggled 'this is a special one, I
could only make 3 bottles of it'. No answer to that so we gamely struggled
on. At V's suggestion, I undertook to chart our route from Cornwall to
Floriers on the blackboard but my brain (and my hand come to that)
would just not get beyond Limoges. Ed was no better (in fact worse, as he
blanked out after Le Mans and so was no help whatsoever. V did her best
to prod my memory but when she started reeling off places like Provence
and Bordeaux, I realised she was as far gone as we were. When we finally
called it a day and had cleared the debris from the table (this by the simple
expedient of removing the glasses – which, given the state of the 3 of us, I
thought was pretty good – then just sweeping the bottles off the table into
a large bin) it was almost midnight and, as V rather unsteadily waved us
off from the door, we realised we had forgotten to pick up the 3 bottles
(which miraculously had remained unopened) which V had insisted we
take with us. We blundered home through the forest and, of course, the
torch gave out half way home. Just as well we had the foresight to leave
a light on in the house as this was the only way we knew where we were
going. Difficult to believe but when we came to the following morning

(late), we came across 3 bottles of wine outside the gate with a little note saying 'You forgot these'. I was full of admiration!

After that, we saw a lot of V – she would often call at the house with little gifts of food, either for us or the tortoises. One day towards the end of our stay, she arrived at the gate with an enormous bag full of freshly picked chanterelles (the bag almost as big as her) and some parsley. She told us to fry the chanterelles with butter and garlic and then add parsley at the last minute – made an excellent breakfast, according to her. This was true as they were absolutely delicious and we lived off them all week!

See you soon

Floriers, 1992

Hi Pand,

Sorry we got cut off – must have been Oscar Tree Frog swinging on the line! I was in the middle of recounting the latest in embarrassing situations but I don't think I'd actually got to the crunch of the matter. I mean this was *really* bad. I told you about Veronique – the stupendous home brewer?

Anyway, Veronique, Sister Marie (Mother Superior) and a few local kids called round to take us off to see the Valley of the Lilies (a beautiful bit of woodland by the river which at this time of year is absolutely stuffed with Lilies of the Valley). We knew the trip was planned but not sure of exactly when and so carried on pottering about, fixing the tortoise pens, etc. An excellent continental habit is 'never go beyond your neighbour's gate unless you are either family or great friends'. We'd assumed this would apply to us being relative newcomers, so always figured we would have time to make ourselves presentable. As it happened, this didn't occur to Veronique and she and her retinue, having no joy knocking at the house door, came steaming down the path to look for us. I, of course, was more or less presentable (in that I had clothes on) but Ed? As usual, he was ...

well ... bare, really. No other word for it. We were down on the tennis lawn and had, just moments earlier, sat down on the bench to survey our latest handiwork (the log pile!). Next thing we hear is Veronique calling out – a couple of seconds in which we managed to exchange horrified looks and then they were there, heading down the path in full view. Nothing we could do – there was nowhere to hide, no bushes to duck into. I was ok but Ed was left high and dry sitting on the bench and trying to look as if meeting a bunch of nuns whilst you were naked was, you know, normal!. You know what it is like here – you have to shake hands, kiss cheeks and all that palaver every time you meet up and this rather left Ed in an awkward position, so to speak! I was literally hopping about with embarrassment but Ed carried the whole thing off with great aplomb – legs coyly crossed, he remained seated whilst politely shaking hands with everyone. It was actually quite weird – you wouldn't have known they'd even twigged anything was odd other than that once the formalities (or, strictly speaking I suppose, the informalities) were over, they pottered off to inspect the tortoises thereby giving Ed the opportunity to streak off into the house and put some clothes on. Seems like I was the only one thinking 'Shit – here we go again!'

The Valley trip was wonderful – we managed to squeeze into 2 cars (Sister Marie's little Citroen and ours) but unfortunately, we ended up with Jeanne – the very precocious 10 year old hell-bent on practising her English and an expert on really crap French pop music! Jeanne insisted on coming back to our house so that she could play the aforementioned crap music again, very loudly, on our stereo. I think we would have probably murdered her except for the fact that her mum is a detective in the local police force! As well as Jeanne, on the return journey, we also had a bag of snails – these were not just the paltry little jobs that plague your Hostas. These were BIG snails – plump, succulent jobs! It turned out that the Lilies, whilst briefly admired and sniffed, were really just an excuse for a snail hunting expedition. Lower down the valley was the river and alongside the river was a nice damp green meadow and in the nice damp green meadow were lots of snails – edible snails and the Floriers nuns love nothing better than snails cooked in garlic for breakfast. Ed and I were given our share, lovingly placed in a plastic carrier bag along with some wild parsley and with strict instructions on how to cook them. We nodded and smiled (as you do) whilst secretly thinking 'Bloody hell fire – what are we going to do with half a dozen ravenous snails?' And what if they expect to stand over us whilst we cook them to make sure we are doing it right? I wouldn't put anything past Veronique. As luck would have it, they left us, Jeanne and the snails to find our own way home – they obviously assumed that both Jeanne and the snails were in good hands. As it happened, Jeanne was fine – earphones, stereo and tapes – which left us free to unstick our snails from the plastic carrier, take some photos and let them go in the garden (with 2 acres the release site wasn't much of a problem, tho I *did* let them go way up the top end!). I'm not sure which of us was the most grateful – us because we didn't have to cook them or them because, for a few hours at least, they must have seen their immediate future as being ensconced in a very hot pan along with some garlic and parsley. They didn't exactly race off when we let them go but there was a very definite air of 'Phew!' as they crept off into the undergrowth.

Despite the wine and nudity, we did have some serious conversations as well. Both V and M remembered the war and the horror and deprivation of Occupied France. Many of the local people took either an active part in the resistance movement or supported it in any other way they could. Though both recounted some fairly awful stories, even then they tend to clam up when talking too close to home and one has the distinct impression that there were a number of people either connected to or still living in the village who were, in those immortal words, 'no better than they should be'.

Sister M had rather an austere look about her (tho she wasn't half as serious once you knew her) but V was always a happy, smiley character. There is little change in M's demeanour when talking of the war years but V's face becomes shadowed and sad. Although they appear willing enough to answer our questions, we've learned not to probe too deeply. In fact, with all the older people in the village (the likes of Emil, the Berengiers, Pascal's parents, etc.), none has much good to say about Bruno or the other few German expats in the area. I don't know whether this is simply the fact that he's German or whether because he could have been old enough to take an active part in the war himself. I've not noticed any outright hostility (indeed, we went to a social evening at Bruno's house and several local people were there, including the Mayor and his wife) just simply the odd comment and a feeling.

Bruno feels that he is well integrated, speaks the language (as he is forever at pains to point out) and to all intents and purposes, he is speaking the truth. France (and the people) have certainly changed in the intervening 20 or so years since we first visited. In 1968 it was not uncommon to have little old men (and women too) shake their fists and spit on the ground as we drove through the villages – particularly in the North and Eastern parts of the country. The Swiss were more friendly and even the Italians accepted us without comment but France was a different matter and quite uncomfortable.

V too has a more serious side her nature, being very involved in the community. Much of her days are taken up with visiting the elderly and the sick around the village – either just to comfort or to take food or help on the domestic side. We went with her on numerous occasions and it was obvious how the people relied on her and the other members of the convent. Better than social services and I assume the nuns from the convent fulfilled their role to the satisfaction of the local people. As at this point, I don't understand everything that is said (well, yes, you're right – I understand very little of what is said but have learned Pass Towels; Boil Water; Baby coming – er, What? Hang on a sec, this is serious stuff Veronique – I can do hatching birds and even hatching reptiles but hatching PEOPLE? No, don't worry Pand – the Baby thing didn't happen but I can see if I continue with the sick trips, it's not beyond the bounds of belief! Scary!

I can't pretend I'm that enamoured of the Catholic faith (or any other come to that) but the Nuns, here at least, are a big and necessary part of the community. Like most things, I guess the little people do the work and the big I Ams spout the dogma.

That's about it for now – it'll be time to go and peer at the Green Woodpeckers soon. They are nesting just a few yards up the track – just short of the abandoned house.

Floriers, 1992

Dear Pand,

I was taking Sudie up the track the other day – we have so little vegetation in the ground for her I am hoping she will pick stuff from the track and possibly into the top field – loads of leaves there. The two of us set off early and all being quiet, I think no one will be along (maybe only the guys in the white van and they are used to it now and just wave and shout 'Ca va?' (or at least, that is what I think they shout)

Half way along the track (ie too far along to turn back and not near enough to Bruno's garden – always a good bet for hiding) and along come a couple on bicycles. The track is only a few feet wide and it is impossible to hide Sudie – in fact, as she is pottering along the middle of the track, I am forced to pick her up and place her at the side (she's too heavy and conspicuous to hold for any length of time) but there isn't enough 'side' to hide a 13 kilo tortoise from view. The couple stop right next to us and say 'Hello'. I say 'Hello' and probably look like an imbecile because I am frantically trying to formulate an answer to the question I just know that they will ask – which they do! I feebly say she is hungry (they tuck their feet in carefully, I note – should I have explained she was vegetarian?) and that my garden is a bit dry and short of food. This is the best I can do in French at this time of day but I try to curry favour by also mentioning that as my tortoise is so big, she needs lots of exercise – I assume that as these people are cycling, they will appreciate this reasoning. They nod and smile while disentangling an enthusiastic tortoise from their wheels and cycle off but not before telling me they are from Paris and are not used to wild animals. I felt a bit sorry for them actually – having seen Sudie and me, perhaps they were expecting lions round the corner.

This encounter should have warned me of the dangers at this time of year! Setting off on my bike for a serious leaf-picking expedition this morning, I got so carried away with chasing cuckoos, I ended up in a part of the forest which I hadn't explored before. It was coming up for midday and I hadn't expected to see anyone about and so was happily pottering along, stuffing leaves in a carrier bag and generally minding my own business. All of a sudden, coming to a gentle curve, I see a woman ambling along the track towards me. I quickly run through all the phrases I might need and prepare to greet her and pass on. No such luck – she is here on holiday from Northern France and wants to know everything – where I come from, where I have been, what am I doing now, etc. etc. She seems interested in the forest and the general flora and fauna and so I am in my element and tell her everything. She is a willing listener and so I explain about the tortoises and why I am tramping the woods picking leaves but then I get carried away and talk about snakes and deer and stuff. We eventually parted and went our separate ways – me feeling really pleased about having passed on some useful information and she looking somewhat bemused.

It was only as I continued on my leaf gathering mission that I began, as you do, to run over the conversation again in my head. I hadn't taken a great deal of notice of her responses but as I made my way home, it slowly dawned on me that I had possibly led this woman astray as far as forest life was concerned. I had the nasty feeling that whilst I was describing my imported wildlife (ie tortoises and parrots), I had given the impression that these creatures were wandering the forest and she being a townie would not know any different! For the next couple of weeks, I shall stay close to home – I dread meeting this woman again in case she wants to know why she hasn't yet managed to spot any of this exotic wildlife roaming the forest. I need to curb this tendency to be helpful – particularly when I don't know what I'm on about!

More soon?

Floriers, September 1992

Dear Pand,

We met 2 hunters way down the track towards Cahors yesterday. Out in force throughout France and from my limited experience, it seems a bit of a casual affair. All the hunting dogs wear bells round their necks – this is to tell the hunters where they are, as the dogs *always* seem to get lost. After a couple of weeks of rain, the stream cutting across the track was fairly high – we stood and watched as the hunters and their dog attempted to cross. By this time we have no compunction about obviously watching, everyone does it, it's a national pastime! Anyway, both men got across but the dog seemed reluctant to get its feet wet. Eventually after much exasperated effort, one of the guys returned to our side of the water, picked up the dog and carried it across – both he and the dog looked pretty embarrassed. I was impressed by this image of the noble, fearless hunting dog. In the spirit of things, I mentioned to the hunter how cold it was – he replied 'Well, it *is* winter' and I wanted to say ' Well, stuff you mate, bet you don't catch anything! '. Instead, I wished him 'Bon Chance' – not because I wished him any kind of luck – simply it's a nice sounding phrase and I was desperate to say it to someone. It's not as if you can say that to the person who sells you bread every day – at least not without them thinking you are totally moronic!

At this time of year, hunters come up the track past our house at the weekends. Always shouting 'Ici' because the dogs spot Morgan and want to investigate. They (hunters and dogs) crash and bang their way through the forest – no game can mistake either their intention or their direction! You can almost visualise all the wildlife rolling their eyes and saying to each other 'Must be weekend again – better make the effort I suppose'.

Sunday mornings seem to bring out the really serious hunters. You see 8 or 10 of them standing around at the side of the road, all very casual in their designer camouflage gear and most of them smoking and popping a drink from the hip flask. That's about the extent of the action – at a push, maybe one of the guys will saunter a few yards into the forest accompanied by a couple of the dogs making a hell of a racket in the process. None of the other hunters take any notice whatsoever and eventually the Lone Ranger returns, squats down and has a slug of brandy. One or two fire off a few pot shots and then it's home to dinner. All terribly macho!

Will write again soon.

Floriers, 1992

Hi Pand,

Just a few lines to let you know that we are alive and well despite the awful weather. We have had a few really hot and sunny days but more than our fair share of rain too. It really has been quite appalling but today it didn't actually rain (having finished from yesterday at about 6 this morning) but was just grey and cold without a glimmer of sun all day. It puts me so far behind in what needs doing and everything takes an age anyway – can't find the tools, right size screws, etc. It's raining hard as I write this so curtailing any further work at present.

I think I forgot to mention before that the trip down was worse than usual – with 2 cars, we didn't even have each other to chat to (or keep one another awake!). Whilst E had the car with the working radio, I had the 2 parrots – not convinced it was a good swap! We got held up at Roscoff customs for over an hour – we thought it was something serious but turned out one of the Customs officers has a son interested in animals so nipped off home to collect him and bring him back to look at all of ours. By the time we twigged this, it was too late and we were too fed up to complain so son had all torts out of boxes (we drew the line at getting the parrots out!) and had a good prod about. I'm all for educating kids about wildlife but at that time of night and with another 600 miles or so to go I would have given the lectures a miss if I'd had the choice! We finally hit the road about 10 pm, drove til 4 am or so and then pulled over for a sleep in the cars. We eventually got here about 6 on Sunday evening.

We've been so busy that neither of us have had much chance to even walk around the ground let alone go for a walk further afield – so much to do and all urgent (of course!) So far I haven't managed to re pot any of my plants yet and certainly not planted any of the outside ones. Having said that, I have a very small patch to the left of the front door which I spent ages clearing last year and planted up with various bits – that has done surprisingly well – the Virginia Creeper is about 3 metres up the house wall now and even the Opuntia cacti must have flowered some time this summer. On the other side, the Wisteria has reached the gutter, the House Leeks all flowered and the wild Dog Rose must have had a good season judging by the number of Hips on it now.

E left Saturday midday to catch the midnight ferry at Caen on Sunday – he stopped at Le Mans on Saturday night – hotels are a much more civilised way of doing this trip but we always need to get on for the animals sake. By the sound of it, he was due for a rough crossing on Sunday night as he said it was blowing a Force 9 and the arrival time at Portsmouth had already been put back an hour. Poor E – it might not be brilliant weather here but at least I am on dry land! Well, no, I should change that – there has been enough rain recently for it not to be accurately descrbed as 'dry land'.

The wildlife is a bit on the scarce side at the moment (probably all drowned!) but on the good days we had 2 common Lizards on the roof plus several green lizards in the garden. Also my favourite beetle – quite large and black but with turquoise 'go faster' stripes around his body as well as a number of other Beetles I recognise from last year (well, not PERSONALLY recognise but you know what I mean). Also one Dung beetle searching hopefully. Plus our ultra blue butterfly from last summer and a large brown and white one too. Loads of crickets/grasshoppers which make a continual noise even on dull days. Some of them live in the house wall and you can hear them all night – at least a reminder that you *are* in a foreign place despite the weather. Our 'hoppers' are back, indoors as well as outdoors – I don't actually know what they are but very sweet and no trouble except indoors one has to be careful not to step on a slow one! Quite a few spiders but not easily seen – a rather smart green one the other day and larger than our green ones at home. Although I have a Spider Field Guide, I don't have a Insect Field Guide for Europe which is rather frustrating. Plenty of wasps which is a bit unfortunate given my propensity to swell up at the mere sight of them and also PLENTY of whatever bit me almost to death last Autumn. Also the odd Hornet or two – looking for a likely winter pad I suspect. Again I am covered with lumps so live on anti-histamine tablets and cover myself with Germolene and Calomine lotion. Helps, but makes me look like the pink and white beast from wherever! Also have several toads – 2 of which come indoors regularly (one tiny and one medium). Not so much getting up to let the cat out each morning as to let the toads out. They are by the door each morning waiting in a very patient fashion!

Only heard 1 Blackbird so far but the Chaffinches are about. No Owls in the garden yet but did see 2 Barn Owls on the trip down – they are far more common in France than England these days and I know there are some around here as I saw them last year flitting through the garden at night. The large Green Dragonfly has been around – spends most of his time perched on the back of the sofa indoors – the sofa is green so can't really blame him!

The tortoises discovered the fruit from the Wild Cherry trees recently which they have been avidly scoffing. At first I was quite horrified to find one of them with red smeared all round it's mouth – I thought it was blood but it had obviously been eating the berries and several of the other tortoises had red mouths and front feet too. So, relief (and another food source – hurray!) One of the Hermann's also discovered a mushroom and tucked into that quite avidly – as there have been no ill effects, I assume it is OK and have made a note of what it looks like. In fact, I seem to recall quite a few of this particular type popping up last year. I counted about 7 different fungi in the garden last November.

Some of the trees are just about to turn but mostly everywhere is still very green. One of the local farms has a couple of Fig Trees on their land – I noticed the other day that they are just ripening and look delicious! Calls for a timely walk and chat I think! The walnuts are almost ready now and although some of the grapes have already been harvested, there are plenty of vines on the way into Cahors which are absolutely laden with luscious black fruit. Most of the Sunflowers have been harvested now – rather sad really as they always looked really smiley and happy when you went past but there are still some huge pumpkins in the fields – they are so perfect, they almost look like film props or seed catalogue photos. Whatever, they look plump and orange and very self satisfied and I hate them because they are not in MY garden!

At the nursery in Cahors, I notice they are selling Lemon and Mandarin trees for about 15 francs (with Lemons and Mandarins on them!) and also a large Grapefruit with fruit on it for about 45 francs. I'm very tempted but we seem to have spent quite a lot lately so I thought I better hadn't. Well, not right now, this minute ... they'll still be open this evening though??

Just had a break from writing this as I remembered a project I had set myself ... namely to make myself an aerial extension for my radio. I found a roll of earth wire here so I've bunged that on the end of the aerial and stuck it out of the window. Got BBC Radio 4 (I *do* miss that every morning) albeit with a certain amount of Arab music thrown in (I suspect I'm picking that up from the south somewhere) but with a bit of judicious twiddling, I might yet get something. The test will be tomorrow morning!

To our great surprise, some shops are opening on Mondays now – previously Monday was just like an English Sunday – totally dead and nothing open (well, apart from the bread shops and the cafes and the bars – you know what I mean). However, I don't think Lalbenque has got that far so I'll go up there tomorrow, get some bread and veg and hopefully post this – otherwise it will be Tuesday!

Will write again soon.

Floriers, October 1992

Dear Andy,

Meant to write to you before but have been a trifle busy one way or another!!

Whilst Ed was back in the UK, V and M invited me to dinner at the convent. Having got all the tortoises and parrots settled, I set off about 7 pm to cycle up there. Not really sure why I chose to cycle but probably because I had some plants for V. The evening started quite formally – I helped lay the table while V put the finishing touches to dinner. A large plate of asparagus (fresh from the Convent veg garden) appeared first and then the main course – an extremely tasty Rabbit casserole. I'd not eaten rabbit since I was a child and was surprised at how good it was. A selection of cheese and fruit followed. Accompanied by a large carafe of local wine, we ate and chatted about this and that.

Dinner over, Sister M disappeared to attend to whatever it is that Mother Superiors do. This left V and I alone with the remainder of the wine plus V's seemingly never ending supply of homemade. You would have thought that we had exhausted her supply last time but she must have had a cellar full of the stuff and had just been waiting for a like minded person to arrive and help her drink it. We were terribly circumspect (to begin with at least) and having cleared the table and washed up decided to do a bit on the blackboard (taking a bottle of some rich purplish wine along for company). Biology was the order of the day but by the time both of us had had a go at placing various organs in a relatively reasonable place on a somewhat rough depiction of the human body and then attempting to name them in both French and English (weird because half the time, she and I were talking about different organs), we got a bit bored. We then decided to move on to plants – a much better bet as both of us at least knew what we were talking about. After broaching the 2nd purplish bottle, it was beginning to tell on us and having by this time abandoned the blackboard (the blackboard necessitated standing up and co-ordinating brain and hand which both of us were, oddly, finding a little hard going), we sat at the table discussing plants – what we'd grown, what we'd failed to grow, what we'd give our eye teeth to grow, etc. etc. Although V had seen our garden, such as it was, I hadn't yet seen the little garden which was her domain in the convent garden as a whole. As one does at that stage in the evening, we thought it would be a good idea to get some fresh air and get me some plants at the same time. That this would have been more sensible (and certainly easier) in daylight didn't really occur to us and so, at around midnight, off we blundered into the garden giggling and nudging each other and trying not to wake the rest of the convent.

As we carefully picked our way along the paths with the aid of V's torch, we collected Geraniums (including a very old French variety – deep red velvety flowers and nothing of the blowsy look of the modern types), cacti, herbs, succulents, grasses, primroses, and all manner of other stuff. By this time, we had managed to fill several bags and even I was beginning to wonder how on earth I could attach these to my bike as well as myself in order to ride home. Having mentioned this to V, she agreed this could be a problem (or at least, I thought she agreed) but she suddenly veered off the path and through a little doorway into what I took to be a cellar of some sort. With the light on, I could see it was a combination of potting shed, shrine and a place to over-winter the more tender plants. The walls were covered with all sorts of items of a religious nature including a variety of Mother and Child statuettes and the benches covered with a number of plants along with the usual gardener's paraphernalia. I think this was V's private little place. Despite something in her distant past (hinted at but I never discovered exactly what) and happily falling in with bad company such as us, she was a very religious woman and this little cellar in this little village was testament to that fact ... However, she is also realistic and having long since noted and accepted our obvious lack of religious fervour, she led me into the far corner to see the array of over-wintering Cymbidium orchids. She knew from being in my greenhouse that I already had a small collection of these orchids and was determined that I should now choose a different colour to those I already had. All were neatly labelled though not in flower yet and I chose a chestnut-coloured one (which I promptly christened Veronique in her honour). After a couple more forays, we finally made it back to the house and, completely exhausted, had a nightcap.

Whilst we were sitting contemplating the number of bags we now had and the inescapable fact that I could not possibly cycle home with all these plants – in fact, by this time, could not possibly cycle home at all – Sister M glided in, took in the sorry spectacle of one nun and one other, both pretty dishevelled and surrounded by the detritus of our night's work and immediately said 'I'll get the car out and we will take P home'. V and I dutifully hung our heads and agreed this would be an excellent idea. So into the little Citroen went my bike, the numerous bags, Vand me and lastly S. Marie who never scolded or batted an eyelid the whole time. Thereby ended another good evening!

Sister M. impresses me greatly – I have the feeling that V is a little wayward (despite being in her 50's) and very impulsive but M seems to have decided that we are good for her – or at least aren't totally bad for her – and seems happy to go along with this rather odd relationship.

I'll let you know later how the new plants get on!

Floriers, end October 1992

Dear Pand,

Thought I'd better start some sort of letter as I keep telling you to write but have done bugger all about it myself!

To get the usual British conversational tactics over to begin with – the weather has been appalling – so much rain I can't believe the world supply won't run out very soon. With our luck though, France has its own personal heavenly reservoir and it will just carry on raining for ever and ever!

I think we have given up the idea of buying a larger house over here – from what we have looked at so far, the prices seem high and given the rapidly worsening exchange rate, I think we'd be asking for trouble.

(yes ok – I can hear you mumbling something along the lines of 'why change the habits of a lifetime' but this is the new me – no more mistakes on the housing front) However, we have persuaded a builder to come round on Saturday to give us an estimate for building on to here. What we were thinking of doing was having an outside room built on to the East end (which we could later glaze in) incorporating a storeroom in which we can site the freezer, washing machine, garden tools, etc. and still have an area almost the size of the original ground floor to make into a sitting area or whatever. Depends what the cost is and how simple it would be to obtain planning permission. Need to butter up the Mayor! The other alternative is to think about buying again in England as we still have all our furniture (and most of our other belongings) in storage at Plymouth.

Unfortunately, in the process of looking at various properties here, we have become embroiled with a manic estate agent who keeps phoning up every 5 minutes to find out if we have been to look at the properties we were given. This isn't always as simple as it sounds – the property details here are always sketchy and the direction to find them sketchier still. I just discovered this evening that we spent an extremely entertaining afternoon looking around a property that wasn't even for sale! I felt a bit of a prat actually but managed to brazen it out in the end. Quite honestly, the house that wasn't for sale looked a much better bet *and* I picked two huge quince and some figs from there as well – much better than house hunting in England Andy! I think I could settle to a career of professional house hunter throughout Europe!

One place we went to look at was just a few miles up the road at Limogne. We were a little surprised that we were given the key to actually get into the house as normally we either just look around the outside or the agent accompanies us. This place was absolutely amazing – I mean, it was just a total junk yard and the outside wasn't much better. It was a big place although you had to shimmy along the walls as every room was full of rubbish and you would have need crampons and ropes to actually see the full extent of each room. When I mentioned the state of it to the agent, she said 'Oh yes, they had a robbery there recently and I forgot to tell you'. I asked her if it was the norm for French robbers to actually leave stuff at the scene of the crime rather than steal stuff – even 2 old cars jacked up on blocks in the yard. I've come to the conclusion that Estate Agents here have no more of a sense of humour than do those in the UK – either that or my particular brand of Estate Agent jokes aren't as funny as I had originally thought!

We've been quite busy here – have now knocked out the brick hearth and moved the woodburner into the corner – that gives us more wall space and we have just been to buy some pine planks to make a run of cupboards and shelves along that end wall.

Right at this moment, I'm sitting here waiting for the Francis Durbridge 'Paul Temple' serial to start on Radio 4 but I seem to have boobed somewhere as I've had it on for 2 hours and the next programme is Norman Lamont at the Mansion House which cannot, in the wildest terms, be considered as entertainment (tho the way he blethers on, it could well be a serial). Either I've missed it altogether or I've got the wrong night. I'll have to come and stay with you soon even if only to get some more books!

On a more personal note, I've had the most appalling cold/flu for the last 10 days. It's ages since I've had a cold and certainly years since I've had such a bad one (perhaps the plant hunt had something to do with it?). Must have got through about half a dozen boxes of tissues and felt really rough and depressed. This evening must be the first time I've been able to use my hands for more than 30 seconds without having to break off and wipe my nose. Still getting bitten regularly. However, the constant munching of anti-histamine tablets does seem to have eased the irritation somewhat.

No signs of the hedgehogs at all but plenty of other wildlife. Having installed 2 rather smart exterior lamps on the house wall, we are now the proud owners of some largish bats which rush round quite busily most evenings. They are larger than the ones we had in Cornwall but so quick I can't see enough of them to identify their make. The Toads still come indoors in the evenings when it is wet and clamour to be let out in the morning. Lots of Praying Mantis and I keep having to rescue them from logs and branches to be cut and putting them elsewhere. There are white ones and green ones of varying sizes (and temperaments) and all are re-arranged very artistically on safer perches. The Beetles are getting a little bit shorter now (well, I suppose the correct term would be 'scarcer' as opposed to 'shorter'- I don't suppose they shrink at the onset of winter as such …). Still plenty of the creatures which look like huge crickets but with long pointed tails – striped either green or brown, quite large and very attractive but unable to find them in any of my books. The house crickets (all now called Skippy for ease of reference) abound and are becoming almost like pets – 'Oops, mind the dog (Skippy)' etc. The local wren has been scurrying about under the cars in the drive; the robin has been around and both blackbirds (presumably from the 2 pairs which nested in the garden last year) along with the usual Jays, Blue and Long tail tits and what sounded like a Screech owl the other evening. Butterflies are in short supply now – the last ones were about a week ago when we spotted both the small blue and the large brown. Plenty of magpies, finches and buzzards about and I have twice seen the flock of Cranes passing over. Also, at Bach (about 5 or 6 miles away) we discovered a large pen of pheasants – next to a Restaurant – specialising in pheasant dishes do you think? The Dragonfly – the huge green and brown job – has, I think, been driven into hiding by the rain as we haven't seen him around for a week or more.

Not many flowers out – the odd periwinkle, cornflower type, but the bright red berries of the Cuckoo Pints stand out in the gloom under the trees. The figs are just going over and there are a few elderberries left. Round about there are plenty of sloes and hips. More trees are now beginning to turn and the colours are wonderful – in some areas just absolute sheets of orange, red and yellow – really quite breathtaking.

Do hope you can read this – crouching on the settee with a couple of hot water bottles does not make for legible handwriting but it's far too complex to get the computer and printer down and set up at the kitchen table. With any luck, the next letter will be printed.

Haven't seen many people to talk to lately (V and M have taken Jeanne to Lourdes with the hope of divine intervention improving Jeanne's health) and in fact haven't felt particularly sociable anyway. The friendly guy – the red car from last visit – now has a white car which confused us somewhat and it was only yesterday that we realised it was him and he realised we also had a different car and that it was us rather than some other weird people. So now we are back to energetic waving and 'Bonjouring' twice a day. Apart from the odd walker, all is quiet. Morgan has renewed his acquaintance with the more intrepid souls who pass along the track and has made a few new friends. He whistles, they whistle back and do the French equivalent of 'Oh look, there's a parrot' and Morgan mutters 'Oh look, there's a frog'. This comment is probably due to this very wet weather and therefore E and I constantly saying 'Oh look, there's a frog' within Morgan's hearing. On the other hand, it could be simply that Political Correctness does not figure greatly in Morg's brain!

We went out to the Garden Centre at Albias yesterday but it was a bit disappointing – not half as much stuff as I had hoped for although we did pinpoint a couple of different palms to put down with Pamela in her little clearing. We actually came out of there with *nothing* – not even a small Bonsai – absolutely *nothing*, which just goes to show how ill I was still feeling and what a bad mood E was in!

This afternoon, in our habitual role of spending money like people with no arms, we bought a Cultivator. As we'd been on about it for 12 months or more, it seemed like a good idea – i.e. buy it now and tailor a possible house purchase in England accordingly. Quite honestly though, digging by hand here is a bit of a joke and we will lose some of the plants if we don't get them in soon. Anyway, the cultivator is quite sweet – has a Hare picture for going fast and a Tortoise picture for going slow – just *had* to have it!!

Talking about buying stuff – I haven't yet bought the bottle of Gin and the Sloes are patiently waiting to be picked. That place we saw earlier (the 'not for sale' one) – its track was literally covered in sloes – millions of them and would have needed 10 bottles of Gin at least. I forgot to mention that it also had an enormous old Walnut tree in the courtyard which further endeared the whole property to me. Shame it was the wrong house!

Coming back from Cahors this afternoon, we noticed a Fungi for Sale stall at the side of the road – first I've noticed but a lot of traffic and too late to stop. Must keep an eye out, especially on the smaller roads and see if any more appear.

Am waiting for a decent dry day to take photos of Curry and Sudie to send to Bernard in Narbonne. He is hoping for an arranged marriage between his male and Sudie. On mentioning this possibility to her, she just said 'fat chance' and ambled off. I'm not sure how that translates precisely into French but at any rate, I suppose I will attempt to be somewhat more diplomatic!

That's it for now.

Floriers, November 1992

Dear Pand,

Melanie the estate agent from Taunton phoned the other evening – the woman must be mad as she keeps giving us details of places which are far too expensive. Like most agents I think she just likes the sound of her own voice – they never actually appear to *listen* (or if they do, the seem incapable of retaining the information you give them for longer than 5 minutes!)

The new run of cupboards and the bookshelves downstairs are now complete and give us much more space in which to hide things away. Oddly enough, the plants have already found their way onto the shelves and you can hear them (the Xmas cactus is the biggest culprit) and the books bickering away all night about who needs the most room! The white Passion flower 'Constance Elliot' seems to have thrived on the ill-treatment it has suffered to come over here and is flowering well – the flowers are somewhat smaller than the common but a rather refined creamy white colour and nicely scented. The purple PF has had one or two flowers open and the red PF has several buds. The Jatropha, despite losing all its leaves in transit has a huge flower spike and several seed pods forming. Obviously bringing it back has made it feel much better! I bought a new Banana plant today (only 49 francs), a different variety than my others but appears to be the same type I have seen planted out in gardens here. If it survives here, it should do ok in SW England. The largest Mexican Hat has a flower spike on – I don't recall them flowering before, just producing half a ton of babies! Flowers aren't open yet but I'll try and get a photo when they do.

The weather continues much the same here as before – apart from 3 sunny days the other week, it's the same old leaden sky with the accompanying downpour of rain. The ground is now so sodden that it is impossible to even attempt any garden work and I despair of ever getting half the plants in the ground. It's difficult to actually 'design' any planting schemes here – it's restricted to what plants you can get in between huge boulders. Anyway, the old 'small at the front, tall at the back' is a bit old hat now – my scheme is designed round what size holes I can dig where! I have managed to get a few more ears of cacti from the cactus house up the track – they're doing well against the front wall. Several of the orchids are showing signs of life but have had to liberate some into pots. Our paths are becoming more and more like muddy streams and the orchids are in danger of being bogged down and driven back into the ground. I've re-planted some into safer areas.

Serge and Angelique have another dog – same make as Coquer (an Argentinian something or other) and, by the looks of it, a similar handful! Went round to Pascal's farm the other day to ask about wood for the stove – impressed by the fact that they not only remembered us but also asked after the parrots and tortoises. Mind you, to the average French farmer a number of torts and parrots holidaying in the locality is eccentric enough to stick in the mind perhaps? Pascal was saying that Bruno (the German guy with the 50 speed Japanese cycle) doesn't speak very good French which cheered me up no end as Bruno is constantly bragging about how fluent he is. The woman in the Bread shop in Floriers has explained how to pronounce Stuyvesant correctly (Stweevesan) which I thought was very helpful of her as of vital importance. Reminded me of the pet shop in Toulouse when trying to buy Millet sprays for Morgan. After half an hour, the woman suddenly smacked her forehead and said ' Oh, you mean Meeyay'. I forbore to remark that that was *exactly* what I'd been saying. There's only so many ways you *can* pronounce Millet after all – I think she was taking the piss! Anyway, I digress … I mentioned to Pascal's sister that Morgan was really very keen on cows and was used to them and whenever they bought them up our way, he whistled and shouted to them. She was quite apologetic and explained that they had been keeping them nearer the farm because of the weather and the state of the ground. I had the impression that she felt guilty about Morgan missing his 'cow fix' and was on the point of offering to herd them up and down the track a few times just for Morg's benefit! I think there is a limit to neighbourly acts even here though. The people who own the holiday bungalow between us and Angelique arrived last Saturday afternoon but I guess they have been defeated by the weather as I haven't seen them out at all. Last year they often strolled up the track. On milder days, Morgan is still entertaining the more intrepid hikers from his spot under the oak tree. One couple in particular last weekend whistled and warbled their way past up the track and a few hours later, back down again – obviously old hands as they started whistling before Morgan did!

Enough for now Pand,

Speak soon

Floriers, January 1993

Here at last is the legible letter of 93 – just as boring as the illegible letters of 92 but at least this time you will know *exactly* what it is that's boring you! Well, that's a couple of lines done anyway!

Anyway, more to the point, did I tell you about the Stripeless Tree Frog – I might have mentioned him in my card. He has been named Oscar and is appearing regularly for a sunbathe at the base of the tree next to Morgan's. He's jolly sweet and now recognises us by nodding his head when we approach and say 'Hello Oscar'. (He's really bright you know!) To be honest, he's about the only exciting thing around at the moment – the Praying Mantis and the lizards all appear to have done a complete bunk for the winter despite the good weather (yes – sun and warmth!) we have been having recently. Even the large dragonfly which used to come indoors and sit on the sofa seems to have given up the ghost. We still have the odd butterfly, bees and other flying, crawling, creeping insects. Indoors now we are left only with the odd leaf beetle and the ubiquitous house crickets (as well as Morgan of course, who now shrieks 'Bonjour' every morning.)

How did your Christmas go with Heth and Kevin – I have a nasty suspicion that I sent you the white champagne and it should have been the pink which is drier and better. Hope it was bearable anyway or if not, that you drunk it by yourself in the dark at home. Went to the south coast for Xmas day – bit of a mistake really. Super weather when we left – blue sky, bright sun etc but when we got south of Toulouse, it clouded over. We were planning to go to Perpignan but once we got to Narbonne, it looked less grey to the left (looking from your vantage point) than it did to the right so we went to Beziers and Valras instead. There was a fair at Beziers and lots of rather cold looking sea at Valras. Valras Plage on Xmas Day was a bit like Bournemouth in the winter (possibly the summer too for all I know). Maybe a bit unfair – there were Bars open and maybe more people about. The sea was rough but picked some shells up (ready to be enshrined as Came from Med on Xmas Day 1992). Actually, thinking back, all the Plages tend to be the same – just lots of holiday villas and apartments on a stretch of sand (tho Valras *did* have a marina) and therefore pretty boring!

The Pyrenees looked pretty good in the distance and stacks of cars heading that way with skis and stuff. Also lots of the shops were open here on Xmas day so it was really quite good. Slightly miffing was that when we got back home, we discovered that the weather had been hot and sunny all day – the torts were all slumped fatly over empty plates and only vaguely raised their heads to say 'Have a nice day then?' Could have smacked them!

It's fairly quiet around here in the winter – only our usual neighbours passing by, tho we did have a new person recently. A middle-aged guy who first came past pushing a squeaky wheelbarrow containing chainsaw and 5 gallon fuel drum … At some point in the forest not too far from us, he spent about 10 minutes getting his chainsaw going and then shortly after, pottered back past with a few bits of wood in the barrow (squeak, squeak, squeak). Came back the next day, exactly the same scenario (squeak, squeak, squeak … Rrrrrrrr … Rrrrrrrrrr … Rrrrrrrr … can't do a chainsaw starting – or not, as the case may be) with, if possible, even less wood in the barrow. Either he has a very, very tiny fireplace and doesn't feel the cold much or it is a plot to check up on Les Anglais avec

Torts and Parrots! Instead of just calling 'Bonjour Monsieur' which is all I'd managed on the first 2 occasions, on the third day, I'd planned to call out 'Bonjour M. Squeaky Wheelbarrow' (in French of course – I'd taken the trouble to look up Squeaky and Wheelbarrow after the second day) but not sure whether he is the sort of guy with a sense of humour. Also, of course, can never be sure if bad pronunciation (or accidentally slipping a page in the Dictionary) may turn my cheery greeting into some sort of dreadful insult which I will live to regret! Anyway, problem solved – never seen him again so that's ok!

We have French TV now – the last TV we bought was in 85 and the technical advances are amazing! This one is a German model – very good, but … it took us the best part of a day to tune it to French channels. Apart from getting the aerial right (you know the old scenario – yep, just hold it like that {300 foot above the chimney} and the picture is fine down here – how is it with you??). The actual tuning is all done on the remote control thingy (a novel concept!). Not a concept we are exactly au fait with! By the time I'd read out the instructions (French, German or Italian – take your pick) and we had translated them to the appropriate buttons (and then had to go thru it another 4 times to lock each channel), we were so bloody exhausted, we didn't switch it on for a week after that! However, having got over the initial challenge of getting a picture and sound at the same time and which vaguely matched, it now provides endless amusement as we try and guess what the news is when I am about 3 sentences behind with the translation – come back Anna Ford – we love you! Even the weather symbols aren't quite the same (tho admittedly it would take a moron NOT to be able to figure fluffy clouds and stuff out in any language) but am not too worried about that. If it rains, it rains – if it's sunny and warm, great!

Mr. Lory's new aviary is wonderful – in fact, we are all thinking of moving in there. It's got everything – shelter from wind and rain, plenty of seating, a little garden, somewhere to put your food, spacious bathing facilities and a sun (safety) porch! Know anyone who wants to buy a small stone house with new cupboards and guest facilities in the grounds?

Serge and Angelique have a second Argentinian Something dog and I found out today they are going to run holiday kennels too. We noticed they had been doing some building at the back of the forge so when they came past with the dogs, I decided to be like a native French person (ie blatantly nosey) and asked them if they were making little houses for the dogs. That's when I learned that they were starting in the 'dog vacation' business. Also, that they (well, not they personally!) will be expecting puppies next year from Coquer and the new dog (Gwappo?). They have 8 kennels for holiday dogs – apparently there are very few kennels in this region – at Limogne (about 20 kms) but not much else. Serge says there are 7 million dogs in France and lots get abandoned. I think quite apart from liking dogs they also need another money source as they say work is very poor – as Painter and Sculptor I don't know whether they work mostly from commission or what but obviously, the recession is biting them too.

M. Bruno (the Germ) poked off back to Germany in October/November and we don't know when he comes back. He has satellite TV now we notice, for all his GREEN outlook. Actually, is satellite GREEN or NON GREEN? Better hadn't say anything I suppose, just in case! Don't know what happens to his chickens – maybe Pascal looks after them.

6th Jan. Right, having discovered the population of France and with Serge's 'dog' figures, I estimate that there are (is, in fact) one dog to every 8 people here. Can't for the life of me remember what the UK dog population is – I know there are roughly 57 million people but not so sure about the dogs. S and A's kennels are up to roof level now (kennel roof as opposed to house roof of course!) so would think they'll be doing visitors by early summer. Re the dog-person ratio, thought I'd do *ducks* next – there are stacks of them about and I'm wondering if I could sell the info to some authoritative body within the EC. There's bound to be a *duck* committee – there's one for everything else after all!

Regarding 'Les Animaux Sauvage qui nibble/rub the tree bark in the garden' …Emile was *really* impressed when we pratted around in the main street pretending to be (as it turns out!) 1) Roe deer adult, 2) Roe deer fawn, 3) and 4) as 1) and 2) but Goat, or lastly 5) a wild White Haricot bean. I also had a little panic when I got home as I did just wonder if I had inadvertently said I *wanted* a wild deer/goat/white haricot bean to keep down the grass! Christ, I sincerely hope not – we've got enough problems trying to keep this lot! Next week, I'm going to look in the Garden Centre and see if they have tree guards – I think they do them for rabbits and probably deer but I'm not at all convinced they do them for Haricot beans. They'd need to be pretty short wouldn't they? This must almost rank with The Woman in Summer (which you may not have heard about) and several other embarrassing episodes.

You will be pleased to know that as well as all the other plants, we now have 3 more – Grapefruit, Lemon and Clementine. Look jolly healthy so we should have LOADSA fruit this year! Have planted the French fig here – after its holiday in England last year, it begged to be allowed to stay here as it said it was sick and tired of going on the ferry. Honestly, you just can't please some figs, can you? The Mexican Hat has finally flowered – I did take a photo but just to whet your appetite ... really pretty in a delicate and refined manner (you could have to look REFINED up as it hasn't figured largely in our letters so far!). Very pale rose colour in large bunches of little trumpets. In fact, I suppose the colour would resemble a pale chocolate rose, if there is such a thing. I've no idea whether they will set seed – seems a bit superfluous really when you consider how they produce and shed babies everywhere. I've heard of a back up system but that would be ridiculous! The Jatropha (obviously conducting an affair with the right insect!) has produced 3 enormous seed pods. These will no doubt just reach the prescribed ripening stage approximately 2 hours after they have dropped off and got lost in the 'cramming into bag ready for the LAST trip – promise!' saga due to take place when various other events come together! Passion flower 'Constance Elliot' (she who thrives on being cut back and stuffed into a Tesco carrier bag) has practically finished flowering. One of the ordinary ones which I (foolishly) planted in the greenhouse has done absolutely bugger all but this could be due to having a Sudie sitting on top of it for several hours a day. Still, at least it won't need a very big bag will it?

The Long Tail Tit flock have returned with a vengeance – there are probably about 25 or so and they seem to turn up in the trees near the house mid/late afternoons. They dash about like loonies but as they sound (and look) nice, I'm prepared to forgive them. Had a Buzzard pretending to be a gate post the other day – it almost flew up my nose when I went to open the gates for the Postman (another little lecture about unneccessary lines on the address). Don't know who was more surprised – Buzzard, me or the Postman! Got 2 wrens now – much like in England, we always had one all year round and then at the beginning of the season, its mate turns up. Both very friendly and will happily potter about even when we are only a matter of feet away.

Ed's just reported that Morgan has said 'Bonjour' again – seems a bit mean to point out that it is now 'soir' when he is obviously trying so hard!

Went tracking the Barn Owls the other night – saw one flash across the road to where another was calling. Only went as far as Bruno's. Looks like he is back now so I suppose we will have to prepare ourselves for the usual homilies – you know the sort of thing as you met him last year when he asked us to do that translation for him.

Believe it or not, I'm *still* trying to get the plants in that we brought over. As well as not being fit weather to plant anything for the first 6 or 7 weeks, the ground is so full of boulders, life really is impossible. If all the boulders were Truffles, Pand, I'd be *so rich* it almost doesn't bear thinking about (note the use of the word 'almost' – I actually think about it quite a lot, particularly when straining to get said boulder/truffle out of a 3 foot hole in the ground!).

Many of the different species of Orchids are showing thru now except, perversely, the Early Purple which should be the first to flower. In the garden, we have I think 8 different types – the 2 we are missing are the Fly orchid and the Spider orchid, both of which I have seen in flower about 2 kms along the top track. This track (which starts only a few hundred metres from our own track) is actually part of a long distance walk which stretches from Bach (east of us) to Cahors and is part of a network of tracks thru the forest. The orchids and other wild flowers are quite prolific throughout the forest – the mini habitats just within a few kms range from dry heath to shady undergrowth. April, May and June are really good months here for seeing the flowers – orchids, wild hyacinths and gladiolus, cowslips, violets, aquilegias and tons more. Away from the forest, fields of wild poppies and loads of other stuff! It really is one of the best times to be here. There's plenty of Golden Orioles in the garden too (they also sound lovely) and our Woodpeckers (both seen and heard). Others include Wren who spends time by the log pile down in the bottom corner of the garden and also by the 'now' log pile next to the house. Then there are Blue, Great, Coal and Long Tail tits, Barn Owls, Buzzards, Kestrels, Chaffinches, a large dark hawk as yet unidentified, resident Blackbirds, Thrushes, Finches of all types plus several others who are just odd sounds in the bushes (really annoying little jobs) and refuse to show themselves.

We have only recently lost our 'house guests' – small to medium toads and frogs who used to come into the house in the evenings, spend a cushy night by the stove and be let out first thing in the morning. Not much different from letting the cat out I suppose! Oh … a biggish sort of spider has just dropped on to the printer – seems keen to know what I am writing. Bit silly really because unless he learned English at school, he won't understand a word! Oops, he's just skittered off anyway and is now crouching on the paper stack with a rather baleful gleam in his eye (eyes?). Oddly enough, we have very few spiders indoors though plenty of different ones outside but, in fact so far, see less spiders here than I did in England. One in particular is intriguing – a crab spider of sorts (they don't always appreciate the time it takes for me to leaf thru my 'Spiders of Europe' Field Guide) but this one changes colour according to the plant I put him on. Well, I find him intriguing tho I have the feeling lately he is getting fairly cheesed off about being moved from plant to plant and having to change colour each time! The other clever job is the Tunnel spider (also bored with my efforts at tempting him out) but sadly no Trap Door spiders – maybe a little way out for them? The other major type is the large Hunting Spider.

I've just finished my letter to Bernard (in French this time) – one and a half pages so can't be bad. Am now expecting him to write back saying 'can we correspond in English please – I can understand it better'. Poor Bernard – he was quite happy with his Spurred tortoise until I told him what Sudie weighed and then sent him her weight chart for the last 2 years. Now he is worried that his is badly kept. Mind you, he was very sweet and did a weight/length graph of Sudie on his computer and sent it to me just before Xmas. He also quite shocked me by saying 'Did I tell you about the other smaller Spurred tortoise I have?' – How do you actually forget one of these. Apparently he got it from someone who was keeping it in a tiny vivarium in a flat in the middle of Montpellier.

Ant and the other 4 babies are out of hibernation now – Ant is a bit miserable, One eye isn't eating much but Hebe is tucking in like a true gourmand. With not much food to pick for them, it's a bit difficult – not as mild in the winter here as the SW UK – so quite a trial to feed at times despite my frantic efforts at growing dandelion, clover, plantain, grass etc for them over the last 2 years – an ancient oak forest doesn't really lend itself to becoming a brilliant veg/tort garden overnight. Still, you try telling them that and all you get are sulky faces and shrugged shoulders (do tortoises *have* shoulders to shrug as such I wonder?)

Bit of celebrity news here – the guys from Pickfords who brought over the big greenhouse and a few other odds and ends were quite taken by the torts – one of them had a video camera and filmed Sudie demolishing a bush in the garden. Curry, being an old hand at the publicity stuff just sat there – presumably the Pickfords guy didn't offer the going rate – no dosh, no action!

Another 2 or 3 months and we will be getting into the casual walker/ serious hiker syndrome. If they are doing The Forest Trail they all come past our gate, tho I suspect the old timers only come up here for the pleasure of whistling at and talking to Morgan. He has a permanent table fixed to a big oak tree just a few yards down from the house and hence about 12 metres from the gate. He entertains all passers by with general whistling, shouting, etc and, for the favoured few, at least one continuous minute of opera. Some are used to it and shout, whistle or sing in reply according to their abilities – others are rather taken aback and only get into the swing of things on the return trip.

A quick update – Oscar Tree has gone into true hibernation (either that or he is so high up in the tree as to be invisible) but the bees and butterflies are coming out some days as the weather is nice – blue sky and lots of sun – up to 61 F today.

We are in the process of building a shed at the side of the house – really to house the freezer (currently residing in half a plastic greenhouse) and eventually washing machine plus garden tools etc.

Well Pand, hope to get your letter soon – meanwhile back to the plants and the carrier bags.

Floriers, January 1993

Dear Pand,

As promised, this is the Truffle Letter!

I'd already told you that Lalbenque (our nearest town) is an important centre for the Truffe Noir de Quercy. The collection and sale begins in either late December or January and continues until March if the season has been good. The Lalbenque market is held every week on a Tuesday and takes up the whole of the main street through town. The start – at 2.30 pm – is signalled by the ringing of a bell and the lowering of a red flag. The official scales are sited outside the Town Hall and are there for anyone to use.

At the first market we went to, there were around 40 stalls – as far as I could see, those selling the smallest truffles were at the Post Office end of the street working up to the larger ones at the Patisserie end. For the first 10 minutes or so, I rushed from one end of the street to the other trying to see what people were doing – some were just going along the street noting, presumably, the prices being quoted. I overheard one guy suggesting a price to a little old man who promptly said something rude and walked off. Others pottered back and forth comparing prices and stopping every so often to bargain. The serious buyers actually picked up the truffles – squeezed them, smelt them and generally discussed their attributes – some were scathing in their remarks – perhaps in the hope of driving the price down?

The street was heaving with people and so the simplest thing seemed to be to pick a likely looking buyer and follow them in order to find out exactly what happens. I chose my prey, a well-dressed and rather elegant looking woman, and followed her from one stall to another. At the fifth stall, she purchased 4 large truffles and I saw her hand over a bundle of notes but couldn't get close enough (at least without the prospect of being arrested) to see exactly the amount which changed hands. I then dutifully followed her to the scales but due to the enormous crush of people, I couldn't see what her truffles weighed. The market was as much a social occasion as a business one – always someone stopped for a prolonged chat directly in front of me and by the time I had politely (more or less!) negotiated my way through, the action was over and done with!

The sellers ranged from typical country people to sophisticated city types – one woman in a fur coat with 6 inch long fingernails (must have been a frontsperson with hands like that – couldn't see her collecting truffles herself). I decided that following people wasn't really getting me very far so made my way to a stall at the Small Truffle end and engaged the seller in conversation. Well, not so much conversation as a rather abrupt 'How much for one truffle please?'. She quickly ascertained my creditworthiness and said she wouldn't contemplate selling a single one – the whole basketful or nothing. This put me in a bit of a quandary – the said basket containing maybe a dozen rather tatty looking truffles. I didn't really want to buy any – only had 50 francs and had yet to buy cigarettes. However, as I really wanted to know the price I confessed and admitted I was a simple tourist (is there any other kind?) and just wanted to know about the truffle market. She then said something which I couldn't quite follow (probably just as well) and then her friend took pity on me and attempted to interpret (her English was on a par with my French so slow going). As I fumbled in my bag in the vain hope of finding a pen so I could get her to write the price down for me I heard her say something which sounded suspiciously like, 'God preserve us from idiots'. I chose to smile nicely and ignore this comment. Meanwhile, the friend was also searching for a pen but she didn't have one either and the seller is becoming agitated and wants me out of the way so that she can encourage serious customers. Persistent to the last, I ignore the frown and ask her if she collected the truffles herself. 'Yes' she says and so I say 'Whereabouts did you find them and did you use a pig?' 'No – a dog – he finds them'. The friend then takes over to confirm that the truffles were found in the forest (slow I may be but I *had* already figured that out – the exact location was what I was after) but was quick to point out 'not any old forest but a special forest'. Just as I was trying to elicit exactly which special forest this would be and did she know of an out of work Truffle dog which I could possibly acquire for a song, the stallholder said to her 'No, this is too complicated and she (meaning me, the foreign idiot) will not understand'. I finally had to accept that I had outstayed my welcome (such as it was in the first place) and my 'Merci, Madame' was accepted with a strained smile and a little handwave. I probably just imagined that 2 of her fingers appeared more prominent than the others!

All was finished by 3.30 pm and the stalls mostly sold out. We were impressed by the number of people attending the market and the amount of buyers from other regions. We had set off for Lalbenque thinking it would be no big deal – we were suitably shocked when we found it difficult to park!

The second market seemed even busier – cars everywhere throughout the village and buyers from as far afield as Finland, Luxembourg and the UK and the French buyers from Bordeaux to Provence and the eastern regions as well as Loire and Paris. One guy in particular caught my eye – huge cigar clamped between his teeth (reminiscent of photos of Churchill) but no tie and his suit was not really snappy – a poor Parisienne or an upmarket local? If possible, there seemed to be even more stalls and a basket maker (sitting by the town hall industriously working away) – an elderly guy but dextrous fingers for sure. He was whipping the canes in and out like no ones business – I was quite entranced! More people about too, although maybe just 'look sees' as plenty had cameras.

By 3 pm or so, most sellers appeared to be wrapping what remained of their goods and taking them away and there were some men going along the trestle tables giving stall holders tickets after writing numbers on them (one I saw was 1100) – best price offered, weight sold? Who knows? The best truffles go within minutes of the flag dropping – the foreign buyers and the big restaurateurs are in there like the proverbial ferret up a drainpipe. The first 40 minutes is the biz – after that, it's just a show. Strangely enough, this weeks market had 2 Gendarmes present – crowd control maybe?

The truffle hunter we came across yesterday must have been collecting for today's market. That was the first time we had seen someone with a pig on a leash   many now use dogs although the postcards and publicity blurbs always show pigs. More 'Aahh' factor I suppose. In fact, we had seen him last week when we went to the PO – he chatting in the post office whilst large pig sitting in the back of his van – presumably the prize Truffle hunting pig come to see where the fruits of his labour were to be sold.

At least I have managed to check out the Truffle scales – they go up to a maximum of 30 kilos – these could be useful! Am thinking of wrapping Sudie in a tea towel (the baskets of Truffles on the stalls are always covered with a tea towel but can I find one big enough?) and popping her on the Truffle scales. She is hovering on the 10 kilo mark (the maximum for our current scales) and I can't keep buying ever larger sets of scales for her. The possible downside is that we would be mugged before we reached the car – 10 plus kilos of truffles (tho a bit of a shock for any would-be mugger). E, being a bit more realistic, says maybe we should just guess her weight from now on. Boring but he may have a point!

I can't remember whether I told you about our other Truffle experience the first year. We really thought we were on to a good thing – invited to a neighbours house for a 'special evening'. Get there, watch a slide show – photos another neighbour took of 'our village in winter', test the new wine (very interesting) but all the while waiting for the big Event. At last, out comes an object wrapped securely in a white cloth – unwrapped with due reverence (and suitable 'oohs' and 'Aahs' from us the audience) and there it is in all its glory – a Truffe Noir no less. E and I thought we would at least be partaking in a Truffe Omelette (a speciality of this region) and after all present had fingered and wondered at this Truffle, we assumed it would head towards the stove. However, much to our chagrin, it was re-wrapped carefully in its cloth and then whisked away by Madame. A family heirloom or something. What a disappointment, particularly as we were living right in the middle of the oak forest and during the season, one could hardly move for Truffle hunters and their pigs or dogs. Later on in the evening, we learnt that this was the first Truffle our neighbour had found on his own property and therefore it was simply brought out and admired (but *not* eaten) every year. Needless to say, we became enthusiastic members of this rather odd Truffle Admiration Society (admittedly in the sly – if not forlorn – hope that we would, at some point, actually get to eat the wretched thing). However, after a couple of years of hopes being raised and sadly dashed, I've come to admire this particular Truffle. It's got life down to a fine art and no mistake – carefully carried into the room (you can almost *hear* the fanfare!), out of the cloth, quick bow round the assembled gawpers and back into the cloth until next year. And our neighbours think we're mad keeping tortoises! I rest my case!

So, there you go – all you ever wanted to know about Truffles and a bit more besides.

Floriers, February 1993

Dear Pand,

This is the home made version of a French birthday card – the shop bought are about on a par with the anniversary card we got from Bub – say no more! I think it is probably going to be a bit late (but not half as late as your present).

Birds more cheerful now – rushing around and getting ready to nest. Mrs. Robin has now arrived and both wrens have been around for a while. Mr. W is visible all year and adores fresh logs to pick over. We collected a few pieces from over the track yesterday, took them down to the log pile and within about 5 seconds, Wren turned up to check them over for things to eat. Lazy little beggar – it would have only taken him a couple of minutes to fly over the other side of the track and sort through them there! When we bring logs up to the house, he comes to investigate and seems not in the least worried that we are within just a few feet of him.

More lizards about each day now but only the common/wall lizards – no sign yet of the large green ones. They tend to be in amongst the trees though and rarely go by the walls as the smaller ones do. I'm wondering whether we will have any buzzards nesting nearby this year. They've been flying over the woods a lot more this year. Plenty of Woodpeckers too – the Greater Spotted but also more Green ones this year – in fact, the Greens seem to be checking out the large tree at the top left hand side of our track – have disturbed them there (unintentionally) several times during the last couple of weeks. Oscar Treefrog seems to have disappeared completely – a real pain as the film his photos were on has been ruined and so no actual proof of a Stripeless Tree Frog in December! Have even taken to climbing the surrounding trees just in case he has decided to become a *high* Tree frog rather than a *low* Tree frog but to no avail. No Praying Mantis as yet either (probably I'm being impatient as it is way too early I think!) but several Butterflies up and about during the last 2 weeks. Also Bees – big Bumble bee types and the basic honey bee jobs.

All may not be lost with the little (big now?) hedgehogs – have found some crap along the path from the Palm garden which could possibly be Hedgehog crap? Stayed down there the other evening in the hope of surprising someone on that pathway but it could have been a bit too cold for much activity as it did, in fact, frost that night. Anyway, they certainly weren't Rabbit, Goat or Haricot Bean craps so *I* think they were Hedgehog deposits. Vast numbers of small squeaky creatures busy making tunnels and pathways everywhere – mice and shrews or voles I think. Also small squeaky creatures scuffling about between the outside wall and the ceiling beam over the cooker – mice I think! Probably the very same bunch of mice which ate the duvet cover last year! Still, all wildlife so into the diary they go!

This was only going to be a note to go with the card but seems to have acquired a life of it's own – tho sadly for you, it didn't have quite enough life to go upstairs to use the typewriter! Am writing this at the same time as watching Jacques Cousteau – he's on every Sunday evening on Channel 1 and this week is poking about in the River Danube. It's gone 6 pm so another hour til dark yet. It's been warm today and we had enough spare time to actually sit out the front for an hour or so at midday – made a change as we rarely seem to get time to just sit! Of course, as we were just sitting, we also opened a bottle of wine with our lunch ... advantages and disadvantages!

By the way, we saw a Hare the other day – the first since you and I met that one coming down the track the summer before last. This one crossed over the road in front of us when we were driving into Lalbenque on Friday. He (or she?) promised to jot us down in his (or her) diary as well!

The Mexican Hat plant still has plenty of flowers – and this 2 months since I sent you the photo. I managed to get 6 seeds from the Jatropha – a major achievement as they are so difficult to fertilise. Also a fruit called a KAKI (can't find anything about it) – I bought it in the supermarket about 6 weeks ago intending to open it up in the hopes it may have seeds in and then promptly forgot about it. I discovered it today and lo and behold, it has a 6 inch long sprout on it and is also producing roots as well! Now bagged in compost and in the greenhouse! I did spot a tree in the garden centre at Escale (Cahors) which was called itself a Kaki Tree (no Latin name of course!) but the fruits looked completely different and in fact, the shoot from mine looks similar to a Passion flower complete with tendrils – so, can't be a tree as such. It's all very worrying Pand! The bit of Royal Fern (of which you are guarding the major part, I hope you remember!) does not seem to be doing much. In fact, that's a blatant fib – it's doing absolutely nothing. Indeed, it's beginning to look remarkably like an ex Royal Fern. I suppose it *could* just be kidding?

After a winter in the greenhouse, the scented leaf geraniums are horrendously leggy but I don't want to chop them back yet as want to get a few cuttings from them. These are the ones I promised you as I now have about 8 different types. The Gardenias are disgustingly overgrown – plenty of buds but these are being attacked by someone's caterpillars (which I remove and place on something hopefully edible outside!). Doesn't look like they will flower in the near future anyway. They will have to remain overgrown for a while longer as I want the cuttings material.

Outside, the orchids have spread amazingly in the last 18 months – literally weedlike (although I never thought I would describe Orchids in these terms!). I think much of it has been due to us making more clearings so some that were hidden have come to light. There are also seemingly vast numbers of young ones too so I guess the hidden seedlings now have more light in which to establish themselves. I have potted up some of the smaller ones in the hopes of establishing a little colony in Devon – they should do well there but if not, I can always bring them back again – they will learn to travel like the rest of our belongings I'm sure! I've already heard the greenhouse plants laying bets on which month they will be bagged up and what duty free stuff they are going to buy on the ferry so they are alright! Did I mention that I bought 3 Citrus trees – Grapefruit, Lemon and Clementine – all of which are putting on new growth now and the Lemon is flowering already – great scent! Only 36 francs each so pretty good value. I know they are old enough to fruit because I saw them in the Nursery last year with fruit on them so – fingers crossed!

As I haven't heard to the contrary, we will get your taps this week (will get the Flexi fittings too as they make life so much easier – we first used them at the Farm and ever since) and bring them over in the summer. The shed is now finished – or at least as far as we are going with it – looks not too bad and gives us somewhere to put all our outside stuff (as well as some from indoors too!). Have made a run of fitted cupboards in the bedroom along the window wall which gives us more space for bedding, clothes etc. Also made desk and shelves on the landing for computer/writing, etc. and recently finished T and G'ing the wall between landing and bathroom so solid now (except for the doorway of course!). Although everywhere looks much better, it doesn't really make the house big enough to live in (as such!).

Am enclosing some photos of the Truffle Market at Lalbenque. Last Sunday, we discovered that there was some kind of Truffle Show but unfortunately we were too late and missed it. It was something like a Syndicate Truffle gathering or the like (perhaps like the Exemption Dog Shows in the UK? I still have no idea exactly what an Exemption Dog Show is). Anyway, whatever it was took place on the last Sunday of the month so we'll look out for the last Sunday in this month and see if anything is happening.

Have the animal papers arrived from the DoE yet? Cutting it a bit fine for March I think. I have a feeling we won't get everything together in time

– then again, why break the habit of a lifetime?

Floriers, March 15, 1993

Dear Pand,

A few lines to say that we are carrying on with buying the bungalow despite being gazumped. It means an extra 4 and half K but it'll cost us that running back and forth if we don't find somewhere else soon.

Anyway, it's just about a mile from Hemyock (the Blackdown Hills) and 5 miles from J26 on the M5. As it is only about 12 miles from Taunton (railway station) as opposed to Williton place being 16 miles, there is literally no difference. The rooms are all a decent size – views are over the Culm valley and Ed says it is nice!

The truffle hunting still seems to be going on apace – we have seen two lots of people over the weekend – both had pigs on leads. Also a quick view on local TV of the Truffe Marche at Lalbenque. What we *should* have done of course is to have bought a pig when we came over in September and had it trained by now! The Marche is still on every Tuesday – I think it continues til the end of this month. Shame we haven't got spare cash to invest in some Truffles!

Wildlife continues to perk up – birds are all as busy as anything and sing until 7.30 pm sharp when the Convent bells ring. After that, they all go to bed. The GS woodpecker is still a regular visitor to our garden – in fact he spreads his favours around (or could there be more than 1?) as I was guarding Curry down at the bungalow whilst she fed on their luscious grass last week and heard a drumming – looked up and there was GSW just about 6 foot above my head. It knew of course that as I was on a feeding expedition, I didn't have the camera with me and so we just stared balefully at each other for a few seconds before it flipped its tail in a distinctly rude manner and flew off down the track.

The weather continues to be excellent – strong winds for the last few days but at least no rain (could do with some now for the plants – smack my wrist quickly!). Lots of lizards out sunbathing and also the little grubs/beetles, whatever, which live in tiny burrows everywhere. I still don't know what they are – even laying on the floor and poking the ground round the burrow entrance doesn't elicit much – they are so quick, I still can't see them properly. Anyway, to be honest, they're getting a bit fed up with this game now – here she comes again – if you listen really carefully, you can hear little squeakings and mutterings – if she taps at the burrow, just ignore her. Far more bees about including an enormous Black job which keeps eying up the house walls and peering into all the gaps. Reminiscent of a mad Surveyor – 'Mmm – bit of repointing needed here' and 'Lord ... look at *that!*'. Oscar Tree is obvious by his absence as are the Praying Mantis but there's more beetles, crickets and spiders now.

Have had to start de-bagging all the plants – again – before they expire as the weather turns warmer. Gave a number of the scented leaf geraniums to V but the rest are looking a bit fraught. Most of the other stuff is ok but Pamela Palm is, sadly I think, an ex Pamela as is the big Eucalyptus (one

I did from seed at Bruntingthorpe) which I planted 2 years ago. Just sown some radish (leaves for torts), lettuce, plantain and dandelion and also some Nasturtiums. The Pergola is now at the side of the house in front of the shed bit and has Mr Lory's Russian vine up one post and a honeysuckle up the other. None of the stuff is really tearing away as yet – the trees take a lot but in a few years, it'll look pretty good! The Cornelian cherries are just about over now but they have been flowering for 2 months and should produce a good crop of berries for the tortoises later in the year if we are still here and if not, the birds will feast on them. Everything else is springing, budding and generally doing a 'Hey, it's Spring – Whoopee' sort of thing. Even one of the violets has 2 flowers open!

Well Pand, as I'm about to run out of paper, I won't invent any more fibs to tell you other than that the dog bowls were very well received by Coquer and his mate and we had a guided tour of the new kennels – beds and heaters in every one (I was tempted to ask how much a kennel cost per night – more comfortable than here probably) and even a couple of holiday residents so looking up. Veronique is working towards an exhibition in Paris next year and showed us the draft of the publicity blurb – I think she plans to put a dozen of her paintings in so it's looking good.

See you in the summer maybe?

Devon, 1993

Dear Pand,

Ed came home the other day. Well, not literally (rhetorically I suppose then?). Got a phone call saying 'Guess where I am '. As this was very early a.m., I didn't guess right – in fact, he was calling from Heathrow. Had to come back to the UK for some vital thing or other for the ship (the Captain maybe – that could be fairly vital I suppose) – anyway, straight into East Midlands airport, stayed overnight at Wakefield and back to Bilbao first thing in the morning. A flying visit as they say! Just think, only 2 months ago we were so grateful for this – 2 months regular income but now getting bored with it all!

Just spotted Thrush – as the trees started to leaf, I lost sight of him for a few weeks – could only hear him. Now I see he is right at the top of the tallest tree which must surely be 70 plus feet – he's obviously armed with a megaphone as I can hear him clearly – to the exclusion of everything else I think. The chaffinch is doing a quick accompaniment on the TV aerial (that is, he's sitting on the aerial as opposed to playing it), the blackbird is having a rehearsal on top of Mr. Lory's aviary and the pheasant is shouting from his hideaway in the east bank. All in all, it's really quite peaceful here!

I'll hope that Ed will be around for a while in August so that I can come up for a few days whilst you are off work. It would be so much better if you had a garden (for you as well Pand – I'm not being totally selfish here). I was thinking that we managed quite well at Twickenham with all the tortoises and the 2 parrots (apart from Helen and the accident with the new carpet – a minor detail) but then again, that was pre-Sudie wasn't it? I suspect now that not only would the Hostas be demolished but the containers as well! She digs so much that I am forever picking up bits of pot, metal, glass, etc. which she unearths on a tiresomely regular basis (rather like the farm in Leicester and the ever present binder twine). I just said to her the other day 'Don't eat that bit of pot as it will … '. Too late, it disappeared. I suspect in a month or two (given the slow rate of digestion), she will gradually produce a whole dinner service. I put, for a few seconds, on the greenhouse floor a gravel tray with capillary matting in it (yes, stupidly I bought *green* capillary matting) the other day and she was out of her burrow like greased lightning. We had a bit of a tug of war but I won in the end. Just think, she's not quite 4 yet! Anna should complain! Perhaps she'd like to swap Jack (and, after the matting, the new baby as well) for Sudie. As Sudie doesn't do sponsored slides (yet), that should clinch things from Anna's point of view surely?

E should be on his cruise now – I think the ship sailed at 5 am yesterday and is due to dock at Santander for its painting and general clean up. He's hoping to get the Santander/Plymouth ferry but as that only runs twice a week at the moment, they may not dock in time – especially if they have any problems. It would be easier than flying to Madrid and then on to Heathrow though.

Strangely enough, I had thought about suggesting that you had a few days down here in September if you couldn't come to Floriers with us. I thought to leave my National Trust card and you could have visited some of the places around here – there's quite a few (and most do cream teas!). It's a shame you can't get the time off to come down but maybe if your finances (or ours) improve, you could get a 1 way bus to Cahors again and then come back with us. Anyway, whatever. Will have to set up an automatic watering system for the greenhouse as 3 weeks will be too long to leave the stuff to its own devices. Still, if you and Gaye were to come down half way through so to speak, you could make sure all was well with it. When E gets back, I'll check the dates with him and let you know.

Well Pand, the sun is just about 2 inches above the hill now so well over the Yard arm and time for a drink I think. It's actually sinking quite fast now (the sun rather than the wine bottle) – either that or a cow has got in the way and is distorting the horizon. Isn't that some recently expounded scientific theory? Cows distorting time and space? Rings a bell somewhere. Actually as I speak, the cows are just having their usual mad half hour – barging about in the bank, puffing and blowing at each other. Better finish now – be a couple of days before I go and post this so will add anything of interest.

Bye for now

Devon, February 1994

Dear Pand,

> Happy B'day to you
> Happy   "   "
>   "   "   Dear Pandy
>   "   "   to you

Well, it's the 10th here – don't care what date it is when you *read* it – that's nothing to do with me! Anyway, you wanted a letter for your birthday – it's not my fault that your card refused to have a letter in its envelope – said it would make it look fat and unattractive – screamed and shouted and really caused a big scene at the P.O. counter so I had to give in and say I'd send the letter separately. Then the *letter* started shouting and bawling and I was *so* embarrassed! Really, I wonder why I bothered at all (so will you by the time I'm finished!). I'll leave the sad, whingeing bits to the end, by which time I'll either have forgotten them or won't have much room left to write them down in.

Plants are doing well now: I have about eight pomegranates, which are looking quite healthy. They are only on their third set of leaves at the moment but at least they look good. Two lots of New Zealand seeds are doing well too: the Kaka (NZ Parrot) Beak have 5 going well (2 or 3 years to flowering size) and the Kowhai – a small tree (v. small at the moment!) which is the national flower of New Zealand. The NZ Flax and the NZ Christmas Tree are being extremely consistent at *not* germinating. The Mango seems a bit tardy as well. Still, it's not going too badly and my Pitcher Plant has grown quite tall now and looks fairly healthy. The Jatropa is flowering but still has no leaves. Have 1 large fig left but now have 9+ new little ones coming.

Friday 21st Feb

Back again – sorry about the short gap – I can't remember now exactly what the hold-up was but it must have been extremely important!

Caught the Yucca chatting to all its friends in the greenhouse today – they were all very happy to see it anyway. I overheard mutterings and mumblings about the need to organise a protest demonstration to the Red Passion Flower's prolonged 'holiday'. If the greenhouse suddenly empties I'll know you've got all the plants holding placards outside your house!

I've just opened your elderberry wine (well, it *is* 10.30 at night) so you must be prepared for a rapid deterioration into waffle before too long. I just fancied a drink and remembered we hadn't opened it so I'd better try and remember to save a glassful (small) for Edward. Anyway, it's jolly nice and the bits of wax that fell in as I was opening it add a certain *je ne sais quoi* (see, it's started already and I've only had a couple of mouthfuls). It's a very pretty colour – a sort of raspberry.

By the way, thanks for the cuttings but I haven't got a copy of the plant catalogue yet. I must look up where the nursery is and take a trip over there. Did Ed give you the V+A article – rather scathing about Mrs E.C.

Curry seems to have been better this past week – this is the 7th day that she has been quiet. I got some live bacteria powder from the vet so that has taken over from the yoghurt now and it seems pretty effective. She still has got one more lot of tablets to take next month though, and as that stuff wipes out her stomach bacteria (as well as the bad guys) we'll probably have to go through it all again. Anyway, she went and munched in the garden for over an hour this morning and had a reasonable dinner this evening so her appetite is improving. Hebe is also getting a bit better now and has a bit more strength when picking at plants. It's very time-consuming getting her to eat though. She is far too small to force feed but will now eat very finely minced food if she sits on the palm of my hand with the food piled round her! At least she has never lost any weight but has remained at 18 grams since early December.

By the way, 2 of my Palm seeds have germinated – I was quite surprised as they take anything from 1–6 months and I only did them about 3 weeks ago. The Jatropa is growing a second flower spike and has finally decided to start producing some leaves. Presumably it got tired of me keep picking it off the shelf every day, poking it and bleating about its lack of leaves. Bought a rather nice Peace Lily last week – from B & Q of all places – it sometimes pays to have a quick look at their houseplants. Quite a bargain, I thought – only £2.99 and a nice healthy-looking plant. I've decided *not* to throw my Coconut Palm away as it seems to have at least stopped getting any worse and might even recover so I'll wait a few more weeks I think and see what happens.

All the snowdrops are well out now and the daffodils are about 6 inches up. Unfortunately Sudie clumped across one lot and I think they are fatally injured – in fact I suspect they will be 'ex daffodils' as far as this year is concerned. Typical, isn't it – spend months and lots of energy getting yourself above ground and no sooner have you struggled to the surface and sunbathed for half an hour than 6 kilos of tortoise lands on you. She also scoffed the garlic shoots and some posh grass growing in a pot in the greenhouse. I'd only just admired the state of the grass the day before – went in next morning and just two little stumps poking out of the pot! Little pig! Also caught her with half the Purple Passion Flower disappearing down her throat this morning. That was supposed to be draped over the Rosemary bush in Curry's section for added hiding place but Sudie had got hold of one end and that was it!

Loads of birds coming in still. I feed them mostly on dried dog food – a bowl of that with hot water on it and the have a wonderful meal along with odd scraps and seeds. They all look well on it anyway. I counted 7 greenfinches the other day – usually we have up to 4 or 5 but obviously word had got out that a new dish was on the menu. The blackbird is always around – rather like the original 'Blackie' who used to come and bang at the back window every morning. The usual other lot still abound – the chaffinches, the 2 robins, dunnocks, Mrs Blackie, the odd thrush ('odd' as in turns up every so often, not an odd thrush!), lots of starlings and Wren who is still about. Haven't seen both wrens together this year. The other week, we had 7 buzzards circling overhead – the most over the garden at any one time. I can hear them most days but don't always see usual lot. As I shall do it myself, it ought not to take long. In fact, if it's more than 6 minutes from Hello to Goodbye I shall consider myself to be slipping a bit!

I meant to ask you when I phoned last – did you want anything in particular for your birthday? Did you have your beady eye on something at the Oxfam shop? Or shall I just get you something when I come across it? I discovered some wonderful plastic bonsai trees in the Co-op the other day – interested?? That's a relief: I would have been embarrassed to take one to the checkout desk anyway.

The Barclaycard saga has taken a somewhat sinister turn (I told you about my reverse charge call to them?). Well, they must have got my uncompleted form and shitty note as they sent me a letter saying 'Thank you for your enquiry [?]. We have requested a copy of the item but it will take two months to get a reply. Meantime we'll credit the amount and show it on the next statement.' I don't actually know what it means but I can hardly wait for the 2 months to be up to find out. There was an item on Newsnight tonight about the Credit Card companies upping their charges to retailers as they are making a loss on the cards – this doesn't come as a total surprise to me I must confess! 90% of their losses probably stem from those cards which have been cancelled. Unless of course it was a subtle threat directed at me personally. I wonder how they knew that I watched Newsnight. I don't watch it every night so that's a bit worrying!

Right, this is getting a bit paranoid (also a bit bad spelling) so must be time to stop and go to bed (after a boiler inspection of course) as it's midnight and Morgan has run out of things to chew. The latest seems to be a great interest in the carpet – as in how long it takes to make a flat-weave carpet into a tufted one – shag pile in one corner actually!

Will phone soon(ish).

Lots of love,

Pippa & Godtorts & others

Devon, May 1994

Dear Pand,

Will have to stop for a while – Corry has just started!

Right, back now! Rosemary plant has been on at me all week ... 'When am I going to Pand's? When am I going to Pand's?' I had to sit her down on the staging yesterday and say quite firmly 'You'll go to Pand's when I'm ready! Do you want to be the only plant to go all the way up there without 12 pages of drivel to accompany you or what?' Lucky for her, she said 'Oh, alright then – I'll do the Or What'. So, now I've got to write 12 pages of drivel – Not a good move I think!

Have just finished the first day of painting the back of the house. Whoever invented this roughcast rendering should be shot (preferably slowly and painfully). Last week did the cleaning (scrubbing the walls with antifungi stuff and then rinsing off) but everything takes ages because there are a million very small people who have to be evicted from the various crevices first. Apart from that, the Great Tit (the one nesting in the stink pipe) is continuously moaning about me working round there. I'm afraid I was really horrid and told him he should have started earlier and then he would have finished building long before I started painting. It obviously didn't go down too well as he promptly shat on my head!

Got some baby Mistle Thrushes – at least 3 hatched out a couple of weeks ago – they must have been the earliest as everyone else is still only tarting up the inside of their nests. There are several Squirrels in the garden this year and have seen a couple of young ones too – playing silly buggers all over the place. The Wren has now built a nest in the honeysuckle at the side of 'your' bedroom window and the Blue Tits are back nesting above our bedroom window. Also 2 Goldfinches around and a Blackcap – none of which came in the garden last year until late summer. Stacks of Slow Worms and Lizards and yesterday, a Snake came tearing out of the greenhouse and down the bank – typically, Helen just avoided clumping on it! Still, I expect next time, it will be holding a little placard above its head 'Please mind your step'. It may have taken a billion years to evolve into its present form but I'll bet it will only take it a couple of weeks to suss out the best way to stop someone clumping on it. This form of speedy evolution will be perfected at Pencross!

Actually, when I said 12 *pages* of drivel, I might have really meant 12 *sides*. 12 pages may well be pushing it even for me and especially at this time of year. There's only about an hour and a half between finishing off outside and going to bed and then another hour after that arranging the rather limited length of wires attached to my new radio and earphones. I lose a further hour from the next day trying to disentangle myself from said wires in order to rise at half six because it is so light and everyone is shouting and bawling and the Pheasants are (im)patiently waiting outside the back door for their breakfast! I think, on the whole, I spend about 2 hours sleeping and the remaining 22 hours faffing around!

Oh, must tell you before I forget – met Frieda and John in Wellington today. Frieda was telling me about the badger which had been in their garden a couple of days ago – apparently it dug up the front lawn quite badly (you know the house I mean – the big posh one with the perfect lawn just down the track?). She did manage to keep a straight face whilst relating this horror story as John spends all his life cutting the lawns (well, the part of his life that isn't spent on drinking rum and raising and lowering the huge Union Jack flag on the said front lawn). God knows what the badger was thinking of – suicide, I imagine! Anyway, the reason I'm telling you this is because it reminded me that I probably forgot to tell you that a badger (could be the suicidal one or a different one) was in our garden a few weeks ago. Tore up the perimeter wire netting at the base leaving a large tunnel to the outside world in its wake. It was mere luck that I looked all round that part of the garden that morning before letting the tortoises out – no particular reason other than checking up on the Elder trees in the hedge – but just as well because even Sudie could have just strolled out through the tunnel without touching the sides!

The little water garden is looking ok – the Cowslips and Primroses have gone berserk as have the Mimulus and Anemones from last year. I've risked it and taken up the black polythene from the surrounding area so will now have to keep an eagle eye out for the return of the dreaded Celandine.

They are pretty and bright but they swamp everything else and there is a limit to how many thousands I actually want in that particular spot! All the Hostas are coming through; the Dicentra (pink and white) are now in full flower and the Giant Rhubarb is already Giant Rhubarbing at the side of the pond. By the way, the Ostrich Fern is sprouting all over the place as is the one in a pot. Do you want to try one again if I can split it later on? The pond had its first casualty the other day – found a little drowned Vole. Sad really – tiny little body floating face down in the water just inches from solid ground and safety – in this case, a branch laying across from the water lily pot to the pond edge. Need to put a sign up! Pheasant's mate (now called Stubby as she has broken tail feathers) pottered off down to the pond one evening after her tea – she was drinking for ages and then suddenly just stepped onto the surface of the water and promptly sank – a great surprise to her for some reason. She's now called Stubby of Nazareth which seems quite apt. Unfortunately, I'd just taken a photo of her drinking and so couldn't wind the camera on quickly enough to catch her 'walking (or not, as it turned out) on water' act.

Left a roll of wire netting against the garage wall quite some time ago and went to move it last week as (along with the old boiler, metal dustbin, etc.) I felt it detracted from the garden somewhat! Anyway, as I went to move it, this very cross Great Tit came out of the top of the roll and started shouting at me. I thought it was a bit odd but backed off and kept an eye on it for the rest of the afternoon. Sure enough, its building a nest in there so, aesthetics or not, the 6 foot roll of netting has to stay. It's getting so I can't do anything anywhere for fear of disturbing someone! If it carries on, I've decided to send out a general memo suggesting that they either let me walk round and do things or they collectively start paying the mortgage and I'll move out for the season. I suspect the post box will be stuffed full of little letters saying 'Ok then – you can do this and that but *not* in the hours between dawn and dusk'. Then I suppose there'll be a separate little letter from the dratted Owls saying ' You know that bit about doing stuff in the hours between dawn and dusk? Well … '

Cuckoos are about now – its great – not quite like Floriers but at least they are here. Actually though, last year wasn't too bad as I saw one several times (or saw several once?). Anyway, this seems a good Cuckoo year so far and have seen them and heard them most days. I actually heard the first one on 20th April (but forgot to write to The Times – in fact, also forgot to buy The Times to discover who had beaten me!). Have discovered that the Cuckoo sits and calls and then, before sneakily flying off to his next position, he gives this silly chuckle. This proved correct time and time again and so I expounded on this theory on my little section of Jan's web site. What happened the other day? Yes, sure enough this bloody cuckoo flew off *without* chuckling – I couldn't believe it. A mere aberration I suspect.

Despite the hard work, I seem mysteriously to be behind with things. Got the potatoes in at least and they are now just showing through. The garlic, onions and shallots are ok but something has eaten most of the radishes. The tiny cabbage are now growing well but haven't found much time to get on with a lot of other stuff. I grew some really good basil earlier on and put them out under a cloche. Unfortunately, one night was just too cold even with the protection and next morning – all basil gone – disappeared off the face of the earth (well, not quite – they *were* still on the face of the earth but in a decidedly horizontal position and looking remarkably like little blobs of green slime). I was extremely miffed, Pand! I've got about 5 plants left in the greenhouse – tiny little beasts – by now they should be great bushy things (got to stop watching these bloody gardening programmes on TV!). Have 10 Sugar Snaps in the lean-to along with Dwarf Beans, Courgettes and Bush Cucumbers and the Sweet Peppers are just at the 2 leaf stage. Doing different Chilli peppers this year (have enough from last year to last a lifetime!) also large Aubergines (rather than the mini type) and also Golden Berries (Chinese Lanterns but edible). A couple of days ago, just finished re-potting about 60 Strawberry plants – now in a cold frame. Unlike last year, no sign yet of early strawbs but still hoping. (Not really vital though as Frieda usually gives me some.)

Have given the big Wisteria another pruning so maybe next year it will make an effort. The French Wisteria which is just tied up against the top terrace wall with a bit of crappy old clothes line, is absolutely covered in flower buds! I think the big one needs digging up, stuffing in a plastic bag and spending 24 hours travelling to Floriers – that should concentrate its mind a bit! I've only managed to save one of the scented geraniums (the lemon one) – so if you have any different, do some cuttings for me. By the way, how is your Pineapple sage? I've got plenty of cuttings of the variegated one – do you want one? Also got some 'French Honeysuckle' (Hedysarum coronarium – look it up in the RHS book – its in there – evergreen, shrubby, about 3 feet eventually) – I thought maybe it would go well in your front garden tub, let me know what you think). Did I tell you – one of the baby Jatrophas is flowering? Only 3 years old so I'm quite surprised.

Consternation tonight – Stubby came for her tea this evening on her own – no Pheas with her. The last few nights, they have both been roosting in the trees behind Morgan's aviary (hence Morgan refusing to come in until 10 o'clock or so when they finally settle down further along the hedge line – makes a long day of it!). Also, the other cock Pheasant hasn't been in today either (this after I scraped together all the loose change in the house to go and buy some more peanuts). So, don't know what's going on.

Made some egg and cress sandwiches for dinner last night but didn't fancy the last one. It looked a bit distressed this morning so I put it out onto the small birds patch. When I looked out, the little birds were all standing around gazing at it. Anyway, I went down to Wellington but when I got back, the sandwich was still there and still surrounded by the little birds though every so often, one brave soul dashed in for a quick peck and then dashed away again. 5 minutes later, the whole sandwich had disappeared (the Jays or Magpies probably) and a cloud of little birds grouching about and muttering 'Well, we *were* going to eat it. It's just not fair'. I got a bit of paper, wrote 'Law of the Jungle' on it and put it out on their patch. After all, someone has to teach them about the ways of the world.

Saturday, 18 May

Pheas is back (with a vengeance I might add). He's taken to turning up even earlier in the morning – around 5.30. First of all, he sits on the front doorstep and jumps up and down and shouts. After a few minutes of this, he then sidles along the terrace to our bedroom window (and jumps up and down and shouts). Once he's satisfied that he's woken me up (he must be picking up some shocking language by now!), he then trots round to the back door and clatters about until the peanuts are put out for his breakfast. Stubby usually turns up a few minutes later so that's another half ton of peanuts gone (and I know for a fact that they go round to Anne's for a bit of a scoff later on!). One of the other cock Pheasants comes later in the afternoon and then Pheas and Stubby come again in the evening. The Robin also comes to the back door with a couple of babies in tow and finishes off the crumbs. Its ridiculous really – you can hardly move out of the house for fear of treading on someone!

I can't be bothered to look back over what I have written (on second biro now!) to see if I told you about the baby owls – anyway, in case I haven't, they are about in the trees on the top slope during the evening, squeaking very loudly. Still only the Tawnies about so far.

At last the other day, managed to spot the Tree Creeper creeping about on a tree (as one would expect, I suppose). Was beginning to get a bit worried as hadn't seen him for ages. So far no sign of the Fly Catchers again (you remember – those very rare River Warblers or whatever we'd decided they were at first sight?). Was hoping they would return as they managed to hatch off 4 babies in the bank at the back last year.

At last the lizards are starting to come down onto the new terrace. I'd been hoping they would eventually try it out during the hot weather as I had felt guilty about removing some of their grass bank. Now all they need to worry about is any number of tortoises reserving the best spots by placing their towels on the sun loungers. Thinking about it, I should take the tortoises' towels away – that'll save any arguments.

Garden stuff is still well behind – it's just getting silly. It's still quite cold at nights and though we've had some hot days, its not sufficient to really push the stuff along. The French 'La Ratte' potatoes are well up now but the main crop (Pentland something?) is a bit feeble. The beefsteak tomatoes (now outside) have their first set of flower buds but they've been at that stage for almost a couple of weeks and are resolutely refusing to open or grow any further. The garlic, onions and shallots are still looking ok but of course, I should have done millions more of them as they are the only things which appear to be moving (to be fair though, this could be due to the fact that they were planted last Autumn!). The courgettes and cucumbers I mentioned earlier are bushing out of their pots in the greenhouse so I'll have to either repot them (which means bigger pots, which means they have to sit on the floor, which means that the Walking Hoover (aka Sudie) will get them) or plant them out. On reflection, planting them out seems the better bet.

(Quick break here as Pheas and Stubby are here demanding their tea) By the way, Morgan now says 'Stubby'.

The Citrus trees are suffering an appalling attack of Red Spider Mite – it's really ruined them, particularly the Grapefruit. Not to be outdone, everything else has Whitefly. Looking on the bright side though, your Canary Island cacti/succulents are doing well. I potted all the seedlings up a couple of weeks ago and most are turning into quite sturdy little jobs. Nothing of the last lot you sent have done anything at all. The white Violets seem to have done a runner but the ordinary ones are ok as is the Laboradorica (the very dark leaf violet). I can let you have some of the Cowslips for your 'Spring Garden' if you want – stacks here now. After the Basil disaster, I've not yet started any other herbs or summer veg (apart from the Peppers and Chillis) – it's too cold to put the stuff outside and I'm running out of space under glass. The heated (tortoise) greenhouse is now so badly infested with Red Spider and Whitefly that I need to get the stuff out, clean it and put it in the Lean-to. However, the Lean-to is stuffed to the gills with things that should have been out ages ago but isn't, etc., etc., etc. Despite all this, I have picked from the Tortoise greenhouse 12 kilos of Tomatoes so far – I don't know whether I will make last year's early total of 16 kilos. Anyway, once these have finished, I have about 25 outdoor tomato plants (if they ever *get* outside!) so barring accidents (Sudie immediately springs to mind – how odd!) should be lots of chutney, sauce etc.

Monday, 27 May

I thought I'd only stopped for something fairly minor but as that was 2 weeks ago, whatever it was must have been more time consuming than I'd thought!

Today was reasonable weatherwise but it's going to rain again tomorrow (and the next day and the next – according to that beastly John Kettley anyway – its obvious he's a Northerner – sounds so bloody cheerful about it! Thinking about it though, John Humphreys is always desperate for rain and he comes from Wales – well, yes, that figures!). Don't know what your plants are like but mine are still slow. The Clematis Montana (the pink job) is out now as are one or 2 of the geraniums and of course the usual standbys – violets, Prims and cows, anemones, bluebells, billions of Forget-me-nots (so many and quite scented). The Giant Rhubarb by the pond now has a flower spike which is almost out – bit precocious as it has only 4 leaves but am not about to argue. Actually, I suspect it might be that it got so dry up until the rain the other week. You know what happens, thinks it's going to die and is desperate to spread its genes.

The Hostas are fully up now (but so are the snails too!). I've planted a few more bits and pieces in the water garden since you were last here so its filling up quite nicely. The Mimulus has really taken off – a vast clump again – despite the bad winter (and latterly at least, some tortoise depradation) it has survived and spread quite spectacularly.

The red Parrot Beak is flowering away happily – unfortunately I can't do much more than glance at it in passing as both Thrush and Wren have definitely claimed that little bit. As it is, I have to whistle in a sort of nonchalant manner whenever I'm round there – just to warn them a foreign object is approaching!

I eventually cut down the early tomatoes in the tortoise greenhouse yesterday – the Whitefly was so bad, you daren't open your mouth in case they flew in and choked you. So now got about 4 kilos of green tomatoes so I think we are going to get a lot of chutney this year (probably you will too!). Amounted to 22 kilos though so not bad. Made a really nice sauce for the pasta the other day – jolly tasty! Have frozen about 3 kilos of ripe tomatoes – just bunged in whole as I didn't have the time to fart around making a load of sauce. I can always do it later and be interesting to see how they come out of the freezer. Also made some Ratatouille (but without the Aubergines as they were a bit expensive – could this be Nouvelle Cuisine?). Miscalculated a bit here though as I bought too many courgettes and then the weather turned cooler so Sudie didn't eat as many as she was supposed to (the only tortoise which likes courgette – mind you, the list of what she *doesn't* eat could be inscribed on the head of a pin – a very small pin) so loads of new style Rat.

The baby Robin seems to have disappeared – after a week or so of coming to the back door with a parent for food, I haven't seen it for a while. The Nuthatch has a nest not far away and the Wire Netting Great Tit now has babies (you can hear the roll of netting squeak every so often!). This last is a bit of a bore really – the netting completely ruins the ambience of the water garden but you know what these birds are like – leave anything remotely suitable laying around and its Ferret up a drainpipe time! Haven't heard any squeaking from the Stink pipe yet – seems rather a long time? All the usual birds are terribly busy but so far the only fledged youngsters have been the Thrush and Robin. Oh yes – a Blackcap was in the other day and the woman up the road said she'd had Linnets in. One Bullfinch has been in on a couple of occasions (same as last year but a bit later this time). While Ed was home, he rescued about 10 baby Pheasant chicks – mum was in the grass verge but the chicks couldn't quite get up the kerb. The Job Centre lady was quite impressed when he explained why he was a few minutes late – you at least would appreciate this sort of excuse.

This is the 4th day Stubby of Nazareth hasn't been around – hope she's got eggs this time. She'd failed to turn up for a couple of days a few weeks ago and then re-appeared so whether something had happened to eggs/chicks? The woman up the road (I *really* must find out her name at least – apart from anything else, it has to be shorter than keep writing 'the woman up the road') said a pheasant had been run over on the corner of our track and the road – no idea when though – hope it wasn't Stubby.

Are you coming down later in the year?

Devon, 1st October

Dear Pand,

Thought I'd start a letter as I forgot to tell you over the phone that another baby mouse appeared on Friday – same colour, same big feet but much quicker than the poorly one. Haven't seen it since and not dead bodies so at least one of the brood (do mice have broods?) made it this far. The light tan Slow worm sends its love; it was hanging about here again and seemed a bit miffed when I just said 'Oh hello, you're back again hey?' instead of kneeling on the floor going Ooh, Aah and poking it gently. It said could I get you to come back again as you made it feel much more important. (Suppose I'll have to buy a packet of those little coloured stars and pin a gold one up over its gap in the wall to make up for my rather brusque attitude lately.)

Morgan has been trailing round almost everywhere with me. Starts at 7am or soon after (mercifully he is wanting a little sleep by 8) and then 9.30 or so he comes out whilst I clean his cage and has 1½ to 2 hours being entertained. He quite likes the sink (has fallen in a couple of times) and has the large orange plastic spoon stuck in your litre fresh milk carton (that was *good* thinking on your part, Pand!) filled with water (to make it heavy and more interesting) in the sink. After one poke round, the airing cupboard (kitchen side) is boring and so is the 'wine' cupboard next to it. The big green watering can was fun for ... ooh, about 3 minutes at least! We now go every morning into the shower to have a warm water spray with the spray gun (which he has now learned to climb up and dismantle – clever stuff). The hair dryer afterwards was a wonderful idea until Morg grabbed hold of the diffuser shield and wouldn't let go. There I was holding a hair dryer with a parrot dangling from the end of it! He also attacked the cleaner when I put it on but I was worried about him getting the flex so there's only one part of the living room floor which gets cleaned every 5 mins – looks brilliant! I spent most of Saturday making him a portable swing: bought a big Dog Chew bar, drilled it out, cut some metal bar, fixed it all up – managed to persuade him on it once and he looked at me as if I was mad: 'Oh go on then, if you find it amusing.' I could have killed him. As it's getting a bit chilly out now, I put him in the big heated greenhouse whilst I'm in there – he goes on his crate at the Babies' end. It was you saying he wanted other animals around to make life more interesting that made me think – we used to have some of the torts indoors more until recently (which is where he picked up 'Curry' and 'Rachel' from). He's still pulling the odd feather out but it's improving (or it could be that he hasn't got many left to pick at). We seem to have an agreement that night time is taken up with chewing the carpet (in the corner between his 2 windows in the living room). He's actually been doing it for ages on and off but I always tried to discourage him, thinking that eventually we would have decent carpet here. However, the other night I thought 'What the hell – better a bald carpet than a bald parrot' and when (or if) we get decent carpet down I'll just use the offcuts to put over where he chews. Besides, there's a limit to what parrot entertainment devices I can come up with every day – if the worst comes to the worst I can always start nicking the carpet sample squares from the shops! I can now see why some parents dump their kids in front of the TV or a computer screen – less wearing on the nerves (and brain).

Nearly 10pm and suddenly Pheasant's shouting somewhere up the bank. I just went out and told him to shut up and he started again. Usually I hear him if the Army guns go off or the quarry's blasting (I'm never sure which it is) but there hasn't been anything like that so far this evening. He came this morning and had his breakfast and then stood under the bedroom window bellowing his head off. I presume at this time of year he is just re-establishing his rights over our garden.

Just had a break here – carpet chewing got boring so we've just spent 20 mins dropping various things into a basin full of water and fishing them out again (all this because I went for a wee and Morgan came tearing down the hall desperate not to miss anything). I myself wouldn't have found the basin that entertaining but you get these weird guests, you know how it is ...

See you soon.

Devon, 1995

Dear Pand,

2 lots of good news for you as a cheering start to a letter: 1) Morgan is back and 2) the chocolate cake is in the fridge awaiting our attention,

Yes, you've guessed – Morgan has been AWOL. I went to collect him after speaking to you and just seconds before I got there the Guinea Fowl started up and gave Morg a fright and he was off. I found him on top of the high hedge round Anne's House after about an hour (and much scrambling and calling from me). A little voice said 'Hello' very nervously. As he was about 12' above the lane and not very willing to climb lower, I decided rather than go home and find the ladders I would do the simple thing and ask Anne if I could use her ladders. Big mistake! She was wonderful – got her ladders out and came down and held them for me while I climbed up. I persuaded Morg to climb across the top of the hedge (about 18" and very twiggy) in the dark – only torchlight. Got him on my shoulder, down the ladders and said 'I'll pop him in the conservatory and run home for his cage.' 'Yes, fine – close the door behind you and I'll chat to him.' Unfortunately, halfway across the lawn with Morgan still on my shoulder (didn't want to try grabbing him in case I missed and he flew off again), Anne closed the ladders with a resounding snap and Morgan took off again – this time into a huge fir tree in their garden. How I managed not to throw myself across the lawn effing and blinding I really don't know. But I *did* manage to reply very calmly when poor Anne said 'Oh Lord, did I make a noise and frighten him?' So, over to the fir tree – at least a million feet in height – climb up and say 'Choccy biscuit' very pleadingly lots of times, but it's quite dark and Morgan just saying muffled 'Hellos' from somewhere the midst of the damn tree. Eventually, I said to Anne if she didn't mind I'd just camp there for a couple of hours and see if I could talk him down (we decided that was the modern term). She offered to make a coffee so I said 'Let me run home and get his cage while you make sure he doesn't go off again.' So I ran home, got the cage, ran back and she pottered off to make coffee. Made it and, horror of horrors, the door slammed behind her and Morgan took off again. If it hadn't been so desperate it would have been funny, I suppose. I can't remember ever having had such a lot of 'bad words' straining to get out of my mouth. I can't stand people being v. calm when the situation calls for sheer desperation. Anyway, poor Anne standing there with 2 coffees and saying 'Well, do you want to drink it quickly?' and me saying 'Er, no, thanks v. much. Think I'd better get off and see if I can find him – awfully sorry about all this. I'll let you know what happens.' This was about 10pm so I pratted about for about half an hour but decided if he had landed somewhere high up he would just be chilly and tired but at least safe and if I blundered around with torch etc. I wouldn't do any good. Next thing was to decide how I could be sure of waking up before first light – answer – don't go to bed at all, that should do it. So I was too pissed off to make my dinner (only a banana mid-a.m.), couldn't concentrate to sit and read (anyway I was so tired I might have nodded off) so I managed to get hold of Ed who said he would leave at 3 (rather than 8). Looked at the marrow and the 8lbs of rhubarb I'd bought that a.m. So I made 2 lots of Marrow Zanzibar, 2 lots of rhubarb wine, potted up the citrus plants into their huge new tubs, watered everything, had about 10 cups of coffee, and kept walking about saying 'OK Morgan' in the hope that he was nearby and would hear me. By this method I stayed awake and vaguely mentally alert (not a drop of drink passed my lips, Pand – some situations are just *too* urgent for drinking!) until half five when Ed came. Made us a cup of coffee and went out yet again. This time I saw an outline in the tall tree above the kitchen – shone my torch and said 'Is that you, Morg?' and this little voice said 'Hello'. So, wonderful, he was in the garden and knew we were there but that's where it finished. Despite my spending the morning on the roof, Morg sat there, warmed up, got his pigeon pals round him and was quite happy. Ed and I were furious, tired and hungry but didn't dare take our eyes off him in case he took off for somewhere else. We were both getting stiff necks keeping watch on this tree a thousand feet above us! Ed disappeared for a sleep and I carried on farting around and watching. Anyway, to cut a long story short, Morgan changed trees at midday to and at early evening took off again and flew miles away. I was so desperate by this time. I thought I'd never get him back. Then we found him in a huge oak right at the end of our lane, but he took off again. By this time it was about 8.30 pm and we were v. cold and hungry (same as Morg, probably) so went back home, got shoes and socks and coats on and the usual seed and Choccy bait. We decided to climb up into the field above us, where I was sure he'd flown (oh, I forgot: in between times we had some Microlights and a hot air balloon flying over, which made *all* the birds take off from *everywhere* – great timing!). We eventually heard this little voice saying 'Morgan' in reply to my calls and in the end I got him on my shoulder. As it was still light enough for him to fly off, Ed scrambled back down the banks and got the cage. After a bit of a struggle I managed to push Morgan into the cage. He wasn't best pleased but at least he was in. 9pm – such a relief! Of course, we still had to negotiate the banks, brambles, slippery leaves, not to mention the odd bit of barbed wire (the farmer's not ours!) before arriving home with Morg and cage intact.

We were in a terrible state by the end of all that. Pity we didn't have the chocolate cake then!

Think that's enough for now ...

Sunnybank, 1995

Dear Pand,

Thought I'd better get a move on and write a quick letter (well, quickish I suspect as it won't catch the post on Monday) as I couldn't remember which date you were actually going to London and this was supposed to arrive before then. Still, if it doesn't, you can have a boring end to your holiday rather than a boring start.

Well, now to list all the exciting things you'll miss because you aren't coming down: absolutely BILLIONS of Slow worms strewn everywhere from tiny new ones to rather largish old ones and all of them saying 'Oh, I thought Pand was coming to look at us – Oh, she isn't? Oh well, we can relax and stop posing around for endless bloody snaps then!' (Nothing to do with me – completely unsolicited comments emanating from under various paving slabs, disused water butt lids and a small square of metal!) Poking Medium Toad who has been living under one of the Torts' compost bags in the old greenhouse for the last 2 weeks – well, alright I'll own up to that. She vanished about 3 nights ago so I suppose that's not really a very good example. Listening to the Great tit parents scrabbling around in the Stink Pipe (much magnified when you are sitting on the loo) and now being deafened by the babies squeaking. Lifting up the old sheet of galvanised on the bank and seeing how many Voles you can count sitting there blinking at you and shouting 'Oy, don't you humans ever knock first?' Watching all the newly fledged birds trying their hand (claw?) at feeding themselves. Spotting the lizards having a quick bask in between clouds. Being frightened to death by Pheasant doing his stupid Flap and Shriek from an innocent clump of vegetation and finally, hearing the Cuckoos day after day and spotting them too. (Not quite as good as Floriers best year but the best year I can remember for Cuckoos for a long time). On the plus side of course, you will miss being squashed at night between the desk and the extra kitchen units; collecting leaves; endlessly counting tortoises; suffering the attentions of Morgan; lifting Sudie on to the scales to weigh her; endless discussions on what we should have for dinner; picking fresh tomatoes (2.5kg so far) and eating early strawbs with Cornish ice cream (half a kilo so far – strawbs not ice cream!). So, there you go Pand – I think the balance is *slightly* tipped in favour of coming down but there's no accounting for people's taste! No, only joking – you can bet your life if you put yourself in penury to come down, all the birds and animals would bugger off (Oh by the way, saw some deer when we went for a walk up to the Monument), the Tomatoes would keel over and the Strawbs would sit there and go 'What – you want me to produce fruit *this* particular week??' The ultimate miss of course is noughts and crosses on the computer while waiting for the builders!!

Well, now to the serious stuff – the Wisteria has bloomed well this year. About 9 bunches (I guess the technical term is Racemes but at this stage who cares?) of flowers which is a vast improvement on last year (about 2 I think). At this rate it'll be another 10 years of careful twice a year pruning before it looks like a proper Wisteria. The Parrot Beak has managed to produce 3 seed pods from its many flowers. The trick will be to harvest them at the right time I think. The summer tomatoes have got their first flowers coming but for some reason the peppers look a bit feeble. The courgettes have completely disappeared – I had 5 out in grow bags and if it wasn't for the bags sitting there, I could have dreamed the whole thing. The potatoes I did manage to get in (the posh La Ratte jobs) look pretty good but seem to have crowded out the spring onions and shallots a bit. The celery is looking good but should have been thinned out of course – this will be the world's first 2 millimetre diameter celery – the ultimate in Mini Vegetables I suspect. The garlic looks ok and if it comes up to scratch that should mean a harvest of around 90 to 100 bulbs. This means that you'll need to take three weeks holiday in the autumn so that I can bring them up for you to plait! Sadly, the French Banana seems to have popped its clogs – a shame as it was a different variety to my original 3. I keep tending it but it's not answering (well certainly not in English or French). The one in the new greenhouse is going great guns again – can't keep up with using its leaves. The 2 in the old greenhouse suffered from the cold but one is sprouting again and the other is vaguely green at the base still. Will have to wait and see for that one I suppose. (Well, you know me – I'll give it 5 years before I'm totally convinced it's not playing!) At long last, I have just finished planting up the window boxes and containers – it seems to have been a never-ending job, and flagging enthusiasm in the last few weeks hasn't helped. Mind you, with the number of containers I've got, it's probably not surprising (length of time and lack of enthusiasm). I shall of course be terribly organised and foresighted and take photos for you just so that you know I'm not fibbing.

Well, I suspect this enough drivel for one week. Hope you have a good time in London and get a few nice days at home too.

See you soon

Cornwall, 1999

Dear Pand,

Did I tell you it's fields out the back here? Directly behind it are horses and sheep, then a huge herd of cows (150–200 I think) and then another field and then after that, over to the left is the sea and the right more fields and woods. It's really v nice country around here – hilly but lots of valleys and woodland. We walked down to the sea at Blue Anchor the other evening – it's only about a mile and guess what – we were walking past the Cleeve Manor estate and who should pop out and follow us along the road – Pheasant! We were really chuffed. Actually there is one at least v close by here – every morning he starts shouting and jumping about in the lane (the lady next door says he comes in the autumn/winter for food – didn't like to say it would be all year round once I'd got my act together) What with the pheasant, the chicken, (and geese and ducks a few hundred yards down), the birds (particularly the Collared Doves of which there are millions), the church bells, it's bloody noisy here – oh for the peace and quiet of Inner London! Even the old people's home opposite seems to be noisy all night, although I suspect it's the staff rather than the inmates. I mean, I don't imagine there's some old person in there who enjoys listening to Heavy Metal rock at 1 a.m. – could be wrong tho!

Been invited to join the Gardening Club and also, wait for it, the Senior Citizens Club!! It's the old lady next door – she gave me the meeting sheets and said 'I know you're busy at the moment, but we'd like you to come.' The Gardening Club yes, I'd already sussed that one but the S.C.?? I know I probably looked a bit rough when she gave them to me, but even so. Anyway, I said in all innocence (well, almost) "Would I qualify as a Senior Cit.?" (hoping she would say – oh no dear you look really young – like 59?!) but instead she said "Oh that's ok – we take anyone." Translated, I took that to mean that they started with a S. Cit. Club and then didn't have that many Senior Cits. So decided to take anyone (well, almost anyone –as proved by her invitation to me). So having rushed indoors and tweezered out every grey hair (leaving about 6 brown ones in the process), I needn't have worried too much – seems like they will accept a 49 yr old (almost) providing she looks about 65 – I seem to fit the bill so there you go. I know I was supposed to socialise more but I'm wondering whether this isn't going just a bit too far?

The next big Event on the Old Cleeve calendar is the Show on 2nd August. Unfortunately, I've already lost the leaflets and info. I was given so it's a bit difficult – you're supposed to enter something but I don't know whether it's a plant or an incontinence bag – I can see I'm going to do really well here!

Speak soon

Cornwall, August 2000

Dear Pand,

Had an interesting day at Dunster Castle recently – went as a backup on one of the Attics and Basements tours – the actual kitchen is wonderful. Now they've decided I'd be a good tour guide (which wasn't what I intended at all). Anyway, saw all the interesting bits, including some of the medieval parts and lots of bats too – in fact saw more Bats in that afternoon than we saw when we went on a special Bat Identification walk there last autumn! There was even a Bat Flap in one part ... what's known as taking your Bats seriously I suspect. I'm aiming for Nicest Person of the Year – was complimented on being particularly nice to a bunch of Belgian and Dutch visitors who I seemed to have acquired during my 10 minute break – actually I was desperate to get rid of them and sit down for 2 mins but I obviously hid this quite well ... just as obviously they couldn't see my face when I eventually got to walk away from them ... as in 'Don't these people realise I'd only come out for a quick fag and not an instant run down on the Civil war/the Bishop of Bath and Wells/Princess Di etc?' I've got a nasty feeling some of them go away with a rather hazy idea of British history but mostly it's only minor details like the wrong

Charles being beheaded (this only comes into it because the one that wasn't beheaded stayed at the castle) and whether the Monmouth Rebellion was before, during or after the Civil War. Let's face it I can't know everything. The fact that I don't know anything doesn't seem to have cramped my style as yet. On the other hand, how many of these tourist buggers know the Latin name of the giant tortoise? Not many I'll bet!! I just wish one of them would ask me.

Anyway, it's the show on Saturday and I have rashly entered 11 classes, so I've now got 2 days in which to sober up and start improvising! The photo on the back of this letter is one I took a couple of weeks ago ... not posed actually ... I'd filled a can with water and stuck it in the porch intending to water my pots of lilies out the front a bit later on. As it happened, Morgan was out playing at the time. I came back indoors from doing something in the garden just a few minutes later to find him sitting on the can splashing the water about so thought I'd take a few pics to send Ed. As the Show Schedule has a class for 'Humorous photos', I thought I'd put this one in. I've also entered '5 potatoes – white'; '3 courgettes'; 2 cucumbers'; flowering pot plant; foliage pot plant; 4 herbs – separately in water (God, they're picky aren't they?); 'any other craft' (i.e. anything other than knitted or sewn – decided to put my bottle gourds in as I had traced the odd colours with brown and gold – that's a craft isn't it?) Well, I think it's a craft anyway and I certainly haven't got a knitted article anyway ... when it comes down to it, who the hell knits 'articles' these days? I mean, do people actually knit cars, house, office blocks?? I think they could be a bit behind the times here. Still, after I've hit the Show with my stuff that shouldn't be a problem anymore ... !!!

Well, that's about all for now.

Somerset, June 2002

Dear Pand,

Did I tell you about my new job a few months ago? It didn't last I'm afraid ...
I did it for 3 weeks and already I was thinking it was not my thing really.

What finally did it for me was the Tortoise living in a roll of lino (I was
appalled as you can imagine!) but a whole catalogue of disasters followed
one upon the other in a relatively short space of time. I'll just give you a
quick rundown!

The woman who said 'Did you tie this horse's halter up like this? – I
must teach you how to tie up a horse' and who also asked me to wheel
her dung barrow up to the dung heap (up a very narrow plank of timber
with unmentionable stuff you could fall into on either side) ... being a
nice person of a helpful nature, I said 'Yes, sure' but she had filled the
barrow right to the top and it was *so* heavy ... I got half way up the plank
and it was very wet and windy weather so the plank was slippy and I lost
my momentum and that was that ... a whole barrow load of dung tipped
over just where it wasn't supposed to be! I then found out that the woman
who queried the horse tying manoeuvre also looked after the dung heap
and she was very particular ... not exactly my best day I think. I tried to
ingratiate myself by saying that it wasn't me who tied the horse up in the
first place (true) but on the other hand, I hadn't actually gone there to tie
up horses (also true).

I then spent 4 hours solid standing in a freezing cold barn measuring out
dried herbs using scales that took at least 30 mins to adjust to any accuracy
each time. That in itself was bad enough but then I had to use a price
labelling machine which came out of the Ark (and that's being generous)
and worked properly on average once out of every 50 labels (the rest of the
time, it took 4 complicated hand movements and a lot of muttered swear
words). There were also 2 other labels to stick on each container so it was
a fairly time consuming job. Even then I guess I could have coped but I
had been adopted by a Sulphur Crested Cockatoo who persisted on being

with me everywhere – if she wasn't on my shoulder she was climbing up my trousers to see what I was doing ... as fast as I filled these wretched jars and stuck their labels on, she'd be there trying to get the labels off. I'd haul her off and put her the other side of the barn and then 5 mins later, this little head appeared at waist level and we were off again! Whilst battling with her and the dreaded jars, I also had a Macaw which came in and pulled everything off the shelves ... I was (naturally!) responsible for everything on the shelves too. You won't believe this but I was actually desperate to get home to Morgan at the end of the day!

At the same time, I was welcoming visitors and taking their admission fees and money for stuff they bought (helped by the Cockatoo which actually raised something like £75 on the electronic till one day by walking on the keys before I could haul her off) In the normal course of events, none of this would particularly bother me but when my boss raised a query on how many jars I'd managed to fill, I mentioned the problems of the labelling machine, the scales, the cockatoo, macaw, etc. and her response was maybe that I should work a little faster. 'Time is of the essence' she said. As I had already the previous week suggested a couple of ways to speed things up (like the fact I could write the price labels quicker than the machine printed them; fill the jars by eye (more accurate than her dodgy scales); banish the cockatoo etc, etc.) I was more than a little miffed. It was soon after that (like about 20 minutes) that I suggested to her that I really didn't think we were going to hit it off and that it would be best all round if she found someone else. We parted amicably (me with a bandaged finger due to my 3rd attempt one day at salvaging the shop produce from the Macaw when he was very keen on demolishing it) and I can't say I was sorry to leave. In fact, I was absolutely delighted. Once I'd decided, I felt *so* relieved, the last hour went quite quickly. It was wonderful to wake up the following morning and think 'Whoopee – no more freezing to death in the barn!' No doubt she awoke in the same mood.

So having got rid of that, you would think maybe I had a bit of free time but in fact I decided at the beginning of March to start selling plants at the local market/car boot sale. Every week now I take around 100 plants and it's hard work trying to get the variety of stuff to attract every sort of buyer. It's pretty time consuming but at least it doesn't involve tying up horses with the wrong sort of knot and I am slowly building up a customer base of people who are looking for something slightly different (as well as those beginners who want advice almost more than they want plants as such). The people I've met (stall holders and customers) are quite interesting too – all local really so know each other to a greater or lesser degree with the usual little feuds and disagreements and gossip.

Morgan of course hates this time of year – even without the extra work of growing to sell, it's always busy and so less time for him. Whilst the weather has been good, he has managed a few days out in his aviary in the garden but he has not taken full advantage. Even a brand new box hasn't impressed him and after a few desultory attempts at customising it, he has spent his aviary time sitting about looking grumpy. Brightens up a bit though when the owner of the horses in the field adjoining the garden comes with her daughter to do a bit of dressage and jumping (daughter quite famous in local horsey circles I gather). Anyway, you know what Morgan is like with any large 4 legged mammal – thinks they exist solely to provide him with some amusement.

The garden is looking pretty good and as I haven't told you about it for ages, I'm going to cheat and include part of a letter I wrote to Joy earlier in the season! Aren't word processors wonderful?

Snowdrops are over in this part of the country and the nodding white heads are replaced by fat green seed heads which hold the promise of another Spring to come. The earliest Daffodils have been and gone but some of the later varieties are still in their prime and offer their heads both to the sun and the early insects. A sweet wave of scent too and impossible to resist leaning down for a closer look (and a sniff too). Clouds of yellow everywhere around here from the Forsythia – as each little golden flower dies, fresh green leaves replace it – an almost seamless transition. The winter Hyacinth are in full bloom – a heady scent which is almost unseemly this early in the year but so welcome. Absolutely covered in blooms is the evergreen Clematis Armandii – its slightly apple scent melds perfectly with the sweet smell of the Choisya bush through which it grows. Even without the perfume, the two look perfect together and will shortly be enhanced by the huge flat flowers of another Clematis (Madame Coulture) – a real beauty. All this takes place in just one corner of the garden … a flamboyant, blowsy sort of corner – the other areas are slightly less 'in your face' but just as attractive in their own way. The Winter flowering

Cherry has hung on to a few of its white-tinged pink flowers and is backed by the dark pink of the flowering Ribes (the latter smells appalling but looks good) and at ground level, that beautiful mid-blue of the Muscari. Elsewhere the delicate flowers of the Alpine Clematis (a rich dark pink) clothe our old Apple tree which is already sprouting, pale pink Azaleas sit proudly above masses of flowering violets and primroses, trailing rosemary is full of flowers, the rich purple and dark pink of Aubretia creep along the ground and the winter flowering honeysuckle sends out a fragrant message every time I walk out the back door to pick some parsley!

The garden down at Chapel Cleeve is blooming too: daffodils, crocus, hyacinth everywhere and so many primroses … ! There are 2 beautiful Daphne bushes – such pretty flowers and the scent is gorgeous. The winter Jasmine is about finished now but already the Fuchsias are growing to take over. The Clematis Montana is covered in buds and the various honeysuckle are sprouting strongly whilst both my evergreen climbing and shrub honeysuckles still continue to flower. The Green (stinking) Hellebores have provided an excellent show this winter and their somewhat pallid colours have been offset by a well coloured red/orange Quince … the perfect combination I think. My twin Twisted Hazels are covered in catkins, the big Horse Chestnut is somewhat gingerly opening its leaves, the Black Elder is screaming for room, the Victoria Plum covered in blossom and smelling gorgeous and … well … it's all just great. Another year, another beginning.

Just in case the above sounds too idyllic, once out of either of the gardens things alter somewhat. Still a sense of burgeoning life but in this particular case it is roadworks – they blossom like some kind of triffid and no matter which road you take, you cannot avoid them. There are roadworks at Blue Anchor bay (replacing part of the Esplanade); at Blue Anchor Railway Crossing (I haven't worked out what for yet); at Dragon's Cross (new bus lay-bys); at Carhampton (rebuilding the stream culvert – for the 2nd year); in Minehead (seafront approach) – laying service pipes for a new housing complex; in Minehead (town centre), re-organising taxi ranks for a new one-way system; in Bilbrook – dredging the Ford (the longest Ford in the UK and don't we know it every Autumn?); in Old Cleeve and Chapel Cleeve. clearing out roadside ditches which would have been best done in the autumn and would thereby have alleviated at least some of the flooding. All this of course just in time for the summer season!

Before I forget, Pand, I saw a Kingfisher on the river at the bottom of Dunster castle the other week! First one for a long time so pretty impressed.

See you soon.

Somerset, December 2002

Dear Pand,

Thanks for House/Parrot and Tortoise sitting the other month (not to mention the plants!) – easier than taking Morgan and Curry up to Chester as we did the other year and wonderful to have an unencumbered holiday too!

Spain was good (apart from that little panic at Plymouth when we thought we'd forgotten all the holiday money!). Covered a bit more of the Eastern regions anyway.

You know we found a buyer for Cleeve Park a couple of weeks ago? Looks like it will go ahead without too much of a problem (I suppose I shouldn't say that remembering the many other fiascos). Anyway, just thought I'd prepare you for the next adventure just so you can't whine and claim you knew nothing about it when it happens!

When CP is sold, we're thinking of buying somewhere in Spain and then selling this house next year and moving out there. Dead simple, eh? Why have you stuck your head in the wardrobe Pand? This WILL be the last move AND will be less fraught with less animals and only 3 or 4 trailer loads of plants. A walkover you might say (well, YOU might not say it perhaps but trust me, it will be!). It was actually swimming lazily around in the heated pool at Blue Anchor that did it – getting older and colder, Spain began to look appealing – southern Spain – sun in the winter and surely plenty of history to explore.

You can come out now – having dropped my little bombshell, I'd better go and do a bit of work!

No doubt I'll hear from you soon?

English Channel, October 2003

Dear Pand,

Bit of a last minute rush (surprise, surprise) The sea being a bit rough, thought I'd settle in a corner and write to you in the hope that my stomach will forget the urge to empty itself! Just been down to the car to make sure Morgan and Curry are ok – give it another hour or so before I go down again. Curry is asleep but Morgan was muttering crossly to himself – actually I think I woke him up!! I think I worry more than he does – you know the sort of thing – do I have enough pockets in the clothes I'm wearing to stuff all animals in should anything go wrong and the boat tip over. At least this time, I only need the 2 pockets so have time to relax a bit.

We left Somerset on a grey day – the Quantocks were practically invisible in the mist and after 3 years of fantastic views and gorgeous countryside, we made our way towards the ferry port and exile. Having now only C and M, I thought it would be easier travelling and as far as the actual physical thing, this is true.

However, there was still the ever-present aggravation of obtaining Endangered Species certificates and veterinary inspections – the veterinary aspect this time not only for Morgan but as Spain (unlike France) also requires veterinary clearance for tortoises, Curry has to be examined too.

The paperwork entailed the usual hassle – what are you doing, what's this, does this tortoise ever stick it's head out and so on and so forth. As no one ever takes a tortoise on holiday from Minehead (or a parrot come to that), there was some flurry over what should be charged for examining them and pronouncing them fit – we eventually settled on the same fee charged for a dog – a bit of a rip off as Curry never stuck her head or bum out and Morgan didn't even bark – you remember that really irritating bark he'd picked up from next door's dog?

Arriving at the Veterinary surgery in good time for our appointment, we discovered that the vet had been called out for an emergency (which is fair enough) but by the time we got to see him, we'd been hanging around for an hour and, intent on embarking on a whole new life in another country within the next few hours, we were a little jittery. He said 'What am I looking at?' and I just said 'a tortoise – seen one before? – shell, head, 4 legs, brightly coloured – look, she moved – she's alive'. As if on cue, Curry crapped all over the table so she was signed off as fit for Spain. Next up was Morgan and the vet had no more idea of parrots than he did tortoises. 'And what's this then?' was his opening gambit. It was probably just his way (at least I hope it was) – after all, there was no mistaking it was a bird in the cage (probably of the Psittacine family) and a fairly cross one at that but we were due to leave that night and I was hopping around from one foot to the other thinking 'For Christ's sake, just get *on* with it – we don't need the small talk – we don't need anything from you, other than a signature and a stamp – Pleeeeeease!!'.

Having been parked in the waiting room in his travelling cage for over an hour, Morgan was well pissed off and refused to rise to the vet's attempts to get him to move off his swing. Knowing Morg, I knew exactly what the problem was – if you take no notice of him when *he* wants to play, when *you* are ready to do something, he resolutely refuses to budge. He sat there like some stuffed Buddha and just glared. The vet said 'He doesn't look very happy – what are his droppings like?' By this time, I was almost incandescent … kept us waiting for over an hour and then wants to discuss Morg's droppings. Fine if he was going to analyse them but we all knew we didn't have the time or inclination for that. I was about to explain a few things to this guy but E. nudged me (you know, the sort of nudge that means – calm down, count to 10 before you open your mouth) and so I took a deep breath and said 'Look, we've been hanging around for over an hour, Morgan is bored, he's not going to get off his swing for you or anyone else and we have to catch the midnight ferry from Plymouth. Does he look sick or does he just look fed up?' As if to confirm my outburst, Morgan suddenly perked up and said 'Oh Shit' (he usually only does that when he has dropped something but at least it proved he was alive) and the vet went 'What?' and I said 'Oh, he's got it muddled up *again* – he's trying to say, erm, well, something'. I long for Phillip, our Cornish vet (you met him once I think) – he used to come out to the house – none of this hanging around in the surgery and always took this sort of behaviour in his stride (the animals behaviour that is rather than mine!). He knew all the tortoises and both parrots and also dealt sensibly with quarantine on each return.

Anyway, we eventually got signed off – precious paperwork in our hands and a thoroughly miffed parrot in the back seat going 'Well, who *was* this guy anyway? Stupid bugger if you ask me. You mean we spent over an hour in there just for you to tell him I was a Parrot? Beats me. Anyway, I thought we were going on holiday. Wake me up when we get there! Mutter, mutter!'

At this point, I admit I did begin to wonder whether this was a good idea or not. Too late though – house sold, furniture gone, now on the ferry with a 2000 mile drive to Almeria in front of us. Miffed parrot or not, we can't turn back without an import licence for Morgan. Which reminds me, I need to find a ferry person to accompany me down to the hold and make sure said parrot is ok.

Will write soon

Gador, November 2003

Dear Pand,

I'm sorry that I didn't get in touch sooner but life has been a little difficult of late! Apart from the physical deprivations, its been harder to adjust than I remembered. The abrupt alteration of lifestyle was something I had forgotten. Takes a bit of getting used to and to go from being with lots of people to being with none is a bit of a change. I miscalculated with my radio too and it will not receive the World Service (which I was relying on) so it's a bit like living in the Dark Ages – not good for a news buff like me! Also of course, no phone and the possibility of getting a line seems remote to say the least. No radio, no TV, no phone, no emails – gulp!!

The weather ... it has been appalling ... torrential rain for most of this first month ... should have bought wellies with me rather than espadrilles (these were wishful thinking I reckon!) The access between here and Gador (main road) is getting worse ... need one of those motors which is amphibious as well as off road!!

Morgan travelled the long distance much better than I had expected actually – I think the fact that he had forgotten the trauma involved in moving to and from France and the added bonus of having his nest box attached to his travel cage helped him to cope. Curry was a doddle (makes all the difference when travelling with just one tortoise as opposed to 20 odd – it is just *so* easy – told you didn't I?). The only fly in the ointment was British Customs at Plymouth – I didn't mention this in the English Channel missive because I thought, like me, you would need some time to recover from the Veterinary palaver. However, didn't we just have to get some real wally who hated birds (well, cockatiels to be specific – and believe me, he *was* specific ... endlessly ... mother-in-law kept cockatiels and he hated them or he kept cockatiels and she hated them ... my survival instinct surfaced and I switched off after a while so I can't say for certain which way round it was.) He went thru the usual ... any weapons, sharp instruments, terrorists, etc. and like a fool, I said 'only if you count parrot beaks' and that was it ... forget the semtex, kalashnikovs (sp?), forged passports, Islamic hitchhikers, etc. ... he shone his torch on Morgan for what seemed hours and said 'Hello Polly' several times in a very loud voice which immediately got up my nose as well as Morgan's. Just as well he didn't look at Curry ... if we had have to have debated which member of his extended family had a tortoise, as well as a Parrot phobia, we could still be at Plymouth now! Where DO they get these people from I wonder! To cut a long story short (tho looking at the above, there's probably not a lot I missed out), we actually made it down here with only one stop (booked into a hotel in Limoges about 3 am for a few hours sleep) so were here late on Friday.

For the first few days the weather was glorious but then the rain struck and we had some horrendous downpours for 10 days or so. Everything was wet, tortoise couldn't go out, couldn't dry any clothes, 8 hour power cuts etc, etc. You can probably imagine how we felt – longing for radiators, cookers, Coronation Street, 9 o'clock news, Newsnight, etc.! Anything in fact that proved we were still in the land of the living!

So ... to describe this house ... shouldn't take long! It's small – bedroom, living room, bathroom, kitchen and cellar room (the latter an extension tunnelled into the hillside in the fashion of the cave dwellings in this area). Our water supply is simply rain water stored in a deposit under the Warehouse (a small room which is between our house and the house next door). We can have water to irrigate the orange trees twice a month but it is expensive averaging out at over £30 for 2 hours water. With 3/4 of an acre and much of the irrigation system in poor repair, it's not such a good deal.

The soil here is very sandy silt so fine enough to smother many plant roots and cause rotting off but rapidly drying out (when the sun emerges) and forming a top crust which sets like concrete – not ideal as you can imagine. Having said that and in case I sound very negative (probably ... its been that sort of month!), both the Bouganvillea and Hibiscus are in full flower and the large Spanish (?) Jasmine bush which scents the air every evening, is in full flower. You wouldn't believe the scent ... it's glorious ... if I could bottle it and send it, I would.

Whilst some of my plants have suffered, many are doing well, particularly the cacti, Palms, salvias and Bananas. It remains to be seen how well they all fare during the hotter summer weather though. We managed to salvage the remainder of the grapes and have 2 gallons of wine bubbling away in the cellar (and that without adding any yeast which we couldn't find to buy anyway!) plus just picking the remaining ripe figs, persimmon and clementines.

I have also got 3 jars of olives soaking in Brine which I hope will be edible in a few months – if not, at least it was fun picking them and I feel I really earned them as the trees are partway up the cliffs and surrounded by Prickly Pear. I also forgot to take a bag with me so just stuffed the olives in my pockets. Typically, I didn't fill my pockets evenly and was therefore slightly overweight on one side so my descent not only lacked grace but I fell into one of the big holes that are a feature of our terraces. If they don't work out, I'm going to be really miffed! Actually, I think I'll buy the next lot ... edible, no stones and a hell of a lot quicker! It's this PYO fetish isn't it?

The cooking facilities here are pretty hi tech really ... we have a tiny 3 burner calor gas thingie (actually its only really 2 burners, both either very high or out, as the 3rd burner doesn't work), an outside barbecue and a beehive oven (as in Pueblo Indian type of oven) halfway up the hillside. We plan to go and look for a proper cooker soon. I can cope with the outdoor method provided the weather is reasonable but as we seem to be living in more or less torrential rain these days, cooking outside loses its appeal somewhat.

As we are a bit up into the hills, there is more varied bird life than the usual glossy Starlings in the towns – buzzards and hawks, Robin, greenfinch, Chaffinch, Blackbird, sparrows, pigeons, Owls, Blackcaps, Wagtails, Hoopoes, Egrets (especially on irrigation days) Jackdaw occasionally and several unidentified LBJ's plus some game type birds (rather like large Grouse) we spotted right up on the top of our western boundary today. We heard them calling but unable to pick out any colouring/markings as they were in silhouette There are still some swallows and Martins about but the Bee Eaters have gone for the winter I think. Crickets (of course), lizards, several different beetles, bees, wasps, flies, butterflies, fantastic moths, various ants, a praying mantis, geckoes (indoors only so far), cute spiral snails and not so cute big snails, spiders (various), a Stick insect (or at least the nearest thing I can think of) and some rather smart creepy type red jobs plus I found a scorpion hiding under a stone the other day ... that's about it so far at this time of year. By the way, that little bird which we saw for a few days feeding on our patio in Somerset not long before we left was a Red Eared Waxbill – usually an aviary bird so possibly an escapee. Don't know what made me think of that but thought I'd pass it on anyway!

Most of our time so far has been spent here trying to get the land in some sort of order and we have done no touristy sort of things other than going to Mojacar (for the bank and computer) and Almeria. The latter is a large bustling sort of city and the port has ferry connections to North Africa ... worth further exploration given time. According to the locals, it also seems to be fairly busy in the hashish trade (tho not much good if they keep getting caught I suppose).

Further along the coast from Almeria is Roquetas de Mar – originally a small fishing port I think but now grown extensively and buildings (mostly apartments/hotels) seem to be thrown up almost as you look. The amount of new buildings under construction in this area is quite phenomenal. I am unsure how much is simply speculative or whether there is truly such a demand. Much of this area is used for growing salad crops, particularly tomatoes and peppers and mostly under glass (actually polythene strictly speaking) ... in some places in a certain light, it looks almost as if the sea has crept inland as the reflection from the poly tunnels gives the impression of a very tranquil sea.

The biggest National Park is part way between here and Mojacar – the Cabo de Gata which we have yet to visit. As well as fantastic scuba diving and massive sand dunes, it is reputed to be the best place in the area to see a huge variety of birds, both native and migratory ... so, it's on our list. At least one advantage here is that all along Spain's coastal (densely populated) strip, it's only a few miles inland before you hit mountains and then it gets quieter and very quickly more rural. Gador (our nearest port of civilisation about 2 miles away), can only be described as a country town (though it does have a mainline railway station) and has few facilities – maybe a good comparison would be half the size of Minehead but only 6 shops! On the plus side, it does have a wonderfully large and ornate Guardia Civil office and lots of sign posts for the Museum (tho we haven't actually managed to find the Museum itself yet, we are *really* very impressed with the signs).

Somewhat against our better judgement, we appear to have adopted at least one Perro de campo (country dog – a Spanish euphemism for feral dogs as opposed to the overwhelming number of stray dogs in the towns and cities which are just dumped). There are actually 3 campo dogs in the very immediate vicinity (for immediate, read our garden!) – 2 of them bitches which have recently pupped and so in fact, we now have one special campo dog plus 6 puppies (would have had 7 but we found 1 dead one) which come for milk every day. Strictly speaking, they are a nuisance because the bitches dig out burrows to have the pups in thereby undermining our already fragile terraces. They also howl all night plus raiding anything and everything not nailed down (one of my hiking boots I had to retrieve from down the river bed and they also demolished a nearly full bag of salted peanuts (Morgan's 'treats' actually) which we had inadvertently left out on the terrace). Then again, what can you do other than offer a helping hand (or carton of milk, etc!) and the puppies (as all puppies) are really sweet and already expect to be rescued if they get stuck in the irrigation channels. I guess they can spot a mug a mile off (especially one that responds immediately to distress calls!! – just how stupid am I?)

There is a Dog Rescue Society in Mojacar and the other day we met the ladies who run it. We had wandered into this small arcade looking for a cigarette machine and we suddenly heard this very English voice say 'If you are looking for a dog, we can help you'. Having spent a fraught hour in the bank next door, my immediate reply was 'Actually, I'm looking for a cigarette machine … I'll come back for the dog later'. It is a charity called PAWS and they have a small shop and are in the process of having a kennel complex built. You can volunteer for shop duty, dog walking, etc. (just like England really!) but sadly, Mojacar is about 65 miles from here so I don't think I'm going to be doing a lot of dog walking somehow.

As for neighbours, we don't actually have anyone living near us. The buildings around are just 1 room jobs that people use when they are working the land so in that respect, we are the only silly buggers actually living here full time. The building which adjoins our house is owned by Antonio and Dolores – they live in Gador and come nearly every day to 'do' (this is slightly worrying because I think maybe I should be 'doing' more than at present – tho I've spotted that today they have pruned their grape vines so, in order not to become the object of gossip, I expect I can't put off for much longer getting the ladders out and doing ours). They are elderly and very friendly (the neighbours that is – as opposed to the vines – tho they are quite elderly too). We are already on kissing terms (which is good) but Dolores is convinced that I understand everything she tells me (and she can talk, believe me!) which I am finding quite stressful! After a quick chat (say half an hour or so) with Dolores, I'm more than ready to lie down for a few hours until my brain gets back on an even keel. Today, I'm still not sure whether we were talking about the campo dogs being pregnant or me … is she expecting me to give birth shortly or what? I can't *wait* for the next conversation (tho I use the word 'conversation' in very loose terms)

One of our other neighbours (from across the rambla) is, according to legend, the local Lothario (not bad going as he must be 70 if a day). He appeared outside the other day at about 11 am having already imbibed half his years supply of wine and insisted on a tour of the house (to see what we'd done … very little!), a tour of the land so he could tell us how to repair the terraces and the irrigation channels (we'd done it wrong!), how to make the wine (hurray, we'd done it right!) and to give us some very complicated recipes involving sardines or codfish, tomatoes, lemon etc. and mud (or at least that's what my dictionary said – I'm taking it that 'mud' means 'mix everything together' but I could be wrong!). He also kept patting me (very heavily) on my shoulder (which didn't do the fracture any good at all) and telling what, in retrospect, I now think may have been some pretty odd jokes. (He also broke off half way thru this lengthy saga to go and pee up the pueblo oven … I was pretty gobsmacked but couldn't think of a suitable comment – not in Spanish anyway!) As I only understood about 1 word in 50 of what he said (but like a true English person just kept smiling and nodding), I'm not sure quite how our next meeting is likely to go – with any luck, he was too drunk to remember much, though that could mean I have to go through the whole sardine/codfish recipe again! I m beginning to think I should imbibe a few glasses before he arrives next time and then maybe we will be on the same wave length?

There is little reason here to mark the days and so it is somewhat surprising to be receiving Xmas cards already – tho the fact that it is pretty chilly once the sun goes down should be a reminder of how far into winter we are – plus the last couple of days we have noticed that the mountains in the Sierra Nevada have plenty of snow on them.

We have taken to scavenging locally for wood to burn in the evening ... we found a couple of old pallets the other day which we are currently using as firewood to eke out the citrus wood ... all very primitive but as people just dump their rubbish anywhere, we have decided to go into recycling in a big way. Today, I found a couple of old paint tins which I can use as plant containers so that was pretty exciting!

We have only been able to access the Internet by using a Cyber Cafe in Almeria City – no chance of a landline here, and doing it by mobile has proved impossible. Am still trying to work out how other people manage to continue working, writing books, etc from these rural parts. Either they have a direct Earth to God link (tell me more!) or they are just kidding and nip back to civilisation every few weeks. I've often noticed with a lot of these Back to Nature in Spain (or France or wherever) books that there seems to be a serious lack of discussion on the more basic aspects of living. I know the Internet or even just a phone can't truly be described as a basic necessity but also – where do these people crap? That is as basic as you can get and I would have thought deserved at least a paragraph or two. Maybe this is just me – having had a closer than nodding acquaintance with most types of cess pits and septic tanks over the years, I tend to think – new house – drainage – does it exist? I can recall more than one place where the Bathroom and Loo was stupendous – a real picture – marble tiles, glass walls, the whole bit but when you investigate, the drain and (worse still) the sewer pipe just evacuated onto the terrace below – it didn't even pretend to run into a septic tank – or even just a hole in the ground!

Anyway, never mind – need to get my mind off drainage (well, that sort of drainage anyway) and concentrate on the water drainage, otherwise known as Irrigation channels – in a mess and few of them working! Unfortunately, the one that IS working is decanting water into Juan's vegetable patch and washing away the soil from his plants. He is not a happy bunny and has asked us to sort it out. As it must have been doing this for years and the previous owner did bugger all about it, I think he is perhaps just picking on us and expecting us to repair 20 years of neglect within a fortnight. I told him we would see to it but at the same time secretly crossed every finger I had behind my back – I mean, who is this guy kidding?

Must go and pluck an orange – will write again soon.

Gador, December 03

Dear Andy,

Just a quick letter (is there such a thing?) to tell you a bit more of the area.

The landscape is reminiscent of the old Cowboy films – not surprising when you think the Tabernas Desert (the only desert in Europe) where they made all those 60's spaghetti Westerns is just up the road from here.

Most of the scenery is very impressive but this area is dependant on growing crops ... mostly salad crops (tomatoes, peppers, aubergines, etc.) and all is done under plastic ... huge areas of plastic greenhouses (if you half close your eyes on a sunny day, these acres of plastic look almost like water).

The coastline is beautiful (tho I think not as interesting as north of Barcelona) but it's the inland bits that are the most impressive. In many parts it is reminiscent of N. Africa – not surprising as the history here encompasses so much of the Moorish influence. Oddly enough, there is one area which we drive thru to go from here to Almeria city ... it's just a bit of wasteland but has one big date palm growing. Out of all this area, *that* says Moor to me.

Almeria itself is a busy bustling sort of city (tho subject to horrendous
traffic jams as we discovered one evening!) and on our way to Roquetas
de Mar, we pass the Port. From here you can get the ferry across to N.
Africa ... just imagine! Ah, Morgan heard me write that – ferry? Ferry??
I'm not going on another bloody ferry for anything! That's the end of that
then – no exploring N. Africa!

Above the sprawl of the new city is the old fortified town (we haven't
yet been thru all of this tho just the little narrow alleys are exciting)
– thousands of years of invaders, defenders, one culture after another.
You can walk on the same path as someone from time past and let your
imagination run riot. Always you are aware of the history of the place
and it matters not if you stop for a drink at a modern cafe ... you *know*
that beneath your feet history marched (or, more prosaically, history went
looking in the shops for a bit of retail therapy!).

If one ignores the tremendous building sprawl that is going on from
Mojacar to Roquetas (and beyond I think, tho we haven't travelled that
far) and discount the modern Urbanisations, what is noticeable is the
Cave dwellings. In this vicinity, a lot of the houses are built into the hills.
Imagine a rock face ... look at it and all you see is a door and a couple
of windows maybe ... the rest of the house is built into the mountain.
Here, we have only one room built in that way – the rest of the house
is, for want of a better word, outside in the open air. This architecture
is guaranteed to avoid the heat of mid summer and remain habitable,
temperature wise, in the middle of winter. Not only that but, with an
even temperature, its great for every stage of producing and storing
juice, wine, olives, etc. Here people truly do still live in caves and who
can blame them?

After 3 weeks of endless rain, we have enjoyed 4 or 5 days of beautiful
weather – clear blue sky and hot sunshine and so we have been able to
get on the ground and pick some oranges (and figs, grapes, persimmon,
custard apple). Most of our neighbours seem to sell their citrus fruit to
the Juice factory up the road but our crop (even off 3/4 acre) has been
so neglected over the last few years, it is not a commercial proposition.
Even so, we enjoy picking the fruit and squeezing to make juice, eating
the clementines out of hand, using the few ripe lemons for cooking, and
trying to make ever more imaginative recipes!

In our immediate vicinity, we are gradually exploring and going further into the hills – just lately we have been sidetracked by the need to feed the Campo dog and puppies and by our scavenging duties. There are no official recycling centres/rubbish dumps here and people just dump all sorts of rubbish anywhere (most recently in our Rambla – not too happy about that!) and so we collect everything which we can make use of. Still, we are slowly getting beyond what we fondly call 'our hill' (the one which houses our electricity life line) – I think we could probably walk for miles but we (well, alright then, I) get carried away with collecting/picking stuff (always take the usual number of carrier bags with me just in case) ... olives, figs, pomegranates, odd bits of stone, sloughed snake skins, the odd stray sheep, etc. I expect once I've decimated the surroundings, we'll actually get to walk further!

Better finish or this will go on forever.

Gador, December 2003

Dear Pand,

Kev should write the 'real' book about living in Spain ... Dolores who rabbits for hours ... after a conversation with her, I need to lie down for an hour to get my brain back. Her husband, Antonio, a really nice guy who is happy for Curry to be let loose in his vegetable patch. Fonso (Lothario – I don't know his real name but either of these seems apt!) who is pretty well pissed at 11 am when he comes over here – I think I probably mentioned him earlier – I'd be surprised if I haven't as each visit leaves me feeling more like a stunned hare than previously.

Between all of them, there is some talk of a donkey. Worryingly, I am unable to really suss out quite what is meant – do I own the donkey and loan it to them? Do they own the donkey and loan it to me? And anyway, for what purpose? Riding it downstream to town when the Rambla and the river floods and the car can't make it? Do I just own the donkey (like a mug) and do bugger all with it? I already had 2 dictionaries and just bought another but none seem to cover the possible lease of a donkey. (Memo to all dictionary publishers here – include some *useful terms*!).

This donkey thing is definitely preying on my mind! Shit … as if I don't have enough problems with Vodafone … I sure can't be doing with arguing about a donkey lease or whatever! Strange place really – rabbits kept in titchy cages, birds in same, coloured pigeons (pink, green, blue – you name it – vegetable dye I think), a dog that lives right next to the railway and seems always to have his bum just on the lines – I mentally cheer him each time I see he has survived. Repairing the road from town is quite simply dumping some sand in the huge pot holes and so instead of falling down known holes *all* the time, we can simply drive up big mounds of sand and *then* fall down unexpected pot holes … it gives us something to think about between the rather scary notice placed at the end of the tarmac road which tells you that you are now leaving the municipality of Gador and negotiating the remainder of the road (ha – did I say 'road'?) leading up to the Rambla turn off. I think it would be exciting if we had an off road 4 wheel drive – at least we would *look* the part.

All the people here are really nice (except the mobile phone people who are absolute shits) and they mostly listen to my appalling Spanish very politely (except for the car park guy who was a real jobsworth in any language). Last night in Almeria, the waitress at the Tapas bar came to an agreement with me … she was learning English and I was learning Spanish. At least we had a wonderful hot bowl of Potatoes and Onions before we attempted, yet again, the horrors of the Internet cafe. She at least was really friendly and made up for the car park prat.

By the way, the following little tale is not something I'm particularly proud of but does seem to sum up the oddities of life here on the edge of the canyons. You will know from the photos and descriptions that the house is built on the hillside … to the front (south) you look over all the citrus and the view narrows between two cliffs, over the old Copper Age settlement and eventually to the coast at Almeria city. To the right, the ground rises steeply (where the Orchids and the Desert Wheatears live and our irrigation water comes from). To the left however is the Rambla and across from this, slightly more open ground on which is sited Lothario's cottage. (He, like everyone except us, lives in town but has a house of sorts here in the canyons from which he looks after his land). Anyway, I was out on the terrace fairly late one morning with the binoculars – not looking at anything in particular but just roving the horizon in the hopes of seeing something worth while. Also, using the binoculars sometimes was a good way of spotting Doggers and the other campo dogs and seeing what they were up to. As I swept over the Rambla and alighted on Lothario's place, I first saw Brownie (the big brown campo dog) in his front yard and then noticed Lothario's Jeep parked there. I thought it strange as usually, whenever he comes up to his house, he always turns up at our house to have a chat and tell us what we were doing wrong, etc. etc. So, without thinking, I played the binoculars over the rest of his ground and my eye was suddenly caught by an odd pinkish shape hiding in the Pomegranate hedge. I was terribly excited because I thought it must be an animal of some sort but was puzzled as to what it would be. As you know, my far sight is pretty bad, even with binoculars but I was so convinced that I had spotted some sort of rarity that we should rush over and check out that I called E and gave him the binoculars and said ... 'Look! ... See that ... What is it? ... shall we go and stalk it?' only for him to hand me back the binoculars after about 3 seconds and say 'Nah – not worth the effort' and I'm hopping about with excitement saying 'Well are you sure? It *could* be something' and he says 'Well, actually, it's just Lothario taking a crap in his garden – the exciting pink shape you saw was his bare bum'. Almost on a par with my claim to have spotted an eagle once in Scotland which sadly turned out to be a plane! Ah well, maybe I'll have better luck tomorrow!

Gador, January 2004

Dear Pand,

Thanks for your letter (and the yeast!) which I collected from the PO the other day. Good to hear from you tho sorry to hear about Betty ... maybe a few weeks rest in Maura's will do her the world of good! Anyway, as you say, driving in nasty weather is no pleasure whatsoever. These days, driving in good weather isn't so wonderful either!

Yes, you are right, Bub was full of her birthday plans (made me feel guilty enough to think about flying back to attend but that thought, although genuine, petered out pretty smartish in the light of the following day (as it does!). I looked at the amount of work here and the time it would take to get to the airport and then the palaver the other end and then I got up and thought 'Hey, who am I kidding?' At least I wasn't stupid enough to suggest the possibility to her so that's ok. Anyway, she says it was her best birthday ever (or at least for a great number of years) so your absence and mine did not diminish her enjoyment (tho I've no doubt she would have loved us to be there).

Thanks by the way for the amphibious vehicle article. Unfortunately due to our lack of correspondence recently, what we are now looking for is Desert vehicles ... after all the horrendous downpour which was literally all November, we haven't had any rain since and are now going mad for water. Bloody typical isn't it?

I'm sorry you were worried that we might have appeared at your door – apart from anything else, returning to England just like that wouldn't be that easy ... importing Morgan takes a few weeks to arrange if nothing else so you are safe for now! Anyway, it's not raining now!!

I was glad that you said you were going to postpone your visit – as February loomed, I was trying to work out how to say it wouldn't be a good idea. Its not that I wouldn't like to see you but its not exactly posh living here. I doubt whether our water supply would cope with an extra person (unless terribly dirty!) and our septic tank (laugh!) certainly wouldn't ... we just spent 2 days trying to find it (cos the loo kept backing up) and finally yesterday spent a very smelly (but satisfying) day drilling various holes in the concrete till we hit gold (or crap if you want to be particular) until we could get a pipe into the actual pit and drain off all the excess fluid ... the loo works a treat now! In our 'stuff this, knock it down, dig it out, just go for it mood' we were very lucky in that we also found the major cause of our water leak. Touch wood, that is more or less solved now. I can't help but think we did all this stuff in France ... Spain wasn't supposed to be like that!

You may have misunderstood about the circumstances here ... the house itself is comfortable enough and the weather since Xmas has been wonderful (too hot some days in fact) and the scenery and walks around the house are just great – once you get used to it, it really does have a beauty of its own. You can walk literally for miles thru the ravines, canyons, ramblas etc. Our last few outings we've met up (accidentally I might add) with the sheep/goat herds which wander back and forth, clanging their bells, across the area between here and Santa Fe. In fact, we were watching (from the safety of our terrace this time) the one man herd this afternoon ... it seems quite incredible to see both man and animal perambulating along what seems to be sheer cliffs. Morgan in his aviary was whistling away (at the same time the guy was whistling his dog) – if we stay here much longer, I'm bloody sure we will get at least some sheep thru the garden ... each day Morgan perfects the various whistles. I'm waiting for a really pissed off shepherd to come to the door and say 'what the hell are you playing at?'.

I discovered my first snake the other day ... we'd been up along the other side of the rambla and for a change, found a gentle (well, gentle for here anyway!) path which wound through the bottom of the ravines. We'd just about got to our 'better turn back' point (we were expecting our 4th viewers for the house) and I suddenly heard a rustling noise which didn't equate with the wind. Sure enough on close inspection of an Oleander bush there was a snake curled up in there. It was impossible to see enough of it to i.d. it but it was really really good!

We've done some great walks here tho I confess I don't really like going thru the tunnels (particularly those which show fresh signs of falls like the one just up the Rambla from here ... it took a bit of faffing and farting about to get thru that one) and I have also discovered (or re-discovered to be fair) a fear of heights! In some spots, I am almost paralysed which isn't terribly helpful. I miss some of the scenery because I just can't look at it ... too busy creeping across on hands and knees! I really envy the goats and sheep ... I really envy the goat/sheep guy ... he seems to walk where I would go 'What??? Are you kidding?'

Good news tho is that even the Shepherd is not invincible ... watching their usual antics today – after the herd had galloped over the hills doing death defying leaps and stuff, one sheep got left behind ... it was in a dip with vegetation and was scoffing away quite happily and quite unaware that it was 'lost'. We were planning to go out to Almeria to the Internet café but kept looking over at it (too far for us to really do anything – unless it proved an emergency – before you wondered!) ... after half an hour or so with Morgan still madly whistling and us debating Internet or not and could we *possibly* get a free sheep and, if so, how much of our water would it want before it turned into something remotely edible, the shepherd turned up and grabbed this recalcitrant sheep by the ear and marched it off over the mountain to join the others. So, no sheep for us! Mind you, Morgan was already muttering 'Well, if its only going to bleat in Spanish, I'm not that keen! '

I doubt I'll match your garden simply for the lack of water. However, I am struggling with mint and parsley and already have seeds up from gourds, tomatoes, rocket, lettuce, spring onion, Morning Glory, etc. Biggest problem is where to put them where they may have a chance of survival. One of my big yuccas already has a flower spike on and many of the cacti are really enjoying life (Euphorbia obesa is flowering away like a mad thing!). The various salvias I bought over here (including the S. confertiflora from Dunster Castle) love it here provided they have a shady spot ... they are all still flowering.

Here at the moment, lots of wild flowers are blooming ... best of which are various euphorbias, White Rock Rose, several geraniums (cranesbill), various succulents and some bulbs too which I can't i.d. The Almond is in full flower and smells superb. There are one or two flowers open on the Citrus but they will not come into their own for another few weeks yet. My new tree aloe (Aloe arborescens ... in the book if you look) is flowering like mad ... beautiful tall spires of red flowers – a real smack in the eye! Apart from these, it's a bit quiet here on the garden front but hopefully more later.

Big gap here as I never got around to actually posting this and the last couple of times at the Internet cafe Freeserve hasn't been available so I have been unable to either send or collect any email. Our last day there was pretty good actually ... just got the server up and everything blew ...!!

Anyway, its now part way thru January and the weather remains hot and dry. Our evenings are spent working out ever more tortuous ways of getting water ... it seems so ridiculous after all the rain we had in November but this is life here. With no TV or radio to distract us, evenings are taken up with Morgan's new trick – he has become enamoured of a broom and so spends his evenings being pushed around on said Broom – brilliant for him but somewhat boring for me after the 10th circuit of this very small house! Probably healthier than Binge drinking but now, after the 15th circuit, I might just question that statement!!

Anyway, we have now partly sussed a way to get the irrigation water (every so often but not to be relied upon!) to top up our water deposit. This cunning method involves lots of hosepipes, muslin and gravel (for filters?) but the main thing is how you get water to run up? So, get a pump?

Days later and I still haven't got around to posting this, so thought I'd add a touristy bit ... (well, not *that* touristy as it's only a few miles away) but we went to Los Millares the other day – the Copper Age settlement just across the River Andarax from us.

Some of the site is still being excavated and cos no one else goes there at this time of year, you have a whole new (or old really I guess) world to yourself ... bottle of water, carton of olives and a bit of cheese and you can sit and imagine what life was like when it was *really* rough (as opposed to now when it's just a bit rough!!). There is, in reality, little to see and the ground differs not a jot from the ground around the house. That very fact of course, made me think and I tried to imagine what our land would have been like a few thousand years ago. So little remains of these sites but in actual fact, strip away the cultivated stuff and it's possible to see – or at least begin to see. The water was there (tho long gone underground like our Rambla); the means of shelter (the numerous caves) tho I am unsure of the source of firewood. Nowadays only Oleander, Tamarisk and Olive grow here along with smaller shrubby stuff although Pines are prevalent once you go towards the Alpujarras or the Tabernas. Eucalyptus grow in abundance along part of the Rambla system and also in groves at Tabernas but they are introduced trees (I gather for their antiseptic qualities – breathing out their own form of insect repellant).

Having said that tho, I've no idea when they were introduced. In fact, I've no real idea which trees as such were growing here in Copper Age time. In fact, I know nothing about this age which is pretty bad considering I am living on top of a designated site!! Will hope to rectify this rather shaming state of affairs when the Information Centre at the site opens for business. Probably Easter.

We also went a little way towards the Alpujarras but it seemed like too much of an adventure after having weathered the Supermarket in Almeria. Actually, the Alpujarras (on the south side of the Sierra Nevada) is only just the other side of the Sierra Gador from us ... standing in the hot sun and spotting the snow on the high peaks is one of the highlights of my day!

BTW, the furry parrot rucksack turns heads wherever I go (mind you, it probably would in Minehead – out here in rural Spain, its a talking point to say the least!). It's very much admired (I like to think so anyway!) Out collecting pine cones the other day at Tabernas, the 2 gypsy women I spoke to couldn't get over it. It was either the rucksack or my poor Spanish they were laughing at – I think it was the rucksack but then again, I could be wrong!! We were collecting the cones – both for Morgan's box and to burn on the fire – and these women were anxious to know what we were up to. Whilst I could easily remember the French word for 'parrot', I couldn't think what it was in Spanish tho I did remember Estufa for stove. Not that any of it helped really because as I flew around the field pretending to be a bird (a lot of realistic flapping of arms and elephantine leaps in the air), to try and explain, I noticed that several other people had ambled over from the nearby village staring and pointing as village people tend to do when met with something totally outside their comprehension. At this point, I began to feel a bit self conscious – well, actually, I felt totally bloody ridiculous and my original audience were going (as I imagine the conversation at least) 'Right, well, either she is a complete dipstick or she is just pretending to be'. Surprisingly, I then dredged up 'Papagayo' (brain probably being stimulated by all that exercise) but I have the feeling they thought I intended roasting a parrot over a fir cone fire rather than letting him have the fir cones to play with in his box.. If gypsies ate Hedgehogs in times gone by, there's no real reason to imagine they don't think we would eat Parrots. Not altogether an outlandish idea when Morgan is being shitty!

I gather your weather is pretty much the usual for this time of year with the normal quota of frost, fog, rain and wind. Here it is still fine and hot but before you get too envious, we have had some really nasty winds – cold off the desert and almost tornado-like, the very dry soil whipping into your face wherever you turned and the wind from all 4 quarters at once. Strong enough gusts to make us wary of what comes off the roof onto our car ... we might be brown but we worry a lot too!

Anyway Pand that's about it from rural Espagna for now ... it might not be mega news but its at least a glimpse of how the other half (namely Me) is currently living!

Gador, February 2004

Dear Andy,

Lothario struck again and our biggest thrill this week was the trip thru the Water Course.

We were quite innocently minding our own business (and relaxing a little after having completed Morgan's new aviary out of Bamboo, 15 foot bamboo pieces dragged up the Rambla and then up to the house – phew!) when Lothario turned up at 5 pm the other day ... 'irrigation is starting again soon ... shall we walk a bit of the course and make sure everything is ok?' (or something similar I think he said!). So, what can we do ... even tho the sun disappeared half an hour ago, dutifully we put our boots on (to do the water course effectively, you need boots and a Mattock) picked up our spade (we don't have a mattock yet ... for shame!) and trotted along behind him, over nasty little thin bits of cliff (look down and you are lost!), thru caves (the third one was literally on hands and knees) and ended up miles away and sitting around on very uncomfortable rock ledges whilst we waited for his friend to turn up and explain (?? hah!!) what he was doing with his grapes (at this point and time, who cared??) We were not only cold and dirty but completely knackered by the time we crawled back thru the last tunnel at sometime after 9 pm and espied our house from the top of the hill – it may not have been so bad, but I'd already been on a hike up the hills in the opposite direction only hours before.

Lothario has promised to show me how to prune the various grape vines – (despite the fact I've done them already – can't wait – He's a bit like Doggers (our campo dog) … arrives silently and you don't know anyone is there until you feel a nudge against your knee – well, when I say Knee, I refer to Doggers of course … Lothario isn't that brave – he just always picks on the fractured shoulder and gives it a good pat before the ritual kissing of cheeks! OK – I'm probably being a bit harsh here – its been a long week!!

Horror of horrors, we have lost Doggers … it must be over a week since she last came and we haven't seen her anywhere about. In fact, I think she was hanging around the orange pickers down the Rambla a couple of weeks ago and altho she appeared very briefly at our door, she has just vanished. I think someone must have taken her because we just haven't seen any sign of her anywhere and the other 3 dogs (Brownie and Shorty plus a very odd bow-legged puppy) are still here. It's all very worrying, Pand … I miss Doggers. I'd like to think someone has pinched her and given her a good home but I'm not convinced! Thinking about it, no one here would have taken her – she's just poked off and it will all end in tears I suspect!

The orange harvest is now upon us … if I see another orange, I will go mad!! Most of the small landowners here sell the oranges to the local Juice factory (so as you down your morning orange juice, think of us!). After a bit, just picking the wretched things wears off … there's only so long where you can do 'one for the crate and one for me'. We don't have a contract this year so we have taken loads of fruit to the Dog Charity shop in Mojacar … they can sell it there and make use of the revenue. Several of the grove owners have skips to load the oranges into … even if you didn't know where the factory was, you can soon find out as they tend to overload the skips and then spill the oranges out all over the road. Here at home, we have orange juice, orange and kiwi juice, orange, kiwi and banana juice, orange ice cubes, duck a l'orange (minus the duck), orange fritters, orange … in fact, anything with orange, we eat it!

At last we have finally managed to install a wood-burning stove in the living room ... just a little luxury! It's burning away happily even as I speak and we are all enjoying it (in fact, we are cooking dinner on it). Being high up, it gets quite cold at night this time of year and there's nothing quite like that sheer heat at the end of the day. We all shuffle up close to it to begin with and then shuffle back against the wall as it starts to warm up. It's really too big for this room but the only one available at the time and we were desperate for something! The little oven at the top does baked potatoes to a T tho and the top is as good as a conventional hob. It saves rushing out to buy a cooker and certainly beats firing up the Beehive oven in the garden!

For the last few weeks, the weather has been perfect ... clear blue sky, lots of sun and hot enough for T shirts and shorts to be the order of dress but the house still needs some form of heating – with the woodburner, hopefully, we have done the business! This bit will be of interest ... we had frost on the car windscreen on Xmas day!! Very brief and the geraniums are still flowering, my orchids remain sanguine (and flowering still) but I'm hanging on to my Fleece ... Tell you what tho ... after all the moaning I did about the rainfall in November, we could do with some now! Our water deposit is already down by a third and as this is our only means of water supply, we are already beginning to get a little nervous (and smelly!!). As we can't get radio or tv, the big highlight of the evening is to go down to the river (just about trickling) and fill up water containers ... am beginning to get quite paranoid ... if we go anywhere and see running water, leap out and fill a container. Honest to God, I will *never* moan about Wessex Water again ... ever!!

Just discovered that the WC leaks (at the clean water end thank goodness) but it wastes water and we are in a very definite saving water mode here! We removed a tile behind the WC just to check if we had a leak and immediately, several litres of water gushed out on to the floor ... we were both so amazed, it was a few seconds of precious water loss before one of us ran out to the warehouse and turned the water pump off. Still, we were quick enough to flip off our shoes so got a free foot wash! I know I said I didn't want to laze about in a villa but this is getting beyond a joke! (Could sure do with a bit of villa living right now!). Although we managed to mend this end of the water pipe (to the cistern), the remaining pipe remains buried in the walls and so ultimately a bit of a mystery. Its driving us mad because the pump (which brings the water from the deposit to the taps – I know you like the technical stuff Pand!) still cuts in even when we aren't running water and so somewhere … we have another leak. Anyway, if it doesn't rain soon, we'll be in … how can I put it? 'deep s**t' doesn't seem too extravagant a phrase in the circumstances. Even the main river down at the bottom of the Rambla has slowed from 2 trickles to 1 trickle and its getting pretty wearing to trot down there to fill up water containers. Am sitting here trying hard to think of something good to counteract the above problems … yep … just spotted him … our resident Gecko has just popped up behind the computer screen … I watch him rather than Coronation Street … accents not quite the same but you can't have everything

Out on another Pine Cone hunt, it was gratifying to see how many posh 4 x 4's were making their way up to the snow line for skiing in the Sierra Nevada (gratifying because we could see there was not a lot of snow up and we need to get our pleasure where we can these days!) Talking of snow, its a bit like looking at Exmoor from the safety of Old Cleeve … I can see it but I don't have to wade through the wretched stuff!

For a short while earlier this year, we are had a surfeit of water in our own Rambla … an overflow from the irrigation system as far as I can make out but that has stopped now. The Campo dogs loved it … they ran around and splashed about and it was nice to see as generally, they have a hard life and to see them having a bit of fun was good (Yes – you are right – we *did* play Sticks and stuff with them!). Now they, like us, have to make do with the little that the river offers.

In case you thought we were slacking here, I should tell you its not only orange harvest but also olives. I'm getting pretty fed up! I can't keep up with all this stuff. Most of the olives I picked seem to have gone all pale and whingy. There is a good way to do them but I couldn't fully understand what Juan said … I tried a mix of French and Spanish along with lots of gestures (yes, rude ones as well) but I think maybe I missed a key word or phrase. I think I told you about my little harvest of Olives and that they were preserving away quite happily? Having peered at them recently, they just don't look as good as I had expected

- well, ok, to be honest they look like rubbish ... what else can I say? Its jolly miffing though - took me ages to get them and then make the brine to put them in. Actually, having said that, I was a bit vague with the brine makeup (all right, not just vague, I couldn't find the scales so just guessed) - maybe that is why my olives don't look too good? Have I got time/energy to go back up the cliff to collect more olives ... make more brine? Should I just go to Almeria and buy them? I think that might be a resounding YES!

The place we bought the stove from had lots of birds - 2 very sad chickens just dumped in a cage on the floor plus some large Quail type birds as well as the usual canary, finch, etc. I really feel sorry for the chickens ... they seem to be the worst off ... I know nothing about chickens really but I suspect they were miserable chickens and I am tempted to buy them even if they do nothing other than potter around and eat some food.

Whilst I'm on the list of Things I Have Not Told You, I think our communication at Christmas was a bit short; non-existent in fact, so I never did tell you about our first Christmas here. Having given you the build up, the reality was somewhat different - 'different' being the operative word here I think!

Xmas day itself was very productive. Morning spent going around the various local industrial estates collecting pallets which are just left out for rubbish (but make excellent firewood) ... dragged into local bar ... (how unfortunate!!) ... wobbly afternoon spent coppicing and dragging home millions of 15 foot bamboo canes which we have a use for. Not exactly traditional Xmas activities I know, but jolly useful all the same. Also rescued a fridge, oil drum and some paint cans from various piles of rubbish (Spain doesn't have recycling/rubbish centres and people/industry just dump their rubbish anywhere). The fridge, laid on its back with the door removed, and filled with compost, will sustain tomatoes and peppers (I hope!), the oil drum cut into 3 sections and the paint drums planted along the pergola and with the same treatment will give my bottle gourds a good start. A discarded single bedstead is on its way to becoming a seat placed at the highest point of our land ... from this, I can survey (and nose at!) all that goes on within everyone else's plot.

The Bamboo is really, really useful tho … just adding the finishing touches to Morgan's aviary (though he has already been out in it on several occasions) using that rather than wood (not easily obtainable here). We've strengthened and elongated the old polytunnel hoops with it and, cut into small lengths, have disguised the paint tin planters. My next project is to make a compost bin and a set of Pan Pipes and if I'm still alive and upright by then, a small trailer for my bike which will then enable me to collect even more bamboo and extra water too (if the river is still running by then!) I'm pretty good at making stuff out of Bamboo and sniffing out water at 100 paces!!

We went down to Roquetas the other day … mainly to use the internet cafe … but also found a small greengrocer and bought some veg there. I have to admit that down in this area, the veg are pretty tasteless. It is all produced locally but because it is forced under plastic for the international supermarket trade, everything just tastes of water. Very disappointing and can't wait to get my own stuff growing! We buy tomatoes grown in Almeria (go past the places they grow) but they are very rough and no taste. The best are exported as far as I know. The agri/horticultural trade here is big business … a lot of the labour is either N. African or E. European and I think much is part of the Black Economy. We also find it difficult to source Free range, Organic produce here … no matter how hard I try to learn the language, the true meaning of naturally produced food isn't always apparent. (Then again, even with a reasonable command of English, its not always that apparent in Tesco's either!). Speaking of Tesco's … the Alcampo supermarket in Almeria is just *huge* – it gives me a pain in the head just thinking about it).

Aside from these little difficulties, the mountains are slowly waking up and flowers are beginning to appear. Wild geraniums are to the fore at the moment but mixed with some local mini Cistus and Broom, Euphorbia and ever present Prickly Pear. There are Cornflowers and also Grasses of various types (some with very big seed heads), various succulents (both large and small leaf), the huge Miscanthus (Bamboo), Oleander (presently seeding), multi-headed crocus, very posh brown/yellow bell type flowers, large camassia type bulbs, tiny geraniums, delicate grasses etc. Brooms and the wire netting bush (can't think of the proper name) are prevalent as are some very smart brilliant yellow flowers (which I've no idea what they are but gorgeous all the same!) The Bouganvillea of course are flowering like mad as is the Jasmine and my Orchid cacti have more flowers on now than ever before.

Now we have passed the shortest day, I am forever looking for new insects ... this period seems to be the optimum mating time for the crickets which is very interesting (though I don't want to be considered a Voyeur!). I have ascertained so far that little cricket perches on big cricket and not a lot will shift them (bit like frogs/toads really – very single minded on the mating front). Blackbirds seem to have already chosen their nesting site ... a hole in the cliffs on our south west boundary but this is the only bird we have noticed making any breeding moves as yet. As the weather becomes drier, the Egrets come up the Rambla more often now ... this evening, three of them perched on top of one of our Orange trees and then alighted on the ground searching for snacks (in this case probably crickets) ... looking out at them, it was almost like the scenes you see in the African documentaries (except I haven't seen hippos here yet but you never know!). I also love to hear the Hoopoes when they come up here ... they are so like the Jays at home ... same cheeky noise and nosy nature ... want to know what is going on (and whether they can have a bit of it!! – perhaps that is why I like them so much – a certain affinity) The Black Redstart is a frequent and welcome visitor and the other day, a group of Long Tailed Tits passed through. Much like at home, the latter spent a couple of days here and then carried on to the next place. We have a pair of hawks which live and work on this immediate area – their diet seems to consist of crickets and lizards, both of which seem to be in plentiful supply at the moment. Latest ones are a couple of pairs of Black Wheatears which live way up the top of the western boundary ... according to the bird book, you can check whether these are Wheatears or Black Wheatears by the fact that the latter often build a small wall of pebbles in front of their nesting hole ... after the olive picking fiasco, I have to admit I'm not *that* inclined to climb up the cliff face and check for pebbles ... I reckon they are Black Wheatears and I'm taking the pebbles bit as read ... to be honest, I can't see anyone that I write to actually coming along here to check so I feel fairly safe in my identification! (If anyone does, I'll just say ... um ... er ... they ran out of pebbles ... sounds reasonable to me).

We also took a little time out at the salt lagoons south of Roquetas and saw Herons, Black Winged Stilts and Marsh Harrier which we were quite pleased about. Not quite the Ebre Delta but still a good walk and birds to see.

More holes are appearing in our terrace walls but I think it is not always the dogs to blame: there are foxes around here (saw a couple the other night, much more of a grey colouring than the English ones) and I think they, as well as the dogs, come here to dig for mice. Sitting out on the terrace the other night, we also spotted a large – very large – mouse – large enough to be a rat in fact – climb up and along the big fig tree. On reflection, I think it probably was a rat (unless they have bloody big mice here). Anyway, am pretty careful not to leave food lying about (dogs, ants and things) so I'm not actually feeding anything.

Gador, March 2004

Dear Pand,

Just a quick update before we get ready to move up to Murcia – have found a place to rent in San Pedro. Unfortunately it is on an Urbanisation but is only minutes from the Salt Lagoons and both the Mar Menor and the Med are within easy reach.

On the whole, Jan and Feb were warm (even hot!) and mostly sunny months but March has been a pig. We had a hard frost one night (tho I think in this little valley it is a frost pocket as a km down the road nothing was affected) which damaged the Bouganvillea, Citrus, Jade trees, Hibiscus, Geranium etc. Most things since then have made some sort of recovery and certainly as I write, the air is redolent with the scent of citrus blossom but the last couple of days we have seen some very heavy rain … good in a way as it has filled our water deposit but rain accompanied by grey skies (bit like England really!) tho as soon as the clouds disappear, the temps reach the low 20's C.

Yesterday, we walked down the Rambla attracted by the noise of water and found the Rio Andarrax (normally just a trickle in the winter) in full spate. Today tho, it is much quieter and almost back to its single trickle. Most of the year it is bone dry and judging by the number of local people who stopped their cars to peer at the river, it's state yesterday was pretty unusual! However, the weather hasn't deterred the migratory birds and whilst the Sand Martins have been here for a few weeks, we now have Swifts and Swallows to swell the ranks. The Bee Eaters arrived here a few days ago – such glowing colours and beautiful voices and vie with the swallows in aerial acrobatics. The Black Wheatears and Grouse seem temporarily to have disappeared but have been replaced by Owls and some sort of 'Mystery Bird' which appears on the cliff tops but which we have been unable to identify as yet (story of our lives … I think my epitaph will read 'She saw but wasn't sure')

The wild flowers continue to enthrall … last week I discovered half a dozen new plants ranging from the tiniest daintiest little job up to my major find which is a huge tightly packed cluster of shortened foxglove type flowers thrusting up thru the ground – reminiscent of a hefty sort of orchid – but oddly in 2 situations and 2 colours. The blue seems to like hiding in the undergrowth whilst the yellow appears in bare open soil. There are at least 4 different types of cranesbill here ranging from tall with pink flowers to tiny with white flowers, both tiny and large grasses, several bulbs and lots of other stuff which I don't know (surprise, surprise!). My main problem has been that I am so far unable to find local info on the flora and fauna of this area – what museums there are, are closed over the winter (ie Sept to April) and bookshops dealing with local nature are few and far between. Our inability to access the Internet precludes that source of information so it is a bit frustrating to say the least.

Insect life is hotting up with the various types of ants busy … most of the time now we are forced into a strange sort of hopping motion whenever we step off the terrace … there's always a trail of ants going somewhere, carrying something either to a new nest or from an old one and whilst a perfectly normal task (such as going to the bin with refuse) would usually take less than a minute, here it takes 30 minutes – not only avoiding the ants but looking to see what they are carrying and where they are going! Sadly the scorpion I discovered earlier in the year has done a runner and

I haven't seen it (or a near relative) since, and I can only honestly so far count 3 snakes. However, a Praying Mantis today was pretty good and I can watch both Common and Wall Lizards most days. Butterflies too are becoming more active – the usual Cabbage White, Tortoiseshell, Red Admiral but also small orange ones and a large Swallow tail type plus Blue and a Meadow Brown (or closely resembling?)

I think I told you that Doggers disappeared for several weeks but suddenly turned up few days ago looking distinctly plump … she's certainly not looking any thinner and the sad conclusion is that she is pregnant again. Its not an easy life for these Campo dogs but at least they survive. Every major conurbation seems to have a Dog Rescue Society (mostly run by English expats as far as I can see) and there certainly is a 'dog' problem here.

Our Grape vines (despite not following Lothario's exact pruning methods!) are enthusiastically bursting into leaf and the Fig trees are full of leaf and new fruit – the latter practically swelling from 1 minute to the next. There will be much to regret in leaving here (greedily now I am thinking of the figs and the persimmon) … the fantastic walks (on our own!), the not-so fantastic walks with Lothario; Dolores' fashion attire (and her unmitigated delight and confusion with my Spanish); the wildlife; the Campo dogs; irritating Juan when we have been unable to tamp down all the rat holes and thereby letting our irrigation water run onto his land; discussing Canaries (birds rather than islands) with Antonio; catching an itinerant orange picker unawares whilst relieving himself (I brightly said 'Ola' before I realised!); trying to understand Lothario when he has been drinking (bad enough when he is sober!) but I *won't* miss the non-existent communication facilities, the endless collecting of 200 litres of water (in 8 litre cans); the regular draining of the cess pit; the bone shaking drive down the rambla every time we go out and the seemingly infinite task of repairing the terraces, irrigation channels etc.

Spain encompasses more cultures, traditions and life styles than you can shake a stick at. It has magnificent coastlines, a majestic hinterland, stunning wildlife, an excellent cuisine and is inhabited by people who are friendly and often helpful to the point of embarrassment. It is also corrupt, full of rubbish, uncaring of it's environment and a miasma of red tape and bureaucracy. So, not much different from the rest of the Ecommunity then!

The building of new apartments, houses, etc, goes on apace here – every spare lot seems to have a crane hovering over it and the speed and density of building is quite breathtaking. Hence modern Spain – the coastline from Cadaques to Malaga and beyond (with a few stunningly beautiful stretches), resemble Manhattan and these days, the tourists cramming the beaches and avidly buying up frontline properties are not just the sun starved British. The sun and sea seekers come in huge numbers from Madrid and Barcelona (a good percentage of Spanish people now own either a country or beach property as a second home) as well as from further afield – Ireland, Scandinavia, Russia and the Eastern European countries and, somewhat surprisingly (to me at least), the USA.

After all the rain we had earlier, it seems odd to mention water shortages but the seriousness of this has recently prompted regional authorities to devise a scheme to divert water to this region from the Ebre River and delta. As you can imagine, the inhabitants of the Ebre, particularly the rice growers, are not thrilled about this idea.

Not that the obvious water shortage appears to figure that highly in the Developers forward planning (well, actually I don't think any of the developers or the local authorities worry too much about forward planning – only as far as forwardly planning which Swiss bank is going to be the grateful recipient of all their dosh!). More than a few Mayors and Councillors are being investigated for corruption (you know, Well, it was funny really – I owned this piece of prime land on which it was forbidden to build – you know, trees, birds and stuff – which, of course, I'm really interested in and worry about – wouldn't sell it for building for the world – but, council meeting, I have to attend and what do you know? – must have nodded off for a couple of minutes and BINGO – my prime environmentally important piece of land has been re-zoned for construction – what could I do? (the holdall stuffed with a few thousand euros placed under my chair was a COMPLETE surprise). I expect it is slightly more subtle than this (this is me now – not the corrupt bugger just in case you had drifted off the plot a bit!) but it really is appalling the way they carry on. The re-zoning of land is even worse than the UK's system of conveniently forgetting what SSSI means but that is probably only because Spain has more land to play with – a dismal prospect. I worry about my part in this but we only ever buy old, broken down places (bit like the

UK) which want someone to live in them and would only disappear from the landscape otherwise (which in retrospect with some of them, wouldn't actually be that bad an idea) so I ease my conscience in that way.

Having said all that, the house we are about to rent is a prime example of development gone mad, but it was the only place we could find in the limited time available which was prepared to let Morgan, Curry and the plants stay!

Will write from there

San Pedro, June 2004

Dear Pand,

Sorry about the non-letters but rather like Gador, it seems easiest just to say that we are moving again – not as far this time so no need to panic about your hols – we can still do Birds, Mud and other stuff as well. Talk about organized – it's amazing! Anyway, I'll tell you about that in a minute.

It is becoming very hot here – getting to 30 plus degrees C by late morning. Being in the middle of a concrete jungle with a lot of building work going on all around, you can imagine the heat coming off the buildings and constant the noise and dust. This house we are renting is not air conditioned and so becomes pretty unbearable at times – particularly the bedrooms on the first floor. We can't wait to get to Los Bastidas which is at least open to country and single storey so hopefully a little cooler.

Which leads me on to my plants and the difficulties in keeping so many is such a small space (2 tiny courtyards neither of which have any method of shade whatsoever). Many are flowering tremendously well but because of the conditions (cramped, potbound, lack of air flow) I have a constant battle with whitefly, greenfly, blackfly, etc. I can't spray because of Curry and the lack of shade in the yards means that it is difficult to time it right without causing more damage to the foliage (I don't think these houses were meant for the likes of us!). Someone's caterpillars have also been stripping the plants and although I've picked some of them off by hand (and taken them up to wasteland to free them just in case they belong to something fairly rare!), I'm obviously missing some. Looking at some of the plants, you'd expect to hear munching noises 24 hours a day but the bugs seem pretty cunning (which is why I suspect Nature does so well despite our efforts to subdue her!).

Having said that, the Salvias continue to do a bomb here – they really do like the conditions (tho not the immediate conditions crammed together) and I am really very pleased with them. Many of the cacti have flowered here for the first time and of course the various succulents are happy here too. Sadly, over the last few months I have managed to lose a few special plants – the Drymis, Pelargonium Cristatum, Passiflora edulis, Senecio but I have, fingers crossed, so far managed to retain the majority. On a better note, the Arauja is flowering and Stinky Stapelia is doing well too (despite Curry getting to it one day and grazing off all the new growth!). My prized Honeysuckle (Henryii) looks pretty poorly but the Ipomea (Grandpa Otis) is thriving. It's all a bit hit and miss. Anyway, if I can just get the majority of stuff to survive until August then I can really get down to it.

I have been gardening a bit by proxy so to speak. Late in the evening when its cooler, we walk around looking at people's gardens (some of the older houses which surround the Urbanisation proper have quite large and established plots). On one of these treks, we discovered a really 'nice' garden – very shaded by big trees (pines, Eucalyptus, Acacia) and with every imaginable plant in, but sadly not met the owner yet. A few streets down, we came across a man irrigating his plot and thru the fence, commented on how well his plants looked – he snipped off a lovely rose bloom for us which we managed to keep for a few days before the heat build-up indoors got the better of it.

We have just spent the morning taking up our excess plants to the house we are buying. Its not far from here (maybe 20 kms but in this weather it feels like a marathon). Our temps here are in the region of 34 to 38 C which is pretty hot!

Have to have a break here ... There is an elderly Spanish guy who is staying a few doors down for the summer – he has sort of adopted me and we discuss his family in Madrid, he shows me photos, etc. As he is on his own until daughter and grandchildren come down next month, he likes to have a chat and I can see him hovering by the gate so better go and say Hello!

This is considerably later in the evening. I have somehow got involved with several other Spanish families on this street and although I truthfully understand very little of what they say, I can pick up enough to vaguely follow some of the conversation. The particular couple of women I've been talking to this evening are also excellent at mime so we were talking about all sorts of things (domestic violence and Flamenco coming into it at one point for some reason). Suddenly Morgan who was sitting indoors but by the open window started to talk. We were standing on the street as it was marginally cooler than indoors and so Morgan was not visible but very audible – you know what he's like when he gets going. My friends looked questioningly at me and I for my sins said fairly dismissively 'Oh, its only my Perro' instead of saying Its only my Papagayo. I didn't realise I'd said the wrong thing despite them looking at me rather oddly. Well, we *had* been chatting for a couple of hours by then so the strain of trying to keep up with them was obviously telling on me! It was only much later that I realized I had actually told them that the small grey bird reciting nursery rhymes and more was in fact a talking dog!

Well Pand, I think you are going to have to wait for the description of the new house til the next letter. Brain death is fast approaching!

San Pedro, July 2004

Dear Pand,

Sorry about the delay but things got a bit hectic!

Anyway now I'll try and describe the house we are buying. It is on the
outskirts of an agricultural town Torre Pacheco. If you have a map which
shows this area of Spain in any detail, you may see it on there – if not,
it is situated between Cartagena and Torrevieja (closer to Cartagena) and
almost directly inland from the coastal town of Los Alcazares and south
west of the city of Murcia. The house itself is about 6 kms from the coast,
is in the middle of an agricultural area and is set in 2,500 sq m.s of ground
(just short of ¾ acre) which is divided roughly into ⅓rd and ⅔rds. The
house forms the south side of a rectangle of buildings with a large inner
courtyard and large area of garden/ground on the south side. The other
buildings consist of barns, an old house, summer kitchen, summer living
room, etc. As the house is attached to another property on the west side,
the ground is split by a right of way on the far side of which is the other
⅓rd of the plot. All the buildings are single storey except the barn which
has a high roof and currently houses a thriving colony of House Martins.
There isn't much of a garden as such but is mostly planted with fruit trees
and vines – Lemon, various Orange, Fig, Pomegranate, Almond, Peach,
Apple, 3 or 4 varieties of grape vine plus some young date palms and a
big Pine tree (this latter good for Morgan as he likes to have pine cones
in his nest box to chew up!) and that's about it really apart from weeds
and dog shit (the owner keeps about 6 dogs and they don't actually go out
for walks. Six dogs times four years in the garden – I'll leave it to your
imagination!!

On a happier note, adjoining the separated plot of land is a property which
houses 2 pairs of Peacocks, some ducks and a dog and belongs to a local
cop! The Peacocks and ducks are a bonus as we miss the chickens and
ducks we could watch out the back at Old Cleeve. It should also ensure that
Morgan perfects his peacock call, as we only had the peacock as a summer
visitor at Sunny Bank and Morgan only ever got as far as the first bit!

We are determined to try and build a swimming pool (nothing ostentatious – just a basic pool) but we have to decide where is the best place for it (and, at the end of the day, whether we can afford it!). Oh yes, we also have a fairly large Deposit (a concrete water store) in the garden which I really want to make into a wildlife pond – it's quite big (perhaps 10 foot by 6 foot and about 3 or 4 feet deep) so it would make a terrific pond.

We went down to Lo Pagan on Saturday night (Lo Pagan is the nearest 'beach' resort from here) to attend the Food and Wine Exhibition there ... it was wonderful tho we came out far too early (we arrived at 9 pm) ... the whole promenade was covered with exhibition tents offering regional food and drinks and each exhibition had its own dance floor – some concentrated on serious Flamenco dancing, others did children and Juniors ... it was hard to work out which dancing floor to watch. The noise was horrendous (according to statistics, Spain is the noisiest EU country) but the atmosphere and the dancing was fantastic. We found one dance floor and stuck with it for a while ... they started at 11.30 pm and even tho we finally gave up at 1 am, they were still going strong. It was all traditional dance so you got the flounced dresses, the castanets, the Spanish shoes, hairstyles, the whole thing! For one dance, they used a smoke machine on our particular dance floor – to begin with it was very evocative but they overdid it somewhat ... we felt very sorry for the little girls (8 to 12 years old maybe) who were waiting in the wings to go on ... most of them came flooding down the steps coughing and spluttering and wiping their eyes! Despite this, the girls came on and did a very creditable sequence – the applause was huge and very well deserved. Feeling somewhat weary, we adjourned to a cafe over the road and spent an hour or so just 'people watching' ... everyone is out ... from Ancients with zimmer frames to babies in prams ... on the whole, Spain uses 24 hours a day ... depending on profession or trade, they start work from 7 to 9 am, close down from 2 to 5 pm and then work til 9 pm and party til 3 or 4 am.

A few days gap here because we have been out and about – mostly trying to organise our move and sort money out. We went down to Mojacar the other day to close off our bank account there and although we left here at 7 am, it was still a hot and weary drive. The temperatures now are regularly reaching the 30 plus Centigrade mark by late morning, so sometimes we don't feel like doing anything too energetic! For a few weeks, we walked thru the Salinas (salt lagoons) every day to the Med beach (and bird-watched on the way) and went swimming for a couple of hours just to cool down a bit but we haven't been for a few days now. July is the start of the 'season' here so everywhere is very busy and the increase in Spanish holiday-makers is very apparent since the schools closed for the summer the other day.

We seem to have spent a lot of time going around the various shops to check on prices for necessary purchases when we move (like a fridge, washing machine, something to sit on, etc.) so yesterday we decided to take a walk on the new pier at Lo Pagan. This takes us along the other side of the Salinas from our normal route and our round walk was about 7 km. On the left of the pier heading out from Lo Pagan beach is the salt lagoon where everyone goes to take advantage of the black mud (said to be good for arthritis, which I think I mentioned to you earlier) and on the right is Lo Pagan beach and harbour. Here the sea (Mar Menor) is several degrees warmer (because it is enclosed) than where we have been swimming but its also more crowded. So we went trotting along there, watching the people smear mud all over themselves and float about in the salt water after which they sit on the benches along the pier before going into the sea on the right hand side to wash it all off. About ⅔rds of the way along, we stopped for a while and used one of the sets of steps down to the sea on the right to sit and dangle our feet in the water and watch the fish. Because of the number of people about, the birds were few and far between but towards the end of our walk we saw the Terns diving for fish and a colony of Swifts making good use of the disused windmill from which to swoop and glide after their insect prey. This area has a large number of windmills (molino de viento in Spanish – so many place/area names have Molino somewhere in their name) – sadly most in various states of disrepair (tho the local govt. are making the effort to renovate some). In this area they were used to pump the water from one salinas to another and inland they were used as part of the agricultural irrigation system.

That's about it for now Pand – are you still coming over in September?

Los Bastidas, January 2005

Dear Pand,

Here in Bastidas, we have the best of both worlds ... out in the country but close (2 kms) from town and we also have some varied neighbours.

Our newest neighbours (in Charo and Juan's old house) are absolutely delightful – Antonio and Manoli with 2 young boys. They own a cleaning supply business in Pacheco – both speak about 3 words of English but as the children are learning English at school, both parents are keen to upgrade their English – good for us! – we've agreed on Spanish one week, English the next.

Antonio is keen on birds (my favourite person already!) and has amazingly grand ideas for their house ... a Jacuzzi, room for a horse and a bird aviary also! I think we will be lucky with our neighbours. 6th Jan was a holiday here so we spent all afternoon next door with these new neighbours drinking Ponche over ice – good but a bit stunning and then in the evening, we went into Pacheco to attend my favourite person (Manuel) 2nd birthday – we bought him a really loud Police car thingie which flashed lights and opened and shut doors – he was thrilled and happily drove everyone round the bend with this blasted thing. Bit of a stupid move on our part really as he could bring it up here – however, I'm relying on him breaking it (or at least the noisy parts) within 24 hours – if he hasn't, I don't expect it will take me too long to do it for him – ooops, sorry, kaput!!

The garden year begins around Christmas – we start to prune the old Fig tree at the far end of the garden – this produces a seemingly endless supply of lush White figs in the summer and provides some much needed shade in the garden. This is a fairly simple task and at the end of the day, we stand back and feel quite satisfied. Hang on tho – one of our neighbours turns up to check whether we have soaked our Broad Beans ready to sow – no, of course, we didn't think of it (being Xmas and all) and stand, chastened, while he tips our carefully saved Fava beans into a bucket of warm water and then, believe it or not, arranged to come back the next day to plant them out for us! I begin to feel like a small child – incapable of even the simplest task!

We bounce out in the morning and think – ok – what's next? It's at this point, January or early February, that the sun starts to climb up the sky and has some real power to it. The grape vines have now lost all their leaves which means its time to prune – recalling my time in Almeria, I set to with the ladders and the secaturs. I'm pretty sure I know what I am doing. No sooner do I get up the ladder to tackle the red grapes than darkness approaches in the form of my oldest neighbour – normally he is a real sweetie but talking grape vines, he turns into a veritable monster. He stands there, plump and gently sweating whilst he directs my pruning – I long for 2 oclock when I know he'll bugger off home for lunch and a siesta - failing that, I wish his wife would turn up – she'd see the funny side and with any luck, she'd drag him home and leave me to it. Meanwhile, he's still directing operations but I'm getting tired and think to deflect his attentions to the rest of my garden. 'What do you think of the citrus?' I say. 'Well' he says 'Did you spray them?' At this point, I am feeling quite brave and so I say 'No of course I didn't spray them – I didn't come here to spray my food and anyway, what am I supposed to be spraying them against?' I wish I hadn't asked as he reels off a whole load of stuff.

In the last few weeks, we have seen more birds come into the garden ... 2 pairs of Blackbirds, several pairs of Black Redstarts (very friendly and appear to take the place of Robins here), Blackcaps, LBJ's (warblers of some type), Egrets, Sparrows, Glossy Starling, Great Grey Shrike, Thrush, Lesser Kestrel, Hoopoe and Buzzard – soon it will be time for the Bee Eaters and Swallows to appear and then we will know it is Spring! At the moment, our Geckoes are semi hibernating behind mirrors and pictures in the house which is a good excuse not to do a lot of Spring cleaning – don't want to disturb them!! It won't be long before they are back outside if the current weather trend continues ... clear hot sunny days and already noticeably longer days. The Death's Head Moth caterpillar I mentioned earlier has done a complete runner – after several days of tracking his whereabouts, I now have no idea where he is ... what a little piggy ... I'd really wanted to see him/her pupate ... another missed opportunity!

This past week has been taken up by a stray dog which appeared here at New Year. It was a bit weird really as we were talking thru the fence to Antonio and Manoli when they said 'Do you have a dog?' We said 'No' and they said 'Well, what's that in your garden then?'. Sure enough, we turned round and there is a dog in our garden! It ran off when we went to apprehend it but the next morning, the dog was back again – only a youngster – less than a year old and very friendly and bouncy. We took him in, bought him a collar and lead and tried to find his owners. No luck – he was undoubtedly one of the many dogs which are abandoned every year in this country. He stayed with us for a week but we eventually managed to rehome him thru an Animal Rescue Society. Animal Welfare here is in its infancy – pet shops still sell dogs and cats despite the huge stray problem, people keep tiny song birds in horrid little cages and baby terrapins and iguanas are sold on the market. I like the markets but it makes me shudder when I see the pet stalls.

The other day we went round to A and M – supposedly for coffee but ended up spending 3 or 4 hours there. They are having a great deal of work done on Charo and Juans old house and we had a very specific guided tour of the planned improvements. Apart from new septic tanks and other basics, we were intrigued to learn that they plan on having several animals including a horse!! Oh, and a Jacuzzi too … things are looking up. With our pool, their jacuzzi and horse, it should prove interesting. Oh yes, they want a bit of a garden too but admit to knowing little about plants. Both speak a little English – about on par with our Spanish and so we have agreed to swap lessons. This is where I find Spanish meals so helpful – always the table is covered with disposable paper – all your waste from the meal is dumped on the table cloth but it is also an excellent medium for writing on – you can do 'in Ingles it's this word and your friends can write 'En Espanol its this word'. The other day, we did 'find the new post office'. The post office in town closed down and moved to some street we'd never heard of and so over lunch, we learned where it was … go straight past the bottle of wine, turn right at the pepper grinder and then make another sharp right at the salad bowl … straight on past the Poncho (digestive) and turn left at the cafetiere and there you are … the Post Office. A novel method of finding your way around if nothing else!

Juan Antonio's birds are beginning to realise Spring is coming – his bird pens run alongside part of our orchard and veg patch and so you can be working away quietly and all of a sudden, a peacock leaps up and sounds off with its ghostly cry – takes a bit of getting used to tho not so bad for me as I remember it from the zoo. Still, I think my beans didn't go in perfectly straight rows due to the sudden 'what was that?'. That's my excuse anyway! I'm actually quite envious of Juan Antonio's patch – as well as peacocks and ducks (he gave me some duck eggs the other week – wonderful!), he has an enormous pool in which there are fish (big!) and turtles – South American I think – we can watch the turtles come out to sunbathe in the good weather. He has been building his house on this land for the last 8 years … so far, it is just a single storey house – bare blockwork inside and out but inside, he has tv, cooker, beds, sofa etc – he uses it for parties and is in no rush to finish it. He has a swimming pool alongside the house and tons of bricks to finish off the top storey but he just doesn't get around to it. The only thing you see above current roof level is one of the dogs (Fat Dog) – he sits up top and surveys the surrounding countryside.

We are still picking oranges … the later varieties are still fortunately sitting on the trees. In all, I think we probably have about 20 trees and whilst they have cropped well this year, I could do without some of them. We have about 6 Mandarin or Clementine trees – the fruit is great when it is fresh but it is difficult to keep – we've been using them with the other oranges to make juice – as soon as they are ripe they need to be used. Currently we have 3 crates of oranges stored and have another 6 trees to pick. The Almonds have been reasonable although I think I need to find a better harvesting method – poking them with an old walking stick is not only time consuming (and erratic – 'hang on – where did that one go?) but only serves to give the neighbours a good laugh … you know the sort of thing … 'and what planet is she living on?'. Next year, I'm going to use nets and try and look as if I know what I am doing! The Almonds tasted jolly good tho – you know the old thing – one for the bag and two for me. I spent hours picking and eating!

The house and garden here is beginning to look better – the garden certainly, altho it will take a year or two to show any kind of definition. I am at last able to grow the type of plants I like in the open tho I have to say the soil isn't in the best condition. Just imagine a plot which has had nothing done to it for 10 years and is covered with the most beastly perennial weeds – in fact, the usual thing! It will look better soon and at least I now have a special bed for my Orchids – I can leave them out all year round – the lazy orchid keeper's ideal! We are becoming experts in irrigation techniques – we can now spot the best priced 25 ml leaky spray at 50 metres! It's a whole different ball game from Gador – instead of flooding the whole plot and sorting out the sluices, this is drip irrigation and a bit more precise. Our water source is a bit complicated (to be fair you wouldn't expect us to have anything simple would you?) and encompasses so many valves, taps, etc., that one wonders whether just window boxes might be a good thing. Actually, sometimes the supply to the house isn't that brilliant – you can either have a shower or fill the kettle! Sometimes you can do both … wow!

Morgan continues to be a favourite – now speaking Spanish – or at least saying 'Ola' but mostly when people are leaving rather than arriving – typical. A bit of a kerfuffle the other week when he finally managed to bite a child's finger – he'd been working up to it for a couple of months so it was a bit of an anti-climax really (tho not for the child … spectacular screaming fit … I was really impressed. Didn't last long tho … the child was back at Morgan's cage within 10 minutes!) As we seem to have an endless supply of daring children, I think it's good for Morgan – gives him an interest! Curry also makes an impact but in a quieter way – as she sprawls on the terrace in the sun, the first comment is on her size and shell pattern and then we get into what she eats – a sure fire way of learning the Spanish names of plants, weeds, veg etc.

Next weekend, we are off to the mountains for a day's hunting. Before you start to wonder whether this is still me writing to you, I should say that we are hunting for wild Asparagus! We've been warned to wear jeans and ankle boots which at first (mountains and things) seemed reasonable … but then I began to think … either this asparagus is REALLY wild and will attack your ankles without the least provocation (and in this case, would I feel comfortable about eating it at the end of the day?) … or more likely from my experience in Gador, the undergrowth can be somewhat prickly and therefore uncomfortable if you go lightly shod. The third possibility is snakes! Spring … lots of snakes getting ready for their mating rituals and not being best pleased when a bunch of heavy footed tourists turn up asking where the Asparagus is! Having disturbed another Ladderback snake in the garden last week, I tend to think we may be guarding against snake bites on this Asparagaus hunt rather than worrying about prickly undergrowth. If you never hear from me again, you will know that my ankle boots were just not quite high enough! Because no one tells you exactly where you are going ... to the mountains could mean anything frrom 1 hours drive to 4 hours drive ... I've given up trying to be exact ... they don't do 'exact' here ... the best word is 'tarde' which means evening or can just mean late ... if you are expecting someone to eat with you, 'tarde' means that they will turn up to eat at some point between 6 and 10 pm. I found this difficult to contend with at first but gradually I am learning! Conversely of course, I can be just as casual but it takes a bit of getting used to!

For the past week, we have been inundated with north-east winds which have been every bit as bitter as those in the UK. The saving grace has been the sun – powerful when it fights thru the clouds and often warmer to stand outside in the sun's rays than indoors. At least tho my Geraniums are in full flower and even some of the cacti are showing flower buds. My orchids remain outside (tho screened with shading) and providing the temperatures do not worsen, I think I shall overcome this winter. On a brighter note, the Jasmine is still throwing out a few scented gems, the dwarf Pomegranate is producing buds, the Lantana is still flowering and one of my cacti has 23 buds! Oh yes, I almost forgot: the Almonds are flowering now – must have done something right. Also, the two big lemons are beginning to flower – if the wind drops, the scent would be wonderful!.

Los Bastidas, March 2006

Hi Pand,

Listen – sorry about your birthday – I can't believe it's 2 weeks since you left
and now it's way too late to send you a card by post. I'll text you tomorrow!

Lots of news even in this short period but varying in degrees of goodness.
First of all, the Morroccan family so keen to buy Tonio and Manoli's house
seem to have dropped out of the picture – no one knows why but there is
at least another prospective buyer on the horizon (this anyway according
to Manoli – I'm beginning to suspect she is a bit of an optimist but no
matter) – this time an Ecuadorian married to a Russian and, best of all,
with a 4 year old child – A and M's house absolutely ideal as just across
the road from the junior school. The downside is that there seems to be
a bit of a hiccup as far as the agent fees are concerned – 2% or 5% – I
didn't really catch the full gist (I rarely do – get most of it but just miss
the really vital part!).

The next news is that Kiga (I think I have the name right), the tiny Droggi
puppy is due to be up here before too long. They plan to bring her up for
a couple of weekends first to get her acquainted with the garden but at
least realise that letting her loose with Droggi for a while will not be a
good idea – he is, as you know, far too boisterous. However, the builder
has been up here and has added lots more bars to the kennel front so that
the new puppy can't squeeze through. Well, that's the theory anyway! So,
yesterday evening, we trotted round to get Droggi and find that his lead
is missing – been taken down from the kennel door, presumably by the
builder but no where to be seen. Either someone has picked it up and put it
in the house or it's been laying around and Droggi has buried it somewhere
(the builders delivered another huge heap of sand – an ideal spot to hide
stuff!) but no lead. So we fed the chickens and played ball, rope and old
clothes endlessly with Droggi but obviously couldn't take him for a walk.
Over the few months we have been walking him, he has become quite well
behaved about not running out of the gate but we hadn't counted on him
being so keen on his daily walk – as we were leaving, the little basket shot

thru the gate and was away – I mean AWAY – like a ferret up a drainpipe! We shot after him thinking maybe Fat Dog and Boxer would hold him up but no … He barely passed the time of day with them before he hared off down the road. I couldn't believe it – the little swine! It was knocking on a bit – after 6 pm so not that long before dark and so many places he could go. I set off down the road and Ed went back to get the car – I spotted Droggi down by the bin (you know where we met the old guy's wife?) but then lost him. Every wretched dog in the neighbourhood was barking so that wasn't much of a clue and I'd walked down as far as the bit between the houses and the old Lemon Grove when Ed drove up and said, 'Get ready, he's coming down the road'. Sure enough, the little sneak was racing straight towards me – 'Oh Hi Pip, were you looking for me?' Luckily enough, I'd got the biscuits in my pocket (poor Fat Dog and Boxer never got a look in as I tore past them) and waved one about as Droggi skidded to a halt. He might well have stopped anyway but I wasn't about to risk it – jammed a biscuit in his mouth and got him by the scruff of his neck – then had to ease off a bit as he very theatrically choked! Yeah, right, I'm about to fall for that? On yer bike!. One hand firmly entwined in his collar and the other shoved under his bum and into the car – no messing! Delivered to the door and decanted without ceremony but not before he vomited enthuisiastically over the front seat. Christ above, he's not even our dog but talk about panic – the whole escape and capture took only about 30 minutes but I dredged up more Spanish in that half hour – you know – on the phone – 'Oh hi Antonio – yep – chickens are fine – Droggi? – yep – he's fine too – No, sorry, he can't talk to you right now – What? Why? Well … he's just not here at the moment – (long pause) Oh alright then, strictly speaking, he's just not here at all – in fact, your prize pedigree dog has actually done a runner and I think I will too' By the time they arrived, Droggie was back and safe.

Just a few days later, Manoli and the 2 kids were here and we went round to give them some oranges and beans. Standing just inside the gate, we were discussing Droggie's tendency to run off when Antonio arrived – between greeting him and saying 'Got to go now – our Trout is cooking', bloody Droggie slips out and races away up the road. Antonio leaps back into the Mercedes and guns it up the drive, Manoli rolls her eyes in sheer exasperation and follows (reluctantly I think!) on foot, we are left with the 2 kids who are desperate to follow their dad and are therefore

hopping around from one foot to another crying ' Pippa – follow Daddy'.
Ed, sensibly, goes off to get our car in the hope of heading Droggie off
and I'm left saying ' Right, OK, I'll go and get some biscuits then shall I?'.
Sneakily, whilst collecting the biscuits, I also whip the Fish out of the oven
(there are, after all, emergencies and EMERGENCIES and my fish rates the
latter I reckon). I get out on to the road with a pocketful of biscuits and
two hyper kids in tow – Fat Dog and Boxer are going berserk thinking
that Christmas has come and I'm using biscuits up like no tomorrow
– poking biscuits thru the fence in the vain hope of shutting them up. A
few minutes later, rather like the Relief of Mafeking, Manoli sweeps past
in the Mercedes and seconds later Antonio comes hot footing down the
drive with a struggling Droggie in his arms. You've seen Antonio – he's
not exactly built for long distance running and he is looking very red
and gasping like an old boiler on it's last cycle. I take one look and think
'Shit, I wonder if he is insured for emergency treatment' and so, not being
trained in First Aid, I take Droggie from him and say 'Relax, I'll hold the
dog, you hold the biscuits and just take Deep Breaths (and please God,
don't keel over on my doorstep). What a bloody performance and what a
picture we must have made … Manoli's stuck under our Fig tree trying to
perfect her 3 point turn in the Mercedes (Antonio's car and his pride and
joy), Antonio is on his back by our gate alternating between gasping for
water (which we give him) and trying to watch Manoli and the Mercedes,
the Ninos are torn between Mum and Dad and the major cause of this
kerfuffle, ie Droggie, is sitting up and looking round quite perkily (tho
a quick turn on his collar soon changes that – spiteful I know but it felt
good!) He should be used to this as when he escaped on Manoli's watch
the other week, she described his re capture as 'I no speak with Droggie.
I catch Droggie and he go Cough, Cough until we are home'. Any guilt I
felt about manhandling him was immediately dispelled!

You went home at about the right time – last week was very cold – it even
sleeted here for a while and in some of the villages north of Murcia city,
there were some quite noticeable snow falls. Further up the coast towards
Denia and Javea, they have experienced some severe storms. We actually
had a frost the other night – such low temperatures aren't a problem but
because it had rained for a couple of days beforehand, the frost was the
final straw for some of the plants. The Rubber plant has suffered somewhat
(tho it will come back), the Bananas have been cut down and one or two

of the newer cacti have thrown up their hands and said 'Well, we're not putting up with this' or words to that effect. Bloody annoying on the whole – you can usually rely on either rain or cold – but not the two together.

Just this last week I have noticed how the oranges smell of chocolate. It's really quite weird and I don't remember it here last year or in Gador (where we had 2 acres of Citrus) the year before. There is a definite chocolatey scent to the oranges now – even just walking past the trees, it is obvious and when you pick the fruit, there it is. I'm beginning to wonder whether I need to go through all that palaver crystalizing the orange peel and coating it in chocolate – just stand in the garden and sniff -!

First snake of the year yesterday – coiled up tidily in the veg patch in the sunniest spot. Looking somewhat scruffy with soil adhering to him so I think his first day out. Although today was much hotter, he was nowhere to be seen – I suspect probably poked off into Juan Antonio's patch. I am mindful of Manoli saying she hated snakes and wonder about the one in the Summer Kitchen. That is a big snake – well, I say is – I assume he is still in there awaiting this year's swallow babies. Though I was miffed he got the second brood last year, I have to admire his tactics – he traversed the fireplace, the washing machine, the hot water boiler, several shelves and miscellaneous rubbish and managed to clear a nest of 5 babies in one night. Not bad going really!

Cauliflowers almost finished now – we are picking tiny heads and leaves for the Chickens. Nothing of much excitement seems to be going in – potatoes is all we have seen at present. It won't be long before the Melon plants go in I imagine – lettuce coming out of our ears of course – you have to get out to Dolores before you find the celery! Failing that, we could always bag a sheep I suppose as they are about as prevalent as the lettuce – though slightly more voracious. Actually though, that might not really be an accurate statement – there are so many lettuce now, they could be said to be eating up the landscape – mad Lettuce marching over the fields and gradually swallowing up everything in their patch. Pity they don't swallow the ever burgeoning population of barking dogs!

As I'm here I should tell you that the Citrus blossom is starting to open – the scent is just wonderful and on those days without too much wind (the Levante wind can be our downfall at this time of year), the perfume is all pervasive.

I know the veggie rustling was a treat for you so I must just tell you about our latest rustling adventure – not vegetables this time but plants. Our prey was a large sickle leaf succulent with huge shocking pink flowers (tho they don't last very long). We already have the same plant which we brought from Gador but the flowers are pale yellow and what we REALLY wanted was the same plant but with the hot pink flowers. Despite several trips to various garden centres, we couldn't find it but – what a coincidence – it grows in profusion along the Torre Pacheco ByPass and (luckily) is widespread at our nearest Roundabout (50 metres or so from the Abattoir). It seemed if we wanted this plant, we had no choice but to gather it ourselves. In order not to appear too obvious, we took Droggie with us as part of his walk – we filled a carrier bag of these plants, most of which had a bit of root on, and casually ambled back towards our house. We were just approaching the Abattoir gates with our ill gotten gains and I was saying to E ' Well, at least in Spain, no one ever queries what you are doing'. I'd no sooner said that when a man shot through the Abattoir gates and confronted us with a spate of Spanish! Droggi of course was of no help whatsoever – whilst he had been a complete pain when we were collecting the plants (snuffling in the bag, getting in the way, etc), he took an immediate backseat when this guy approached us. Although we'd not actually murdered anyone, taking something from outside your own plot immediately makes one feel guilty and straight away I thought 'Whoops – we are just about to find out that the roundabout belongs to the Abattoir and we aren't supposed to rustle stuff'. Whilst at the back of your mind you think there can't possibly be a problem, the guilt complex comes to the fore. The man in question didn't appear to be swearing at us but the only words I could translate with any surety were 'Great plants – over there – and then I lost the gist of the conversation. Our new found friend realised we didn't completely understand and, with a gentle pat on the shoulder, he bade us wait a moment, vanished into the Abattoir compound and climbed up into the cab of a huge articulated lorry with number plates showing it came from Seville. We watched him climb back down and walk over to us carrying a plastic bag carefully in front of him – he was coming to show us that he had done exactly the same as we had – he'd snaffled some of the Hot Pink plants to take back to his garden in Seville. The only difference was that whilst we had just shoved ours into carrier bags, (only being 5 minutes from home) he had been more circumspect and had wrapped his little plants in damp paper towels to ensure their survival on the long trip to Seville. I was 'so' relieved that I treated him to a description of exactly where and how we were going to use these plants in our garden! He seemed impressed by the idea of meeting fellow snafflers and once Droggi realised there wasn't going to be a confrontation, he was all over this guy – yes, yes, I am a nice little Spanish dog – I didn't realise you were friendly, etc, etc. Quite embarrassing really as the guy almost had to fight him off! I've an idea Droggie would have quite happily travelled to Seville with his new friend if we hadn't dragged him away.

Remember that really, really healthy crop of Broad Beans in the veg patch? Big bushy jobs with loads of flowers coming? I'd been going up every day, talking to them (with the odd conversational aside to the Peacocks and Ducks) – you know the sort of thing – Hello Favas, how are you doing? Good Fava, nice Fava – come on, grow, I want to eat you – well, maybe the latter sentiment might not have gone down terribly well with them but they were coming along wonderfully nevertheless. Even one of Antonio's mates remarked on how good they were looking and I was beginning to get really excited! Just as I was wondering whether Torre Pacheco was into Fruit and Veg shows, disaster struck!! Over one weekend, we had horrendous winds and my little Fava plantation was totally flattened. I couldn't believe it – all that energy and effort I expended on them (not to mention the conversational ploys) and there they were, Flat Beans as opposed to Broad Beans! I felt slightly better when I read in the paper that some people in Alicante had lost the roof off their houses (most of the houses being less substantial than this one I presume!) but still upset about the Beans!

Still, all things come to those who wait as they say (who ARE they anyway? Magic Bean Gods or what? We all say THEY without the least idea of who we are referring to). Anyway, the Bean Gods being kind with the weather, we now have Broad Beans coming out of our ears – brilliant young and raw in salads and just as a snack but they are beginning to overtake us.

The Mange Tout are not so prolific and I am having a daily battle with snails (which are hiding in the lush broad bean crop and sneaking out on forays) and some patchy deficiency which turns stuff yellow. The Peas are coming along and I am keen to get a good crop of these. I don't know whether you will remember but every big party meal here is always accompanied by fresh pea pods. Every place setting should have at least 6 good pods (at an average of 9 peas to a pod, that means each person should get through at least 50 peas – as you may also recall, that is probably about the only real green veg you are likely to see in the course of a 6 hour meal!) Growing good peas to give away is becoming a bit of a challenge!! Bit like an Epitaph isn't it? 'Here lies Pip and her Peas (and Parrots and Torts) – endlessly searching for the Perfect Pod'

Enough of the boring stuff – our swallows arrived very early this year – part way through February and although there are not as many yet as last year, our pair came back unerringly to the Summer Kitchen. Oddly enough, they have completely ignored the nest they built and used last year (the one on the Fluorescent light above the door) and have opted instead to build a new nest on the old Chimney breast. I've no idea exactly what memories swallows hold (obviously enough to return to the same nesting site year after year) but for them to so obviously ignore their old nest makes me wonder whether they associated their loss of the 2nd brood last year (the snake) with that particular nest. Anyway, they seem happily ensconced on the new nest (which seems to contain far more grass than the previous nest) and it is the usual thing now every day – we approach the summer kitchen at a crouch whilst calling 'Anyone in there?' Usually in the day time, now the nest is complete, there isn't a conflict but on the odd occasion, as you creep in through the door, a swallow zips out and parts your hair! At night, you can go in and the pair of them are sitting snugly together, either in the nest or on the chain to one side. They look at you rather blearily but apart from the odd chirrup, they take no notice.

Another red letter day today – Lizards mating!! I'd gone up the Veg patch this morning to get some old vine prunings for Morgan's box. Having gathered several of these into a bag, I then detoured to look at the Peas and Beans. I managed to pick a handful of Mangetout and as I walked around the edge of the Bean bed, I saw what appeared to be a tangle of vine prunings with a lizard in the midst. On closer examination, this proved to be not so much as a bunch of vine prunings and a Lizard but a bunch of vine prunings and TWO Lizards entwined in courtship – still as statues once my shadow (inadvertently I should add) fell across them but with no intention of shrieking and running off. Having watched them for a few minutes (voyeurism?), I then stepped round them and watched them for a little longer from a different vantage point. If Lizards are anything like Snakes, the actual courtship ritual can take hours and hours – I'm not quite sure at which point I arrived on the scene – it could have been at the 'Hello, I'm Justin, saw you earlier, really fancy you' stage or it could have been at the 'Jesus, this is my pillow, my bed, my apartment – who the hell are you? Whatever it was, when I went back to look a couple of hours later, there was nothing there – just a bit of flattened grass. I expect this is why someone invented the word Transient? (or One Night Stand for younger viewers)

The Blackbird is being a bit silly again and nesting in the most inappropriate place. You may remember last year I told you that it had 3 nests in all – the first (in the Orange tree next to the cactus garden), it never bothered to complete, the second (in the furthest Orange tree) produced 3 babies which at their plump, just feathering stage, were then abandoned and died and the third and last in the Red grapevine at the end of the garden from which 3 babies fledged. This year, the first nest was completed (very posh and natural and only a tiny bit of a Mercadona plastic bag woven in to show this was a Spanish Blackbird) but was made in the very lowest part of the Echium bush. 3 eggs were laid and the male Blackbird was busy everyday in the courtyard digging, poking and such like. The other day, one baby hatched but when we didn't see the parent bird searching for food, we sneaked a look in the nest. By this time, all 3 eggs should have hatched but when we looked, the baby had disappeared and the remaining two eggs just sat there. I imagine they will nest again and will hopefully go straight for the grapevines which seemed the most successful last time. I've only just today tied these vines down onto the ironwork and have religiously pruned out those spurs which have more than one shoot. However, I've left the ones to the East to trail down and therefore hopefully give the Blackbird some cover should she decide to return to last years successful nest. What with trying to keep the birds, geckoes and Crickets happy, rescuing snakes, trying to keep the swallows happy, it's all getting to be a bit much!!

Oh, Shock, Horror – next doors Chickens are no more!! The field picking was getting a bit sparse once the Cauliflowers and Brocc were finished so we gathered a load of Sow thistle from the garden one day (weeks ago I guess now – this letter is getting ridiculous!) especially for the chickens. Went round to get Droggi, and thought it odd that the chickens weren't clamouring for their fresh greens – walked up to the pen – no chickens, not even a feather! It was a couple of days later that we saw Manoli and asked where they were – they'd decided to get rid of them because the sparrows kept going in there and pinching their food and making a mess. The simple answer to that of course would have been to have meshed the Chicken pen in properly with small gauge wire (which we suggested months ago when Antonio spent a weekend up here with an air rifle popping off at the Sparrows). That would have been my plan but then again, I'm not Spanish! It would seem that a more simple idea was simply to get shut of the chickens – no effort (other than the wringing of necks) and the benefit of a quick Barby and anyway, chickens are 10 a penny and you can always start again. I must admit we were pretty upset – we'd grown attached to the chickens and half the purpose of our recent walks with Droggs was to collect food for the chicks and watch them leap up and down when they knew they were going to get fresh greens. We also liked listening to them – it did seem rather abitrary just to snuff them off like that. And we have to buy shop eggs now apart from anything else.

Did I tell you about the guy who phoned us a few weeks ago – said he was a freelance agent and had spotted our House for sale advert in Fred and Diane's shop and could he list it? So, why not – we checked him out with Diane and she said Yeah, he's a bit weird but he does seem to sell stuff. The weird bit was certainly right – he's a very strange character but he has brought us 4 viewings – one of whom came twice and went away saying they would make us an offer but we haven't heard since. His name is Graham Cross and he lives, I think, on his own except for a dog (which regularly feasts on sheep heads – his neighbours must love him) and half a dozen cats. He seems not to understand what you are saying (though he is English) and is forever bemoaning the effort he puts into his chosen career. You can actually see the words you are saying to him going right through his head and leaving it with nothing in between to catch even a nuance of what you are saying – he's actually interesting from a purely academic point of view or at least he would be if I was conducting a scientific experiment as opposed to trying to sell a house.

Anyway Pand, I'll explain further in the next letter – it's getting too late now for my brain to work properly – there's a surprise then! Or I'll pen the rest of it if I don't get to the Post Office tomorrow ...

Los Bastidas, April 2006

Dear Pand,

Sorry not to have been in touch recently (what's new then you may ask?) but I was saving it until I could tell you that we were moving. As it is, I cannot be absolutely sure but I think its going to be in a couple of months.

I can now confidently (phoo – my best derisory snort!) report progress as such – not progress like you and I would know it but that A and M's bank is starting to do the paperwork! This reminds me of the need to do our paperwork! I have Cites Endangered Species papers but strictly speaking and especially with the Bird Flu thing, Morgan really should have a new vet certificate – God almighty, can you imagine getting the right office in Madrid to tie up with the right office in Paris and getting the paperwork here? Doesn't bear thinking about. Curry is ok – she doesn't need a vet certificate to go into France. With no idea of dates, Morgan's veterinary certificate is pie in the sky anyway. A blanket and a roll of beak sellotape I think – if no sellotape, I can picture it now ... 'Anything to declare Madam, guns, illegal immigrants, drugs or such like? No, absolutely nothing – apart from the trailer load of plants and minor stuff like that' and *just* as we cross the barrier – the blanket covered lump in the back of the car goes 'Ola' and everyone freezes – the Customs guys because they think – Mm, well spoken terrorist and us because we think Typical – good old Morg!

Nope, you're right Pand – Morgan won't let us down!! Actually, I've got a new ploy which should work – we ran out of the home made choc digestive biscuits but have since discovered some rather sticky Jaffa Cakes – Morg really really likes them (tho he only picks off the choc and the orangey jam and leaves the bare sponge on the cage bottom – rather like so many tiny beached whales adrift on the sand) – I shall stuff him full of these as we approach the border and with luck, the blanketed lump will simply be emitting satisfied munching noises and the orangey jam will be enough to make any comments indistinguishable from my non stop gabbling – wonder how long it takes to learn to throw your voice? Effectively that is!

The garden birds have been fairly hit and miss – the Blackbirds are now on their 4th nest and still seem not to be happy. They have tried one Orange tree, one Lemon tree, the Echinacea and the latest is one of the Bouganvilleas in the car parking bit. We've had eggs, tiny babies but nothing to full term. A sad story for the swallows – our personal pair came back this year – early actually as part way thru Feb. they went straight back into the Summer Kitchen but ignored last year's nest on the Fluorescent tube (the one the snake cleared out) and started to build on the big chimney breast. Did the nest, did the eggs, and we had 4 babies and then late one afternoon, we went in there and tragedy – nest on the floor, parents panicking, 3 dead babies and one just barely alive. Quickly banged up a little shelf, gathered up what we could of the nest and put the live baby back in and kept watch. We couldn't work out whether the chimney breast was too smooth and the nest had just come adrift or, more likely, Snake had been up to his old tricks but this time, on a smoother surface, had actually brought the nest down with his weight. Either way, the one baby was being tended and fed by the adults for a week or so and then suddenly – nothing. Baby disappeared. Too early to have fledged and anyway, we would have seen it round the Patio so can only surmise that Snake, having been denied his earlier meal, crept out and polished this last baby off. Since then, we have tried to make places for the adults to nest again in the tank room and the garden room but they seem not inclined to start again (and who can blame them). As it is, they continue to roost in the Summer lounge in the heat of the day and at night but that's about it They still come in the house (into the big lounge) and settle on either the Rhino Horn (a favourite judging by the amount of swallow grub on there!) or the blades of the ceiling fan.

On a happier note, I think there is a pair nesting in Droggi's posh kennel – a nest and eggs in there last time we looked. There is a Cerin nesting in the first Pomegranate tree in the orchard but no one seems to have bothered with the Almond trees this year. It's a poor show but I think that's really all we have nesting this year – you've probably got more than we have! The Hoopoes have been about in the garden and fields but I'm not sure where they are nesting. Bee Eaters continue to overfly the garden and fields – so far, I think they are less in numbers than last year. The Lesser Kestrel which was so frequent the latter part of last year and earlier this year must have moved off further inland to nest as we haven't seen it for ages – same with the Buzzards and the Black Redstart. One minute they are forever around and the next minute – gone!

Had a bit of luck with the Frogs this year – at least one in the Broad Bean patch and another in the old orchid bed (since converted into a garden for Curry – complete with little pond) but as it gets hotter (into the mid 30's C) and drier they seem to have bogged off again – I assume to Juan Antonio's turtle lake. The young Praying Mantis which we assiduously fed with flies for a week or so repaid us by eventually running off up the house wall never to be seen again! At a loss as to what we did with our stunned flies, we soon found a way to use them – there is a colony of Ants living under the step of the Office door and they have been thrilled to bits with a constant supply of flies. If the ants aren't out and about, it just takes a smart rap on the door step, park your fly there and within seconds, they send out people to collect it. Having donated 60 paperbacks (just thinking of getting rid of that many books sends me into convulsions) to a shop which runs a lending library and there being not much on TV, the Ants are a good bet! Before you start to panic, I have of course saved my good books – it was just getting ridiculous – hardly any furniture but boxes and boxes of books. I'm actually looking forward to getting somewhere where the post is decent which means I have the chance of getting some books via the Internet – got a list as long as my arm but need to make reasonably sure they will get to me – no point doing it here – lucky if you get half your post!

The big Ladderback Snake emerged from its winter quarters in the Balsa last week – I was standing looking at Curry the other morning and caught a movement amongst the Rosemary and Geranium bed. There are some old Cerinthes in there and although they had done really well over the winter, with the high temperatures they were beginning to fade and I had simply tied them up a few weeks ago to get the last look of them before cutting them down. (In case you had forgotten, these were the Cerinthes from the Independent offer or, strictly speaking, they were the children of). Anyway, the largest of the group was about 1 metre or more high and the movement I spotted was the snake climbing up into them – I just saw his backside so to speak.

Enough of this now,

Speak soon

La Flotte, 18th July 2006

Dear Pand,

The problem with moving is the sudden cessation of communication although after all these years, you should be used to it by now (the proverbial bad penny springs to mind or should it be the prodigal sister – maybe not – I don't expect either of us has a fatted calf prepared and even if we had, I don't expect we'd be prepared to fling it on the Barbeque?). Anyway, I'm back now so will endeavour to give you some idea of our last few weeks in Spain.

Spent most of June trying to finalise the sale of the house and came to the conclusion that Spain (or at least our bit of it) must exist in a parallel universe – you say things to someone and you see the words leaving your mouth and heading towards the other person's ear – you watch and, yes, sure enough, those self same words you've just spoken zip across and enter that other persons head. You actually SAW this so you know, without question, that it happened. The recipients then nod and say 'Si' and 'Claro' and 'Entiendo' and 'No Problema' and so on and so forth, even unto infinity and you are lulled into that state of mind whereby you think – OK, that all seems to be fine – we all know what we are doing and how and when we are doing it. Perfect. No misunderstanding and so we can all go forth and carry out The Plan! Seemed reasonable to me!

Having valued Bastidas (house and land) and had a full copy of the Escritura in early April – the Bank said 'Hey – no problem – the property is good, Antonio and Manoli are good for the finance … let's go!' We check rigorously with A and M (because this sounds like a dream come true) and they confirm – yes, yes, it will be possible for us to buy your house at the end of May and so you can move to France at the end of June. So we started looking for 6 month rentals via the Internet but soon realized that finding an available, and suitable (thinking of Morgan, Curry and plants) property to rent for a few months wasn't going to be particularly easy – summer season was fast approaching and everywhere was getting booked up.

At the beginning of May, Antonio, having called for us at the house and then scoured the neighbourhood before eventually tracking us down at the market in Pacheco, screeches to a halt within inches of us (nicely done but a bit nervewracking) and says – Lets go to the Annual Horse Fair at Fuente Alamo. When we buy your house, we want donkeys or horses for the kids. Tho I think this might be putting the cart before the horse (or Donkey or even house), the offer is tempting and so we pile into his rented car (the Mercedes, as I understood, being somewhere for valeting in order that it can be sold and another, more work like vehicle, purchased in its stead – ready for the Campo lifestyle at Bastidas – but that's another story … God, how many 'other' stories are there I wonder?) Once in the car and heading toward Fuente Alamo, almost the first thing Antonio said was 'Don't worry, everything is in order for buying your house – it's all going to happen – the Bank has spoken'. This sounded reassuring.

Anyway, we spent a couple of hours checking out all the various horses, donkeys and mules for sale but thankfully, Antonio didn't buy one. Whether this was simply that he knew it wouldn't fit in the car boot or whether it was the result of the phone call he received from Manoli while we were half way round the Fair, I'm not sure. I didn't intend to eavesdrop, and in fact couldn't hear Manoli's side of the conversation apart from a really loud squawk at one point which I roughly translated as – Don't you bloody dare buy any more animals – are you completely mad or what ?! We've got Dogs, Chickens, Quad bikes coming out of our ears – we do NOT need a Donkey – well, not yet anyway. Judging by Antonio's placatory response, he got the message!! (tho I think Manoli's afterthought of – Not

yet anyway – rather left an opening a mile wide for Antonio to drive
through at a later date – bad move Manoli!)

A week or two after this, we found a house to rent in France (La Flotte)
but we needed to say when we wanted the rental to start from. Bearing in
mind our previous conversations/agreements with Antonio and Manoli, we
trotted down to their office to tell them about La Flotte and to check that
they were still on course to buy Bastidas so that we could arrange to rent
La Flotte from the end of June. A couple of quick phone calls and heads
nod – 'Si, no problema – the finance is assured even if we have not sold our
town house – the Bank has written this in blood and we trust them. That
alone should have alerted us – as soon as officialdom says No problem (and
even worse, mentions Written in Blood), you know there IS a problem or
at least, there is very shortly GOING to be a problem – but, there you go!
Go through the rigmarole yet again – the sale will be finalized before the
end of June? The Bank is happy? Tomorrow they will give you a date for
the Notario? (Si, si – keep calm – everything is ok). At this juncture, with
the problems next door we are desperate to believe everything is ok and,
in fact, we DO believe it! (After all, if this IS a parallel universe, we should
just be able to wind things back if anything goes wrong! – I think I'd been
reading too many Terry Pratchett books!) so, there we were in the office
saying OK, we plan to leave for France at the end of June and rent this
house at La Flotte whilst we look for somewhere to buy. You understand
that we have to arrange this now, like today? (Si, si) and we also have to
pay 2000 euros for a security deposit ('si, si – we understand') and another
900 euros for the 1st month's rent ('si – es normal') And we have to sign
a contract to say all this is taking place but it needs to be by fax because
we are running out of time so can we use your office fax to do this now
('Si, si – no problema – anything you need'). I persist and say – You just
confirmed you are ready to buy Bastidas next week? You're sure? Because if
you have any doubts, you must say now – this is SERIOUS stuff. Another
phone call and the Bank says – Yes, we arranged the finalisation at the
Notario for the 2nd week in June.

So, we took the plunge – faxes back and forth and Antonio and Manoli
looked on approvingly whilst we signed our lives away (tho we didn't
actually realise that at the time) and we all went off for a celebratory
drink. This then degenerated into a search for Champagne (to really seal
the deal) back at their gutted house in Bastidas. Apart from anything else,

this entailed the trauma of beating off Droggi and Kiga (we'd failed to walk them that day and they were miffed) and having blearily to fix the batteries on to Little Antonio's latest electronic gadget (for some reason, we always have to do this – I'm not quite sure why).

The end of May arrived and no one having confirmed a date for the Notario, we catch Antonio and Manoli on one of their visits to the house next door and ask 'What's happening?' (we didn't actually pin them up against the fence but they got the drift nevertheless.) They say 'Well, the guy who is buying our house has taken the Escritura and is examining it but anyway the bank say that with all the mortgages involved, it is better that we sell our house at the same time as buying yours'. Cue sinking heart! I tried not to panic but, in fact, failed dismally! Chickens coming home to roost with a vengeance and not even Chickens we knew (I think the Chickens had been 'offed' by then – I'm sure I told you about that).

By this time, we had engaged a transport company to take our worldly goods to France and, as is always the case with removal people, we were assured ' everyone wants to move now – we don't have another window (how I hate that expression!) until September so, do you want to go at the end of June or what?) With the mad construction next door (already 2 floors and a roof terrace directly overlooking our courtyard at the back and no help from the Ajuntiamento), we dismissed the 'or what' and went for the end of June. (I should add here that this particular removal company insist on giving you a crap ornament whenever they collect/deliver your goods – the guy said 'Oh yes, in case you think we have left something behind, don't worry – we always leave a little reminder (I can't recall much at this stage but do remember thinking – Hells bells!) so that you will remember us and think – and these were his words not mine – Oh yes, that was Trans Spain who moved us – I must immediately recommend them to my friends (or enemies – well he didn't say that last bit but he may just as well have done). I mean, we just spent the last few weeks getting rid of all our useless crap (saving the useful crap of course) and this guy was going to give us more! And WE were paying HIM – Hang on a minute Pand whilst I go and find a wall to bang my head against!! Actually, I think I'll just go for a walk. I have the feeling this letter is beginning to take on a life of its own. Will finish the Exodus From Spain in my next letter.

Bye for now

La Flotte, 12 July 2006

Hi Pand,

I know I've spoken to you a couple of times since arriving in France but as there is a limit to how long even WE can converse on the phone, herewith Part 2 of The Exodus from Spain.

It was executed in the best manner – ie sneaking away at midnight!!! Only because it was so hot really – the trailer stuffed with all my long-suffering plants (or, more correctly, filled with muttering and squabbling carrier bags) – the cacti are whittering and the Jatropas are loudly and firmly saying – Pip, we should be on top, we are delicate and special but you've put Stinkey Stapelia on top and it just isn't FAIR and a loud voice from the bottom somewhere complaining about being squashed, can't breathe and Are we nearly there yet? I feel sick!).

At this stage, I can't be bothered with the faffing around and so put the trailer cover tightly over them – the muffled shrieks I will ignore because with Morgan and Curry yet to deal with, I know we've still got at least a couple of hours work (which, in reality of course stretched to about 6 hours!) and we'd planned to have a last swim in the pool – a sort of good bye swim and hopefully cooling our brains before the trip!

Antononio and Manoli (along with little Antonio and Manuel) had been with us for most of the afternoon and evening which we spent going through the vast amount of paperwork we had each accumulated for this momentous transaction. After making us pose for several photos (on our own and with them – pretty embarrassing as we were grubby and dishevelled and they were cool and clean!), they eventually left around 10 pm or so and told us to phone them whenever we were ready to leave and they would come and wave us off. At this point, both we and they were still under the impression that the sale would go through within the next few days, so we were all pretty cheerful. As they had sold their house in Pacheco (bit of a gap in passing this info on to you I think) and had nowhere to live other than our house (theirs next door being gutted and not habitable) so they were going to move into ours and so were already eyeing it up with a proprietorial air.

They were worried about how to look after the Pool and so E and I between us spent an hour we hadn't got drawing a huge diagram with instructions (in Spanish as I had the foresight NOT to have packed the dictionary!) of how Manoli – you note Manoli's job rather than Tonio's! – should clean and maintain the pool. Having finally got our act together, we called them up soon after midnight and they came out to the house to see us off – a somewhat prolonged leavetaking and all very tearful but finally we exited thru our mini Palm grove – dignified other than Morgan shrieking Hola – typically just that bit behind the time! Ringing in our ears was Manoli's request that we phone as soon as we arrived in France. She had prepared us a mini picnic – big flask of coffee and some cakes to eat on the way -also included, rather sweetly, was a reminder of her mobile phone number so that we could talk to her while we ate the cake!

So, roads quiet at that time of night as thankfully was Curry and, surprise, surprise, even Morgan (for a while anyway!) We had just negotiated Benidorm and its surrounds and were congratulating ourselves on a rather smooth getaway when the mobile phone bleeped. This about 3 in the morning so took us all by surprise. It was Manoli sounding very panicky and what with just entering one of the numerous underpasses and Morgan doing his phone conversation bit, I found it hard to understand what she was saying. Knowing that once we had left, they would stay at the house for a while deciding how they would rebuild it, what they would rip out, etc, we had left them a bottle of champagne and some nibbles so at first thought she was just ringing to make sure we were ok (or maybe that we really *were* leaving the house in their hands and weren't about to sneak back to Bastidas and ruin their grand plans!) Anyway, I check behind me – yes we have Curry and yes I KNOW we have Morgan – check wing mirror – yes, we have the trailer – can't be anything desperate surely. They have house, gate and garden keys; they have paperwork for house; they have money for bills and conveyancing fees – can't be anything serious! So I say Hang on Manoli – we are on a road where we can't stop – we will call you once we find a pull-in.

Find somewhere to stop (luckily too late and too dark for anyone to spot the animals) and call Manoli. After the usual greetings, the where are you, are you ok, is the coffee still hot, have you eaten the cakes, etc we get to the business – You forgot to leave the Power of Attorney for Pedro to sell the house on your behalf and to receive the black money says Manoli. I say I thought that was OUR copy – the Notario *said* that was our copy and he made one for Pedro. No, no – there is no copy – did not Juan Paolo, to whom you paid an arm and a leg to translate for you, tell you to leave this copy with us – I didn't like to say anything at the time because he spoke English and was very professional and then at your house this afternoon, I forgot to remind you but we HAVE to have this document. With Morgan squawking Hola and E (not being privy to the conversation and therefore not realizing anything was wrong) saying – Tell Manoli the cake is wonderful – I can think of nothing other than to reassure Manoli that everything is in hand and I will send her the document post haste as soon as we hit France (which at this rate will be several weeks from now!!) After marching round the car park for a few minutes thinking ... we've spent the last 5 weeks patiently waiting in various office, filling in this form and that form, done everything necessary, accumulated a mass of paperwork and STILL we've left something out. Unfortunately it's not Morg! Cool down a bit and climb back into the car only to find Curry must be psychic and has grubbed in her crate – probably the thought that she might have to go back to Bastidas and the University Vet clinic? Climb out of the car and clean Curry up. Climb back into the car only to find that somehow, in all the excitement, Morgan has unhooked his water bowl and now has no drinking water! Climb back out of the car, unload some of the stuff which was meant to stop Morgan from eating the back of the passenger seat, re-fill water bowl, load stuff back in, climb back in car and, sigh of relief, eventually set off again.

Somewhere between Benidorm and Barcelona we pulled in for coffee and a rest – at the end of June, it is very warm and having worked hard to clear Bastidas, we hadn't slept for 24 hours and were tired enough just to sleep in the car. It seemed like only minutes before we awoke to a car park full of holiday makers – it is now the 1st July and the start of the holiday season. There was no one here when we pulled in but now its swarming and we have to uncover Morgan (Hola to anyone who passes within yards) and, even worse, let Curry out so I can clean her crate – you know how much

Curry can do – the tap and rubbish bin are of course placed well beyond where we parked in the middle of the night and means an embarrassing couple of runs by which time Curry has woken up, is warm and the minute my back is turned, rushes off to investigate some intrepid motor caravanners. I try at first to disown her by saying Yes, I saw this tortoise trundling around earlier on, but then relented and said I thought I knew who the owners were and would take it back to them. Scooped Curry up and trotted back to the car only to find a squad of school kids on an end of term outing had discovered Morg in the car and were chatting to him quite happily. I am too exhausted to say other than Hello, yes, this IS a parrot and yes, this IS a tortoise and shouldn't you be getting back on your bus now – look, its going to start up – it's going to go without you! Horrid I know but there are limits and I think I've just reached them.

We hit Barcelona sometime around mid day and whilst we are negotiating the traffic – Ed driving, me with nose stuck in map and Morg making unhelpful comments from the back seat – the dreaded mobile bleeps again. Ed is saying – The phone, get the phone; Morgan is saying Hola, si, si, ok and I'm thinking – God, there can't be anything else wrong SURELY? So I let it ring a bit and then answer and say Hello very quietly (sometimes if people can't hear you they just put the phone down which would be good?) Anyway, it is Nicole – the person who owns the house at La Flotte to which we are presently fleeing. She hasn't heard from us and are we still intending to rent the house? The very thought of not having a bed at the end of this jars me into life. Yes of course – sorry about the lack of communication – we are this very minute making our way towards you – right now we are in Barcelona – sort of! OK, she says – normally it takes 3 hours from there but having exchanged a few emails with you, shall we say 6 pm? Looking at the map, I think maybe she usually does the trip by Concorde but as we are travelling by road I settle happily for 6 pm. As it happens, we arrived at La Flotte about quarter past 6 but only because we misread her (rather crap) directions.

Running out of time so will finish this later?

La Flotte, 14 July 2006

Dear Pand,

I thought the removal day (or days as it turned out) deserved a letter on
its own and will serve to remind you how sensible it is to remain in one
place for at least 5 years!!

Technically speaking I suppose it's not you who needs the reminder, it's
me.

Only briefly touching on the actual move (not the travelling bit – just the
move!) when we spoke on the phone, here's the full story!

On the day when it comes to move, (which is 3 or 4 days before WE
actually leave Bastidas), no one from the removal company has appeared
by 8 am. This is somewhat disconcerting as we have to go the Notario
(with the Translator, who doesn't drive and lives a million miles away and
we have to collect, and blah, blah, blah) in order to arrange the Power
of Attorney which will enable Pedro (employee and friend of Antonio
and Manoli) to sell the house on our behalf, collect the black money
and immediately hand it over to Antonio who will, as our arrangement
stands at the moment, meet us in Barcelona and hand it over to us at
a later date with the legal money being transferred by the Bank on the
day of the actual transaction. Hope you are following this – I'm not
sure that I am!

Anyway, no sign of removal van so we phone and enquire – 'Ah' they say
'someone has put a brick thru the windscreen of the very vehicle we are
intending to use to transport your goods and so we are running a little
late'. Feeling somewhat fraught, I say 'Ok, I understand your problem but,
to put it brutally, when the F++++ are you actually going to get here?' They
seem a little miffed and say 'Well Madam, if you feel like that, with no big
van we will have to make several trips in a little van, collect all your stuff
very carelessly, drive back to our depot, dump all your stuff even more
carelessly into our warehouse and take it from there and this will take us

most of the day – if you were thinking of buggering off by this afternoon, I'd forget it if I were you!' By this time I was not only worrying about what crap ornament they were going to leave with us but just simply worrying! Morgan was already in his medium cage (the big one being dismantled and packed away) and eyeing up his small travelling cage with some disfavour – Are we really moving AGAIN then?

Mid-morning and a couple of guys turned up with a mini van – they neither looked nor sounded like the professionals we had been led to expect. In fact, they were just basically a couple of guys who hadn't managed to find employment more suited to their talents, which (as we discovered) were pretty minimal and certainly didn't run to furniture removal! They seemed to consume a fair amount of beer (ours that is) while we moved stuff from the house to the terrace and they wandered around scratching their heads and doing that dreaded thing – you know, when you get a builder in for something really simple and he walks round giving that nasty whistle thru the teeth all the while saying – Well, dunno about this – until you could slap him round the head and say – Look, this is simple – can you do it or not? No, I suppose I'm exaggerating a bit here – they weren't *quite* that bad but bad enough for E and I to go on strike after a few hours and pointedly plonk ourselves down with a glass of wine (or possibly two – this was a BAD day) and say – as WE are in fact paying YOU, we thought we'd take a break.

Eventually it was finished and, as per the contract, we expected our belongings to go off to the storage depot in San Pedro and be delivered to us in France not more than 5 days later. This we had arranged with some foresight – we had 3 days left in Bastidas (albeit without furniture and stuff but could use the facilities at Antonio and Manolis house next door – gutted but the big party room in the Patio was equipped with everything essential to camping) so we weren't too worried. Give us a couple of days to get to La Flotte and our furniture should turn up within minutes of us being settled and ready for it.

You know that saying – Ne'er cast a clout til May is out? For Clout read Furniture and for May read July! I don't really know why I thought the furniture removal would go smoothly – after all nothing else had! But then again, working on the Law of Averages, as everything else had gone wrong,

SOMETHING (like the furniture removal) SHOULD have gone right but possibly I've got the theory wrong? Who knows?

Suffice to say, the removal company arrived at La Flotte some 10 days later than promised with our stuff – well, that is to say, they arrived with *most* of our stuff, just forgot the 2 double beds. By the time we'd finished unloading (again, oddly, E and I seemed to be more than pulling our weight), it was late and dark but as we got towards the back of the vehicle and were happily saying – 'just the 2 beds then' – there was one of those horrible silences – you know, the sort of silence when 2 happy, anticipatory persons say something which obviously fails to connect with the other 2 bored, how-long-is-this-going-to-last persons. 'Beds? What Beds?' they say (and at this stage, they haven't even left us the bloody crap ornament which I was always going to fling back at them anyway – every move, I get rid of crap – I do not need new crap, that sort of thing). Although we cannot really believe it, a close examination of the truck shows that indeed, it's now empty – no beds lurking in there.

E and I repair to Ferry's half completed Tower, climb up to the top, and SCREAM very loudly. Once we have done this, we very sedately clamber back down the unfinished stairwell (not a problem on the way up, we were SO incensed!) and set about trying to resolve the missing bed thing. A gallon of black coffee at least enlivens one of the removal guys to say ' Yeah, I remember you had beds in Spain'. Once we have recovered from this startling observation, we say 'Yes, yes, relax, think back, take your time – remember, the beds were on the terrace, along with the fridge freezer which you seem to have scratched to hell and back – no, no, sorry, don't worry about the Fridge – it is at least HERE – just relax and think Beds – what did you do after taking the beds from the terrace? Put them in the van? And then what? Well, yes ok, AFTER the 10th can of beer, what did you do? Beds remember? Biggish jobs with soft bits to go on top – yes, that's right – MATTRESSES – ring a bell? Relax – just imagine a calm blue sea – beds floating on it – where did those beds float to? San Pedro possibly? Storage depot Come on … just think! '

Despite all this amateur hypnotism, the final result was no beds (well, I suppose we knew that anyway – not being able to transfer the beds physically, it seemed a bit much to expect such a duff bunch to produce them mentally) but we had hoped at least to find out where the bloody things were!

Knowing at what point to accept defeat, we then moved on to the next tactic – When could we expect our beds then? 'Dunno, Ma'am -they could still be at the depot in Spain or they could have moved on to the UK but we will sort it when when we next come up this way.' Oh right then, no need to worry – that is REALLY encouraging. Would this be this year or next do you think? No, don't bother to tell us now – let it be a surprise why not! Stupid bloody people!

Happily, these guys were trying to find their way to Rodez that night, no doubt intending to wind up some other poor suckers. Strangely enough, I knew exactly how to get there (from the Floriers era) but as they didn't know the area, under the guise of being helpful, I got our big map out and went to great lengths to show them the best route. It goes without saying that I sent them the longest, hardest way round – no beds, no ornament even, – so no directions! Why should I care?

The beds finally turned up last week – delivered by a guy whose brother lives in Todmorden! Yes – I couldn't believe it either, especially as this guy with the beds spoke with a very strong Scots accent but swore his brother has some connection with Tod. Tho I have to admit, he did get a bit shifty eyed when I said 'Wow – small world – my sister lives in Tod – what was your brother's name again?' Brother lives, works, terrorises Tod but our friend made it clear that he 'doesn't have a lot to do with him'. You will probably know him then from the Job Centre? The mind boggles – here we are, in the foothills of the Pyrenees at least 20 km from the nearest village and some person turns up with our beds claiming intimate knowledge of Todmorden. If the bedroom wasn't so hot, I think I'd go and lie down and try starting life again!

Well Pand, that probably covers The Move – the really awful bits I've no doubt told you over the phone. Next letter should be all sweetness and light. Did I tell you about the snake which attacked me?

Will write soon

La Flotte, July 2006

Hi Pand,

Good to hear from you – sorry about the interruption – a Belgian guy came to ask whether we could accommodate a strange woman with 2 horses for a couple of nights. As this was fairly late at night, I didn't have enough wits about me to say 'Yes, of course, no problem – she can sleep in the living room with Morgan and Curry and we can tie the horses up round the back and that'll be 50 euros on the nail'. Instead I said 'Dunno mate – I know no more about this set up than you do – you want a strange woman and 2 horses in your house, feel free – other than that, phone Nicole or Ferry tho as one lives in Narbonne (about an hour and half from here) and the other lives equally as far in the other direction, I wouldn't hold your breath in getting a solution to your problem before the night is out'. I mean, who do these people think we are? We might sort the pool out but sorting out accommodation for strange horses is asking a bit much! Anyway, they trotted off back to their little house (but, oddly, complained to Nicole that E had no clothes on when they came to the house – worried about his daughter with some man wandering around with no clothes on.) The fact that he came to our house late at night and his daughter, accompanying him on this woman and horses question, went straight round the side of the house to talk to Morgan and gave Ed no more than a passing glance leads me to think that Dad noticed more than Daughter did (apart from the fact that E went and put his shorts on as soon as he realised we had guests!). Anyway, this is the guy who sits by the pool and smokes either nasty cigs or cigars and so today, I made a point of going for a swim and theatrically coughing (tho I do still have what's known as the 'Murcia Cough') every time I got to the edge of the pool nearest to where he and his wife sat. In the end I had to admit defeat – I stayed in the pool so long, I started to wrinkle and my throat was sore so I gave up and came out, carefully dried myself and said very sweetly 'Hope you enjoy your evening' and staggered back up the hill to the house.

Our new best friend is Manuel German (despite the name, he IS actually French) – he keeps the 15 or so horses on the land and seems to have the run of the place with his endless tractors and broken down bit of agricultural equipment (and the ubiquitous binder twine of course) – it was he who promised us some timber to make Curry a secure place but having promised to bring us the stuff last week, we have heard nothing since. When I was talking to him, he totally understood my Spanish (having ascertained that I spoke only Castillian as opposed to Catalan) and so I was thrilled to bits – I could *talk* to someone. However, the fact that he understood the Spanish should have warned me – when someone says 'I'll do this' the fact that here in France they say 'Demain' as opposed to 'Manana' means the same so I don't really know why I fell for it again. Curry's pen aside, I have to confess that Manuel can be pretty impressive. Just standing talking to him, he is a little guy, scruffily dressed, greasy hair and an enormous beer gut – however, seeing him on a horse leading the herd for their evening feed, he looks totally different – in fact, he looked the part enough that you saw him and immediately thought 'Gaucho' – leather chaps and a very jaunty hat and even the beer belly sat well with the horse – and he can ride, no mistake! So, I'm impressed (but not sufficiently impressed that he has not yet delivered the stuff for Curry's pen!).

Which reminds me to tell you that Curry is much better and pratting around quite happily. In fact, the other night, she escaped from her pen and we were going frantic trying to find her. After all, there is 40 hectares of ground here (the only thing that kept me sane was the knowledge that Curry couldn't have gone that far!). We had Ferry and two of his workmates searching the area for hours. Half way through this, Ferry said to me – but I saw her there at the base of the Tower, eating dandelions – I thought you were keeping an eye on her. This wasn't a good thing to say to me because I was SERIOUSLY worried. Look Ferry, you and Pauli were farting around by the tower and said you would watch her so don't give me a load of crap excuses – I *said* I was going to make the dinner – we did the Donkey – we're only asking you to watch a tortoise for God's sake!

After about 3 quarters of an hour, I eventually discovered Curry round the back of the house and, as you do, shouted OK Stop – got her! As is normal with a tortoise hunt, everyone piled round and said Where is she then? You know Curry – blends in like no ones business and so I took a lot of pleasure in saying – There she is. And savoring the blank faces – Where? Here, I say – pointing to a clump of dry grass, Are you blind or what? Bit unfair really – Curry had sneaked into a large clump of drying grass – the brown and yellow of which suited her colouring to a T. Ferry says But I walked past there at least twice and didn't see anything. I say, with some satisfaction – Well, you may be able to build a house but quite honestly, you're rubbish at tortoise hunting!

To be serious, Curry had one nose bleed about 2 weeks after we got here but since then, nothing. It is still hot and dry here but nothing like as dusty or such a fierce heat as in Spain. It's not ideal for her as she doesn't have the vegetation she is used to but it is certainly an improvement. I'm really relieved and hopeful that the nose bleeds are at an end.

Now we have 3 French families here for 3 weeks of squads of kids screaming about round the house. We had a few problems to begin with (we were feeling somewhat delicate in the brain department what with the aggro over the Bastidas sale or non-sale as it turns out), but after a couple of days we have come to an understanding – in the late afternoon when it is cool enough for Morgan to sit outside, the kids can come and talk to him (very sweetly, they bring their chairs over so that they can seriously chat) and the same with Curry – they can look and stroke but the rest of the time they keep to their own bit and don't bother us. It's a bit peeving that we have to sort this sort of thing out as Nicole had promised us peace and quiet.

Mind you, I think Nicole doesn't know much about what is happening here anyway – she's very much into making lists – which I can empathise with – but she doesn't actually seem to get much further than that. Not terribly helpful when we are her tenants. However, she does speak Dutch, German, English and French fluently which is an aggravation in itself – sometimes, if I feel particularly annoyed with her, I speak to her in my excruciatingly bad Spanish – just for the sheer joy of hearing her say 'I don't speak Spanish so I can't understand you'. Naturally, I don't let on that not many Spanish people would either. Very petty I know but it makes me feel a little better! I also greatly enjoyed her description one day of a stray dog which she called a Strolling dog – just as good I thought, so I didn't correct her. At least that night I went to bed happily thinking Well, she might speak four languages but a STROLLING dog? At least it is not just me – Ferry (Nicole's husband) is not as fluent in French and is quite often wont to say Well of course, if Nicole was here – she can speak FLUENT French ... and then some rude Dutch expletive follows! We're getting to like Ferry!

I'll write again soon

La Flotte, 22 July 2006

Hiya Pand

I know we spoke briefly (or not so briefly?) the other day – or it could have been more than a few days – am fast losing not only the will to live but also the ability to keep track of dates, days or anything else.

The clouds of butterflies which so enthralled me were obviously just sent by the devil to make me feel better – it worked to begin with but as I couldn't find the book to identify them, that soon wore off. It's all very well for these butterflies to flutter and entrance – Oh Come on Pip, just a bit further – but the little beasts just dance about and I think, yes ok, I'll just walk to the next butterfly and before you know it, I am deep in the woods with no water bottle (after all, I'd only intended plodding up the hill to see if there was any post – there wasn't – only some stuff for Erhardt). However, there are sneaky little creatures who rustle away just out of your vision and it is so quiet as to seem a bit creepy. I'm investigating very closely some really good spider webs and suddenly something shrieks and leaps up a few feet away – I can't see it but heart pounding, I wonder if it is safe to go on. I've been told that there are wild boar here and, without my water bottle, I'm not convinced that I can deal with an encounter of that nature. I don't suppose it is a wild boar shrieking but then again, after 3 years in Spain where things are rarely what they seem, I don't feel that certain!

Did I tell you about the Toads? Originally one toad which was hiding in my bag of compost. Trying to rescue the plants we had bought up from Spain, I was innocently re-potting some of them late one evening when it was a bit cooler. As I reached into the compost bag, I felt something that certainly didn't feel like compost but thought – what the hell – you often get bits of bark or something similar in the bags. Reaching in a second time, the bit of bark suddenly lunged up at me and I'm thinking 'Help' and the bark is thinking 'I'm going to be killed' and between us, we are panicking like mad. Leaping back to a safe distance, a quick slurp of wine gives me enough courage to look into the bag and reassures me that the satanic bark is in fact a toad. As the toad didn't have the option of Dutch courage, it sits there in my hand gulping nervously and obviously worried for its future. We come to an arrangement by which the toad comes into the living room and snaps up various insects. After an hour or so of this, I'm beginning to wonder just exactly what the surrender terms were … 'You can stay in here for ever and we will never shut the door or what?' Anyway, mindful of my responsibilities, I made a house for this toad (a female I think by the size) – a large upturned clay bowl with a load of compost in and surrounded by our little solar powered lights so as to provide drive thru fast food in the evenings. She shot in there quickly enough and I thought 'cracked it – pet toad – no problem'. The next night however, another toad shows up and knocks at the door then two more and I'm thinking 'can't really be doing with all these toads indoors – apart from anything else, Morgan is peering at them and obviously worried in case they climb into his cage. Curry also is looking at them with a sort of proprietary air – France? Frog legs? Yummy. As you know, she enjoys snails and once she knows she's back in France, it's always possible she is going to get a taste for Frog (or, correctly, Toad) legs. I wonder if we need to offer her some garlic so that she can do the whole bit properly! No, only kidding.

As it happens, the problem is solved because when we walked back from the swimming pool (a bit of a joke I will explain later) the other night, we saw on the path outside the front door a snake and in it's mouth was our Toad! We were, to say the least, a bit surprised as was, apparently the snake. Before we could do anything (not sure what we would have done anyway), the snake released Toad and slithered back into the undergrowth (the undergrowth in question being Curry's temporary pen which is a bit worrying!) and we were left staring at our toad which was bleeding from the encounter. We washed out the wounds on the Toad's back and it crept off – thinking about it, I have no idea whether this was a venomous snake or what. Since this encounter our toad population seems to have shrunk somewhat and so now our evenings are spent wandering around the buildings here looking for toads. It's a bit miffing because it was so nice to have them around – we haven't had toads since Devon.

Did I tell you about the donkey here? On our first full day, we found this donkey which had somehow inadvertently walked in some old vine cuttings and was wandering around with 2 large pieces of vine wood trapped around its back leg. It was caught so tightly, there was no way to get the wood off without creeping under the electric fence, and indeed, creeping under the donkey, to release it. E talked to it and I lay under its belly and did the business and it ambled off quite happily. For the past week, it has seemed amiable enough – when I walk up the track to look in the post box (an exciting affair at the moment as you get post every day – well, when I say you get post every day, it's only if someone sends you stuff but it's such a novelty that even junk mail and letters for Erhardt are exciting – tho only exciting by proxy so to speak! – I haven't yet got to the desperate stage of steaming open Erhardts letters – only because they look like bills I should add – but at least I can contemplate on the 10 mins walk back why anyone would send anything to someone as boring as Erhardt and try to work out from the postcode or logo who is writing to him and why. One of these days, I'll either just bluntly ask him or, perhaps a more subtle plan, I'll stand there and say 'This looks important, I think you should open it now – I have, luckily, a knife in my pocket which you can use to slit it open and tell me something thrilling – failing that, the knife is sharp enough to slit your throat and then I don't need to keep trailing up and down with your boring old post '. Still, I digress – this was supposed to be about the donkey and it and I have a vague understanding – I walk past its paddock and it looks at me ... I say 'Hi there – remember me? I'm the prat that rescued you from the vine wood' and it ambles over and looks me full in the face and says 'Yeah, right, prat rings a bell – tourist are you?' and I think 'Yep, this donkey has some sense'.

Anyway, total excitement the other evening – the track in front of the houses has recently been laid with gravel (well, that's a kind way of putting it – what they've done is chuck a whole load of pea shingle down – several inches thick so like walking on Chesil Beach but without the thrill of the fossils, and the poor Dutch couple who have come on holiday have a hell of a time wading thru the stuff with the baby's push chair) and so every sound is magnified. So sitting here last night about 10 pm and there is a very determined plodding noise up and down in front of the house. Look out and there is the donkey – presumably bored and wanting a bit of company. As you can't get anywhere off the track here without hitting a 3 strand electrified fence, I'm amazed that the donkey has found a way through. We rush out to question him but at the same time, he is trying to rush into the house – bit of an argument ensues as Toads are one thing as house guests, a full grown donkey is another matter!

We eventually win and having bribed him with a bucket of water, we are feeling mean enough to knock at the house where Ferry is sleeping and ask what are we supposed to do with this donkey? He rushes out and says 'I'll phone Manuel German – you look after the donkey and we will sort this out'. This is all very well but the donkey, having had a drink and now realising it is the centre of attention, makes a beeline for my plants and starts to make threatening chomping noises. Having left loads of things in Pacheco just to get my plants here in one piece, I am not too happy about this and go back to Ferry and say 'Don't just phone, we need to do something now'. So he disappears in his motor and comes back 10 mins later and says 'I have made all the escape routes impassable, the donkey will not get out'. 'Terriffic' I say 'That's not exactly what I was worrying about'. Whilst we are all standing around discussing the pros and cons of donkeys (the holidaying Dutch couple have come to their door by this time – I think they imagine we have laid this on as some part of the holiday entertainment), the donkey takes the hint and pokes off into the dark somewhere. We think this will be the end of the matter and have just made ourselves a bedtime Hot Choc when Floris (Ferry's son) comes tapping at the door and says 'My father says you speak Spanish and therefore the Donkey should understand you – will you help me get him back in his field?' To be honest, I couldn't think of a cutting enough response so, like idiots, we found some rope and went wandering off to get this blasted donkey – which had, by this time, strayed down into the yard where the horses are fed. There are no exterior lights here so E, I and Floris went stumbling down the steep track lit by one little torch. The donkey had found some spilled food and was reluctant to be captured – it led us a merry dance thru an old outbuilding before we managed to catch it and bung the rope round its neck and even then, it wasn't that keen on going back to it's paddock. Eventually, with 3 of us shoving it up the bum, it finally condescended to move but not without first fixing us with a look of injured innocence as if to say 'Well, stuff you – I was only looking for a bit of entertainment'.

Having installed the filtration system on the little pool (just a bowl in the ground), flyscreened the whole house and rescued the donkey, I'm not quite sure why we are paying to live here – should be the other way round. (Tho Ferry and Nicole have offered E a job if we are still here in a couple of months – heaven forbid!)

The house sale in Pacheco gets ever more complicated – when we left, the sale was imminent – now 3 weeks later, we find that the bank has not yet approved the mortgage. That's an abridged version of what is really happening – whatever difficulties there are in buying/selling a house in the UK pale into insignificance so that should give you some idea. All our efforts to find a house here to buy are wasted so far without the guarantee of a sale in Spain.

Every day is a surprise – some pleasant like the 2 Woodpeckers in the walnut tree outside here the other morning – chattering and messing around and attacking the tree and chucking bark about with great abandon or the baby Praying Mantis climbing about on one of our Yuccas (could be one we inadvertently brought with us tho they are in this part of France too) or the pair of Black Redstarts which come to the waterbowl to bathe every evening – others unpleasant like the price of petrol and cigarettes and food in general and finding we haven't sold the house! Just little things like that!

You will be interested to know that we are going to look at a house on Monday (this we arranged before we heard about Pacheco) – it is near the medieval town of Albi not a million miles from Cahors. An old stone farmhouse which has recently been renovated (tho the attached barn is yet to do), quarter acre of garden (tho only lawn as its a holiday home) and a 2 acre field close by with a stream. It looks really pretty and reminds me of the holiday houses further up the track in Floriers – you remember, the one in particular from which we liberated the cactus ears and the other derelict one which we went into (I was about to say 'broke into' but don't remember actually jemmying any doors – anyway, even we wouldn't have done that would we? If I remember correctly, the front door practically fell apart in our hands!).

I think we will probably end up in that area – this part of France is very expensive and according to Ferry (the house owner we have most to do with) this is set to become a second Provence with house prices reflecting that. More about that in the next letter.

Anyway Pand, it's dark now and I should check my Toads and see if the Glow Worm is about. I forgot to tell you about that. There it was, glowing away like a mad thing on the wall of the Dutch tourists' house. I hadn't seen a glow worm since we were at Sunny Bank so it was really exciting (tho miffing that it chose the Dutch house to glow on rather than ours – I said 'Look, do you want me to tell Andy about you or not – if you do, just stop faffing around and come and glow on our house.' I suspect it was dazzled by the thought of endless supplies of Edam or something. No, that's horrid isn't it? The Dutch family are actually very nice and daughter Inez (5 years old with stuffed rabbit) is already my firm friend – we go looking for the baby rabbits which abound further up the hill around the old machinery (and yes, there is yards and yards of binder twine too – what a surprise!). The baby rabbits incidentally are a very dark brown, almost chocolate coloured – prices being what they are here, it would be cheaper to suck on a baby rabbit than a Kit Kat (tho Kit Kats are probably easier to catch – it crossed my mind to send Inez under the tractor to try her luck but then sense prevailed – she is always dressed in pristine white which isn't conducive to rabbit hunting and I figured her parents might suspect something). So we just watch them – I think about chocolate but no idea what Inez thinks of as she has only got as far as 'Good Morning' in her English lessons at school. Possibly she thinks 'Why am I standing here, dressed in white, with a strange woman and watching these little rabbits dart about – I could be at home watching a violent video'. Who knows what 5 year olds think about – I can't remember that far back!

The house here is unbearably hot – the end one of 5 houses converted from what was originally an old farm I think. The buildings sit East to West on the slope of a hill and surrounded on 3 sides by steep woodland, fields, etc. It is a very pretty setting but the main facades face south (and ours being an end, also has an East aspect) – the sun is fierce at this time of year in fact almost seems as hot as Pacheco. There is not an atom of shade around the house – the only shady bit is the valley bottom if you can negotiate the Colditz type fortifications set up to keep the horses in (and, at the same time, the tenants out). We have 40 hectares they say and all of it is yours whilst you are here and you think, yeah, yeah, how do I get to it without knocking myself out on the electrified fence – I mean, they have 3 strands from approx 1.5 metres down to less than a metre. I have to say these are the first horses I've ever known with the ability to Limbo dance.

The house is 2 floors but Ferry and Nicole have decided not to put shutters on windows or doors. 'Why?' I say 'This climate needs some protection from the heat in summer and from the cold in winter – 99 percent of buildings in France have shutters – that's France. 'No' they say 'We think shutters are so ugly and they will spoil the look of the building' and I think, Try living in them – maybe shutters won't seem so ugly then! They are crazy – they are also Dutch which may explain it – there seems little point in building houses which look nice but make no concession to climate and consequently to the overall comfort of the inhabitants! I confess I am also amazed that they have made no use of solar panels and were also very disparaging when a client they are building for had the temerity to demand guttering and down pipes. Again, the reason for no rain water goods on any of their buildings is that it detracts from the look – so huge puddles where the rain pours off the roof and no rain water for our plants. As I say, I find this attitude very peculiar coming from Dutch people – I'd always understood they were very environmentally conscious. Well, that's another myth blown out of the water!!

Tell you about the Albi house next time.

Love to you

La Flotte 12 August 2006

Dear Pand,

Not quite sure exactly where we are up to at the moment but I distinctly remember us talking on the phone – I think it was a couple of weeks ago but not sure.

So ... Manuel German ... my new friend ... speaking to someone who understood me has quite turned my head! Anyway, we discussed the young Hare which has been hanging around here lately – sits on the doorstep and peers at us and then scampers off briefly under the car and then back again to the door ... the toads and also the snake which practically ate the toad one night (I think I told you about that) ... the rabbits (those choclately coloured ones ... the foxes (one of which we have just seen sniffing round the car this evening) and other bits and pieces. Having lived in this area for most of his life, he's very knowledgeable about the flora and fauna so a good person to chat with.

Apart from the obvious house selling and buying problem am now suffering an Orchid crisis – I know I'm going to whine here but in the immortal words of Victor Meldrew, 'I just cannot believe it'. These orchids have been the length and breadth of England (more or less), they've been to France when they were young, they've been on the ferry, they've spent nearly 3 years in Spain and now back here in France, they've decided to have some sort of crap infestation. Have just spent 2 days cleaning them with detergent and water and still they are whimpering and saying 'Ow, Pip – we want somewhere to live – done the grand Tour and now we want to settle down'. Such is the agitation that it is spreading to the other plants – the Lemon Eucalyptus has suddenly realised that there is life outside a Tesco carrier bag and even the house leeks are whittering. Every morning I patrol the trays and check the plants (this sounds like Animal Farm), and every morning, the muttering seems louder. I can see their point – *I* want them to be settled (so does Curry because then she can eat them) – once they are in the ground I won't have to keep worrying about the voices in my head. Well, maybe not strictly true – I'll probably still have voices in my head but if the voices aren't plant related, then I probably won't worry! I can feel myself veering off into the unknown here Pand – I'll just go and get a cigarette and a glass of wine and calm down ...

I can't write much about the garden (what garden?) but the other day I did spot a complete field full of wild flowers (I imagine they are grown for seed). There isn't an awful lot here at present but certainly plenty of Sloes. I gather there are plenty of Fungi here come the Autumn and should we be unlucky enough to still be here, I will of course investigate (and pick!). The basic growth doesn't actually differ much from what we have been used to tho far more deciduous trees as well as the ubiquitous pine. To be fair, it is not the best time of year to see stuff – very hot and sunny and everything burned to the ground. The fields of sunflowers tho are just as I remember them – vast swathes of golden yellow and the odd blood red poppy making a statement. Sunflowers seem to be the most optimistic of plants – they turn their face to the sun and think everything is wonderful. I hesitate to say 'Hey ... tomorrow someone is going to come along and chop you down'. How awful – I sound like the Grim Reaper ... no, that's not quite true, I *feel* like the Grim Reaper ... maybe not the Reaper bit ... just *Grim*.

Enough of the boring stuff ...

It being some 15 years since I actually last made a comment on the French propensity for hunting, it seems only fair that I should attempt to offer a slightly more up-to-date view of this sport. The average Frenchman, like the average Spaniard is still completely hooked on this pastime and so, whether you agree with bloodsports or not, it really is a part of the rural life here.

The guys still line up on the side of the road – their camouflage gear has, to my eye, become slightly more chic but much to my amazement, the whole sneaky camouflage thing is negated by them topping it off with bright orange fluorescent emergency worker vests and matching baseball hats! This safety wear has, I understand, been forced upon the hunting fraternity in order to try and lessen the number of hunters shot and killed or seriously injured each year by their fellow enthusiasts. Once someone worked out that an over excited hunter armed with a high powered rifle (and not a fantastic amount between 2 ears) could create a bit of a problem and wipe out a percentage of tourists, the hunt as such is finding its parameters somewhat curtailed. This was probably a good idea originally but you've only got to look at the number of deer and wild boar queuing up in the local hunt shop to get fitted for fluorescent vests and hats to realise that this is not exactly a foolproof scheme! Well, not from the hunters point of view anyway.

Our European neighbours don't go as far as meeting outside the local pub and downing a few stiff gins before the fun starts – they tend to favour the spread out and use the hip flask technique. On the face of it, it is hard to know which tactic works best. England still has foxes and France (at least our little part) still has a healthy population of Roe Deer (a number of which regularly cross our paddock) and an even healthier population of Wild Boar.

As in the UK, the tide is gradually turning against the hunters here but it seems to be based more on a safety aspect than a revulsion against the actual hunting and killing of some unsuspecting creature. Eventually, I'm betting on the noise pollution laws to solve this problem – the racket from the bells which the hunting dogs wear is unbelievable at times. I guess the hunters don't actually need to expend much ammunition – they probably bore their prey to death with a few choruses of The Marseillaise as rendered by 20 dog bells!

Apart from the wildlife I've already mentioned, there are 15 horses here – well, I say horses but in fact we have to pretend they are cows. Morgan has never liked horses but, as you know, has always had a soft spot for cows. As the nearest cows are something like 15 kms from here, we all pretend that the horses (which trundle by the front door twice a day) are in fact cows. When he sees them, Morg gets quite excited and doe shis old routine ... 'Come on' ... 'Hey up' ... 'Come onnnnnnnnnn' and of course then breaks into the sheep routine with all the whistles and you think ... what the hell ... if he thinks they are cows and is happy, who cares? Most of the horses don't give a stuff but there are one or two stroppy buggers (we've met them down in the valley) who loom over the electric fence and look at us and Morgan as if to say 'Who are you calling cows then?' Morgan of course then goes in his box and makes Cow noises very loudly and we are left dealing with extremely irritated horses. What can you say? Sorry – not personal – I didn't *say* you were a cow – it would just make my life easier if you could pretend to be one ... give you a Euro? ... Whaddya say?

As of this minute, we have a new batch of holidaymakers – Nicole is supposed to have told them that we are living here (as opposed to holidaying) and expect some privacy (after the Japanese sightseeing tour which really pissed us off). The new tourists have only been here about 3 hours and I have already removed their dog from our house twice and am beginning to wonder which part of 'Bugger Off' they are failing to understand. (I have to admit, I am tired of looking in all the various dictionaries – German, Dutch, French – to be honest, I always thought 'Bugger Off' was more or less international). It could be that because one hand is busy entwining itself in a collar, the internationally renowned gesture has fallen short a bit – my sense of balance is not good and I cannot do both hands, so to speak. I think I need to practice!

By the way, the house at Albi was completely crap – a round trip of 400 kms totally wasted tho it confirmed we didn't want to be in that particular area. There doesn't seem to be a lot in this area and we are going to look at a couple of places west of here next week. If you look on your map, find Toulouse and then go down and to your left towards the Spanish border and you should find St Gaudens – around there. The Pyrennees should give you a clue – just keep to the right or, technically speaking, north.

Will write again soon

La Flotte, 8 September 2006

Dear Pand,

At last!! A bit later than promised but look at all the pics! First of all, I hope you have managed to at least vaguely pinpoint the house site on your trusty atlas. In fact, I confess I thought it was in the Haute Pyrenees but I found out when we were at the Notaire on Friday that the address code is 64 thereby denoting that the house is in the Pyrenees Atlantique! You learn something every day. Actually, at that point in the Mountains, the demarcation between the 2 departments is a very fine line.

So ... where to start Probably to try and explain in a bit more detail exactly where this place is. The house itself is about 3 or 4 kms from the village of NAMONTER – a little itsy bitsy place but with a junior school, a Tourist Info Office (which, naturally enough, was closed when we were there), a fairly clean public loo, the Mairie, a well planted and shady car park and, presumably, a bread shop somewhere! A pretty little place. Some 8 kms further is the market town of VIC EN BIGORRE – a town probably not dissimilar in size and make-up to Todmorden. Big Market Square (market is on a Saturday) with a mixture of old and new housing spreading out from the centre. One supermarket on the way out of town which, in keeping with the population closes every day for a 2 hour lunch (except for Fridays and Saturdays). The land in this area is mostly small agricultural – maize seems to be the biggest cereal crop with sunflower and some tobacco. Interspersed with tracts of woodland, the whole is in some ways reminiscent of the South West UK – rolling hills, small fields, small farms, loadsa cows (which Morgan is ecstatic about of course!) and extremely pretty villages where not a great deal appears to go on. The difference of course being that, in some areas of the region, you have the magnificent backdrop of the Pyrenees. Sad to say that, unlike here, we will not have the mountain views but even so are still going to be an hour and a half or so from some of the best ski slopes (tho why this should interest us I don't really know!).

Should we ever feel the need (not beyond the bounds of possibility) LOURDES is only about 25 or 30 kms south of us. The nearest big town/ city is TARBES – with chemical and engineering industries and a major agricultural market, this is probably about the most prosperous town in this region. More to the point, it is the home of the Jardin Massey – supposedly one of the best parks around here and containing masses of rare plants and such like. Let's hope it's easier to suss out than the Palm Gardens of Elche!!

So that, though somewhat briefly, tells you where it is. The next thing is 'what it is'. Basically, it is (or was) a farm which as far as I can make out is about 200 years old. It seems to be pretty typical of the region and, rather sweetly, is classed as a Fermette. Disappointingly, this doesn't translate as being a little farm – simply that originally, it was a single storey building with all the living quarters on the ground floor and storage in the roof space. Many of these houses have been renovated to make use of the roof space and that is what has been done with this one. The amount of roof space varies from place to place – at least with ours, there is head room, tho a few cunningly placed trusses in the bedrooms makes you wonder whether to spend a few quid on safety helmets! The house sits part way up a hill and faces East over a bit of a valley with excellent views of the local ruined Chateau on the opposite hill. The ground, which extends to 3700 sq mts (just short of an acre) is mostly to the East and North and consists of a big courtyard, a part-walled and well laid out (tho overgrown) veg garden and a small field which at present contains 3 donkeys! Apart from one or two scrappy bits, the garden also contains an enormous Barn (constructed mostly from river stone) and an ancient Pigonier. The house is also River stone construction (tho rendered) and about 150 sq ms in total so more or less the size of Bastidas.

On the ground floor, a hallway and stairs – to the left is a living room with the most enormous fireplace and to the right is the dining room which then leads thru to the kitchen which in turn leads thru to the Veranda (semi conservatory in our language) with a teeny weeny bathroom next to the dining room and behind the kitchen (very odd feeling!). A biggish pantry leads off to the left of the veranda and next to the veranda is a wash room and then a store room. Upstairs are 3 bedrooms and an even tinier loo and washbasin. Anyway, hopefully, you will get at least a good idea from the photos (tho bearing in mind that there was a great deal of indiscriminate use of wide angle lenses there – particularly in the hallway – notice the fish eye appearance of the right hand wall?!)

Anyway, more to the point, we loved it immediately and got on really well with the owners right from the word go (as well as eating most of the produce as we walked round!). Jean Claude is I think, a Cabinet maker (or if not, he gives a very good impression of it – the furniture he has built looks pretty professional to me!) and Nicole is a Professor of Physical Education (might have to start doing a few press ups or something!). They rescue stray animals (which currently consist of the aforementioned

Donkeys, some rather smooth looking Goats and a rather nervous dog), grow vegetables (and judging by the amount of jars of interesting looking stuff also know how to preserve things) and enjoy the wildlife. Jean Claude has just spent 5 years building their house and a couple of apartments on the hill above 'our' house, Nicole plays the Piano, Accordian and Drums and they jointly own a boat (based at Cap Breton) from which they indulge in sea fishing. Judging by the photos they showed us, they are pretty successful too – whacking great Tuna and stuff! As I said, we really got on well with them (despite the lack of a common language) and they have asked us if we want to spend 2 or 3 days there next week (along with Morgan and Curry) so we can start working on the garden and get to know the place. We've also arranged to rent the house until the paperwork is complete so with any luck, we may actually be able to move in there part way thru September rather than have to wait till everything is finalised (which, at the moment, is liable to be 1st December).

Not much more to report on the house as such but the trip over there is interesting (tho not particularly recommended at 5 in the morning – the time needed to view houses and still get back here at a reasonable hour in the evening). Having said that, we've now seen the whole route from before dawn to well after nightfall as last week when we went to do the initial paperwork, we couldn't get an appointment with the Notaire til after 5 pm. Once we'd crawled out of there at 6.30 or so, we still had 4 hours driving before we were back here at La Flotte.

Re the quick text, you will know that we finally managed to complete the sale of Los Bastidas after 2 nail biting months here. E went back down to Pacheco a couple of weeks ago to collect the Black money from the sale. Despite A and M's entreaties, I didn't go – for one thing, there's no one here to look after Morgan and Curry so that's a no-no for a start. However, I'm glad anyway that I didn't go as they have totally eclipsed the garden. Even now, I do not understand why they have done it but done it they have. Everything has been ripped up and dumped in a massive pile up in the orchard/veg garden. They have, surprisingly, left the Citrus trees in situ and the Palms I brought from the UK but everything else has gone – Honeysuckle, Kiwis, Bottle Brushes, Bamboos, Araujas, Grape Vines, Jasmine, Passion Flower, Ornamental Grasses, Agaves, Cacti (old and new – fabulous flowers – no difference!), Rubber Trees, Rosemary,

Thyme, even Pelargoniums and Geraniums, succulents – the whole lot has gone! They now have the ground more or less as it was when we bought the place – Citrus trees and bare ground (tho full of weeds again I guess) – nowhere for the birds or anything. I could kill them! Even they rather shamefacedly admitted to Ed that I would have cried if I'd seen it – that's putting it mildly – I don't know that I would have even spoken to them before I killed them. I think they think that next year I will have got over the shock as they are determined we go back down for a holiday. Bring the Tortoise they say – no problem – poor Curry had little enough to eat when we were there nurturing patches of grass and stuff for her – I can't imagine what they think she will eat going for a holiday! Finely barbequed spare ribs I suppose! It just seems such a shame to have finally got the birds coming in and even, briefly, a frog (one of Juan Antonio's strays I suspect) and to have made a bit of an oasis and then for them to casually destroy 2 years work. Worst of all, they didn't give the plants to anyone – just dumped them in a huge heap to be burned.

Anyway Pand – new house, new garden – this time next year should see a good harvest one way or another!

Namonter, January 2006

Hi Pand,

As usual, I cannot quite remember where we were up to last – I assume one of us is going to phone the other at some point but can't quite recall which (or who?) or when. Anyway, seemed a good time to start yet another letter and fill you in on what has been happening since we last spoke.

We have spent the last 2 days demolishing the open fireplace and canopy in the Dining Room so that we can put a woodburner in. The middle of winter is probably not the best time to undertake this job but as it was getting a bit silly sending good wood up the chimney (and needing somewhere for Curry – gone are the days with state-of-the-art heated tortoise pens), we decided to make a start. Plus the fact that we found a stove of the same make but smaller than the one we had in Spain for only 550 euros (plus a couple of hundred for the flue of course) – it seemed a good bet when most of them here start at 800 or more. So here we are – Day 2 – cleared the fireplace, along with a couple of cubic metres of cobbles and associated rubble and this evening decided on a break and wandered up to Nicole and Jean Claude. In fact, we got no further than the Goat field and found both of them slaving away in the semi dark – Nicole feeding the Goats and Jean Claude clearing ground with one of his numerous machines. We'd actually only meant to go up and ask them a couple of questions but Jean Claude pre empted us – one hand guiding the machine and the other making the world wide gesture 'Come and have a drink' – so there goes another evening!

The first bottle of local champagne takes care of getting over the day's work and with the 2nd bottle, we are happily comparing prices for construction materials and watching one of the dogs practically turning somersaults for biscuits. By the 3rd bottle, Jean Claude is telling me how much my French has progressed (at this point, I think maybe the 3rd bottle was a mistake!) and we deteriorate into our usual routine of repeating everything we can think of which, in one way or another, has a pronunciation difficulty for me – this involves Frogs, Foxes, Woodburners and various other things tho my Toads gets full marks each time. Pity I can't hold a conversation based solely on Toads! Anyway, having vaguely ascertained where the Plant Nursery is (as opposed to the Garden Centre), borrowed their Infra Red lamp and shade for Curry, arranged the time to collect Adrienne to go to the Market in the morning, found the best place to buy floor tiles (there isn't one – just need to look around), we finally drag ourselves away after 4 hours (this was just for a casual drink – nothing serious!) and stumble and slide back down the hill to the house. We were terribly independent and refused Jean Claude's offer to drive us back via the road – bit of a mistake – what is in reality (and in daylight) a simple haul up the hillside through the woodland becomes something slightly different in the dark and with your fair share of the Champagne! All manner of stumbling blocks not to mention, in the latter part, 13 goats peering at us and saying Ya Boo, that'll teach you to tell me to leave your plants alone and other pithy little comments. It was on this walk back this evening that I had the brilliant idea of using the 5 tons (grown in immensity since last mentioned!) of huge cobblestones we had removed from the fireplace to make one of those Polynesian ovens – you know, big pit in the ground lined with stones and then make a fire. I could picture it SO well – heat the stones to a major degree and then slow roast all 13 goats with Isabelle and Opaline on top! Oh God strike me down – what a horrid thought – well no, not a horrid thought as such (quite an attractive one actually) but maybe a bit mean?

Interestingly enough, both Isabelle and Opaline stopped speaking to us last week because we put up a temporary fence to stop them getting to the south side of the house and walking along the terrace (for want of a better word) and eating the plants in the window recesses. Now of course, they just walk up the drive, up the steps and stare in at the windows, calmly watch Morgan (by now bouncing up and down and shouting I'm going to tell Pip) and start to eat the plants! – they know they can get a couple of mouthfuls at least before we, alerted by Morgan, can rush out and tell them off. There are so many ways in here, its impossible to keep the little buggers out and when you go and tell them off, they just look at you – Hey come on – Chill out – so we're eating everything that's growing – what's the problem?

The other day, the dreaded 3 (Isabelle, Opaline and someone beginning with C) came down the hill like a plague of locusts and started eating all the Holly berries. I was in the middle of doing something and had a bucket in my hand and noticed them gaily stripping the berries. Trotted over to tell them to bugger off and never thought about the bucket. They did of course – Yipeeee – Pip's going to feed us and came rushing over – What you got then? Lets see – that's a BIG bucket etc, etc. Huh – its empty – how could you DO this to us?? So that was a waste of time then! I've tried prodding them with a stick (gently of course) but it has little impact – in fact, it would be fair to say it has no impact at all. These aren't the thin ribby Spanish goats but fat French upper class goats and the stick (actually not a stick but an old Foxglove flower stem which was to hand at the time) probably didn't even get beyond the fur. Whatever, anyway, they either didn't even feel it or just turned slightly and said Just a bit higher and to the right–--yep, thats it – hit the spot – Oh sorry – did you want me to move or something? I think I'll probably just give up. I think I'm expending more energy jumping up and down in frustration and running indoors to say to E Did you just SEE what those bloody goats did? They keep Morgan amused I suppose but I am gratified to note that they are frightened of Curry – Oh my God, did you see that stone moving? Wah, wah … its the Mad Stone come to get us!! Just need another 2000 tortoises and I could probably cover the perimeter reasonably well. Mmmmm – perhaps forget about the fencing as such and use Tortoises?

What's your weather like? I spoke to Nicole this morning when she was feeding the donkeys and she said (worryingly I thought) – Even being this close to the mountains it doesn't get so cold here and I thought WHAT? We had several frosts in November and December – all of which were harder than I've experienced since leaving Leicester. I waited for her to laugh and say she was only joking but she didn't so I clumped off feeling somewhat depressed as it dawned on me that it probably WAS this cold here! My plants are all geared up for warmer climes – most of them have taken a quick look outside and just said You ARE joking? What can you do? They'll not shift out of the Verandah and even in there, it gets too close to freezing to keep the majority happy. Everywhere you turn, its the same old thing – Didn't want to come here in the first place; Can't we go home; But Pip, its chilly here; Yeah, yeah, love the mountains, love the trees but its BLOODY cold! Anyway, despite that, the Orchids are flowering away – I've cut 3 sprays already (2 yellow and one Cream and Red) and another 9 or 10 to go. Also the Papillon Amaryllis is flowering again – something of a surprise because I'd hacked it about to give a flowering bulb to the La Flotte Nicole and I thought it would take a year to settle down. I wonder whether it will do so well next year though – it really seems to relish the hot sun for a good part of the year to bring it into flower. There isn't a lot of variety in this garden – 3 or 4 shrubs, Iris and some Aster and then mostly it is annuals like Marigolds, Californian Poppies, one or two Sweet Williams and Pinks, millions of Foxgloves Primulas and Violets. A lot of the trees have been debarked by the Donkeys and/or Goats but there is a wonderful Oak Tree down the drive which is estimated to be about 300 years old. It really is a beauty and looks incredibly majestic (would look even more majestic if the old Mobile Home was moved from underneath it!) Also a large Camellia – double pink flowers – Adrienne says she planted it nearly 30 years ago. I've been cutting the odd flower for indoors for the last 3 or 4 weeks.

The garden birds are now becoming enthusiastic users of the Seed Feeders and the Fat Balls. The regulars using the feeders are Robin, Great Tit, Nuthatch, Greenfinch and Chaffinch and of course, Sparrows. Other birds, like the Long Tailed Tits, tend to be a bit spasmodic. Plenty of other birds in and around the garden – Blackbird, Redstart, Wren, Rocksparrow, Jay, Crow, Magpie, Red Kite, Buzzard, Thrush, Treecreeper, both spotted and Green Woodpeckers and Wagtail. Within a short distance there are Heron, Doves, Partridge, Lapwings, Kestrel, Egrets and loadsa Ducks. We also have our own little herd of deer (Roe deer) which quite often potter up the back drive, thru the yard and into the paddock. The first time we saw them was a proper misty November morning and we watched 4 of them very delicately picking about in the paddock. With the valley backdrop and the early morning mist swirling around their feet, they were the very picture of Yuppie Nature! No – they DID look pretty and natural. The fact that WE knew that 50 metres down the road, the guys from the local hunt were waiting for them spoiled our view somewhat but as the Deer didn't know they were about to become so much Venison Steak, I can only assume it didn't spoil their early morning enjoyment. Would you believe they shoot Pheasant here too? I'm amazed – in 3 months I have only seen 1 pheasant – either they are bloody good shots or they are lousy shots and have been trying for this one Pheasant for years! I think I might go for Pheasants rather than Chickens and train them to go to my boundary and wiggle their ears and do big raspberries (and possibly also teach them to say – Well – Stuff you!). No possibly not. Knowing how Macho hunters can be, that might just be pushing it – a big raspberry from fairly deep undergrowth would probably be sufficient to cheer both me and the Pheasants! If I can't get Pheasants, a fairly realistic tape recording might be in order.

Anyway Pand that's about it for now

Namonter, January 2007

Dear Andy,

Just thought I'd bang off a letter to you now because a few things to tell you before I forget.

Actually, whilst I think of it, what I DID forget to tell you ages ago was that we had an earthquake here!! It was soon after we moved up here for good – say early November – and we were sitting in our accustomed place in the Store Room (where we used to sneak off for a cigarette!). All of a sudden, the walls of the house vibrated and our chairs shook (not quite enough to spill the glass of wine but worrying nevertheless) and we thought ... Hell ... what's happening? Having gathered our wits, we went back into the house to find Morgan sitting very very quietly on his perch and refusing to speak (unusual to say the least!). Adrienne came tumbling downstairs from her bedroom saying that Capucine (her little dog) had also gone very quiet and nervous and did we know what was happening? This a bit worrying as she has lived here for 30 years or more and we'd only been here a few weeks. Anyway, Adrienne was glued to the TV news that evening and we discovered that there had been an earthquake at Lourdes (about 30 or so kms south of here) which had registered 5 point something on the Richter Scale. When we spoke to Jean Claude a few days later, he said we shouldn't panic – according to his information, the tectonic plates met somewhere in this area but he didnt think it was too close to our house. Being a bit of a stickler for exact information, I said Yeah, yeah,

I REALLY believe this but what do you mean by Not Too Close? Are we talking miles, kilometres or inches here? Just give us a vague idea. When he stretched out an arm and said Here more or less, I was dumbstruck – what it amounted to was that the Donkeys were in the earthquake zone but we (supposedly) weren't. However as this only involves inches, I can't say this reassurance particularly cheered me up. So there we are – right on the edge so to speak! I give up.

So what I was really writing to you about was the market. This takes place every Saturday morning at Vic en Bigorre (our nearest town). It's a mixed market – the market hall as such is open sided but roofed and the stalls spread out into the surrounding streets. Thinking about it, probably the same size as Tod market but with the added excitement of livestock! Not big livestock – just chickens, ducks, rabbits and little stuff like that. Oh and some Turkeys too but they seem to have had their day now Xmas is over! I keep looking at Chickens as we have a Chicken house here (well, we also have a pigeonnier too – a few Fantails?) but I just can't decide which chickens. I see people walking away with chickens tucked under their arms – I just need to be brave enough to buy some! On Saturday, we were walking up the road towards the market and spotted a little guy trundling towards us. He was short and swarthy and had this huge chicken tucked under his arm and they appeared to be deep in conversation. Unusually, the chicken didn't have its legs tied together (the usual mode of transport to and from the market) and it wasn't struggling or squawking so perhaps not a bought chicken? It was as if the guy had got up that morning and just casually said to his chicken Hey, shall we go up town this morning, look in at the market, have a beer or two, see what's going on – you know, just make a day of it!? It was such an enervating sight – I can see, a year hence, taking my own Chicken for a day out in Vic! (No point trying to do it with Morgan – he's more likely to let me down in the conversation stakes. At least no one NORMALLY expects a chicken to hold a deeply philosophical conversation although, naturally, I would expect MY chicken to!)

Having said that tho, Morgan is improving – not only saying Bonjour (tho not always at the right time) but also now I think he just starting to say Au Revoir (I think he learned this very quickly the other day when we were inundated with the French version of Jehovah's Witnesses – can you believe it? they latched on to Morgan – he was in the Veranda at the time and they came round that way and he, stupidly said Hello – How are you? and they were in here like Ferrets up a drainpipe. Oh, do you speak English and oh that's really good because we have learned English just to enable us to bring the word of the Lord to you blah, blah, blah – my name is Mary and this is Caroline and blah, blah, blah. I say No, No you have the wrong person here, I really don't want to be rude but!! Its a shame really – they are always such NICE people – like the Mormons I met in Honolulu but they always seem physically unable to take No for an answer – in the end, you are almost forced to say which of these 2 letters do you have trouble with – is it the N or is it the O (or, on a really bad day, is it the F or the 0) which is giving you a problem?

What is your weather like at the moment? Here it is unseasonably warm with the sun being hot enough to sunbathe under so to speak. I'm a bit wary tho because having suffered some very hard frost in November and the first half of December, I don't trust the weather to continue in its little mild spell. The mountains now have less snow on their slopes than was evident last month – they still glisten and wink at you every morning but you can tell that their heart isn't really in it at present. They are no doubt pretty fed up with the Yuppie Skiers crying What, no snow? Looking at the mess of crappy cheap ski resorts on both sides of the mountains, the lack of snow is perhaps not a bad thing entirely tho all those mountain dwelling animals (other than the skiers) which have taken the trouble to grow thick white coats for the winter are all now wandering round and muttering Well, not much point really is there? May as well get your old red coat out Gladys – bugger spending good money on a new white one!

Do you remember when we used to see a dozen or more Buzzards circling over the garden at Sunny Bank? Always late Winter/early Spring? We are now seeing the same spectacle only this time with Red Kites. Yesterday, we watched at least 10 of them circling round and round above us for most of the afternoon. When they first approached from the direction of the little lake over the track, they were low enough in the sky as to almost present a prehistoric outline. For a few seconds, it was as if the Pterodactyls had come back to life – really weird! Morgan loves them of course because he just assumes they are Buzzards and whilst they are not directly overhead, he is out there enthusiastically yelling Come On Then but the instant they come over his head, he zips into his box and does very quiet halfhearted

Buzzard noises but all the while making sure he leaves nothing of himself poking out of his box. Once they have faded away up the hill, he's out again looking all surprised and saying Oh, have they gone then? Well – you know Morgan – most things on 4 legs at ground level are acceptable (even better if a few whistles activates them) but Pterodactyls? – a bit scary!

Thank God no one thought to buy flying lessons for the Goats and Donkeys this Christmas. Bad enough with Isabelle and her pals on the slope behind the Verandah – teetering there on a three inch ledge and forlornly saying – Well, its not OUR fault – we only wanted to get at those really, really nice red berries and if you hadn't been SO horrid, you would have let us approach the easy way from the drive. As it is, we have to balance up here and cause all sorts of damage while waiting for you to give up and go back indoors before we can REALLY start to seriously ravage the bank.

I think I'm about to suffer from Goat Rage!!

Love for now

Namonter, February 2007

Dear Pand,

You will find enclosed your Birthday card – late, of course and also not really a Birthday card (the printed 'Merry Christmas' being a bit of a giveaway I suppose) but, in fact it's not too bad a card – I know the Robin (or I should say the Rouge gorge – just returned from Elisabeth's where we did Birds That I Have Seen or similar – will explain later!) is a frequent visitor to your garden and having at last managed installation of Sat. TV (first Corry on Sunday after 7 months!), I see your weather is going to be snowy so I guess the card will be apt enough provided you get it before the snow melts. Anyway, Happy Birthday Pand!! !!!!!!!!!!!!!!!!

I think it's a while since we've spoken (am still trying to get to grips with this new computer – French programme … Wah!! And French keyboard … Wah, Wah!! Tho *have* found what passes for an apostrophe but tiring and messy so assume you can place them where necessary yourself – same for inverted commas Im afraid) so a bit to catch up on. Where to start?

Weather I think as that is always something we have in common. Well, needless to say, bit of a shock here – gets cold and frosty and all that rubbish I was trying to avoid. The first frost – and probably one of the hardest – was on the 1st November and that knocked a lot of stuff on the head. There were 4 or 5 frosts in that month and then December, on the whole, was pretty mild and quite sunny. January started off well but then lots of grey days and some freezing fog and then on the 25th, it began to snow and continued for 24 hours. It took a week for the last vestiges of snow to disappear! The mountains of course looked very pretty and, I suppose, so did the garden and the surrounding valley (if you like snow that is) but it ruined the Camellia tree which was pretty annoying. This Camellia (a dark pink semi double) had started to flower in late November and was looking really luscious but the snow and freezing temps finished off all the open and part open flowers – now a fairly disgusting muddy brown colour. However, there are still loads of buds on (in fact, there are several flowers out now) so, fingers crossed that there will not be any more really hard frosts, there should be quite a show over the next few weeks. The tree is more or less just that – a tree – planted about 30 years ago and about 4 or 5 metres high with a spread of a couple of metres. Just before the snow came, one of the spring Iris had dared to flower – it had about 12 hours of life before the snow and freezing temps got it. In fact, Id only really just spotted it and was talking to it and encouraging it and the next minute practically, it was an ex Iris. Bloody annoying! The weather is still mixed – grey and horrid or suddenly warm and sunny but of course after the snow, the soil is wet and claggy and difficult to work. With the cold weather, I've lost some of my plants – the Jatrophas and a tree Aloe being the most desperate losses. They were kept in the Verandah but the temperatures dropped so low, they just keeled over! I've managed (I think so far anyway) to salvage one Jatropha but you know what Cacti and Succulents are like – you tend not to know sometimes that they are dead beyond redemption until the warmer weather arrives.

We've had various bird feeders around the garden since Christmas to try and encourage the birds in from the surrounding woodland. Peanut holders; seed feeders and fat balls and its been pretty good. Loadsa birds which leads me on to where we were earlier on this evening – at Elisabeths house for our (supposed) weekly French lesson. So far, to be honest, its been such hard going that we were desperate to give it up but as she is a neighbour and useful for info apart from anything else, we've persevered. The biggest problem is that we have to contend with the 2 children (hyper active??? Phew!!!) – they join in, which is great but they get so excited and shout and interfere that most of the time, we cannot even hear what Elisabeth is saying and the kids insist on wanting to play and talk to us (in dialect sometimes which is a problem) and they are SO loud and banging around and shrieking Pippa – look at me! – difficult to concentrate. However, this evening, after 10 minutes listening to Aline blethering on, she and her brother went out to play and so it was reasonably peaceful (apart from one or other of them bursting back thru the door and bellowing Pippa, rabbit, rabbit, rabbit, etc and Are you listening to me? in a rather peremptory tone – that's mostly Aline – 5 years old, very sweet but a bit of a pain in the arse if you are trying to concentrate on one thing! Anyway, this evening, Id typed out a list of the birds we had seen here together with the French translations as given in my Field Guide with the intention of getting the correct pronunciation and then writing it phonetically. A reasonably easy exercise you would imagine but no such luck – the first stumbling block was that I had mis-spelled Oiseaux and added an extra U somewhere. Elisabeth took some convincing that this was simply a typing error – a teacher of English by profession, she can be a bit patronizing at times to say the least. (The other week, she even asked us if we had a French Dictionary for Gods sake! I constantly expect her to ask us whether we have our Dinner Money or whether our Mittens are securely taped to our coat sleeves!) Anyway, having spent ages doing this bloody list, I then find that she says Oh, we would NEVER call it that – that sounds SO stupid – no one in Namonter would know what you are talking about and also, you haven't said whether it is Le or La or Un or Une. I tried to say I had enough trouble typing the list anyway – I figured I could work out the sex later! Elisabeth also doesn't have much of a sense of humour – well, she probably does, just not quite the same as mine! Anyway, what with one thing and another (drifting from the subject in hand, talking with Aline and brother – his name is something like Guillum but I just can't pronounce it to Elisabeths satisfaction and so I dont call him anything – just Hi You!!! How are you?? Give us a kiss! which both he and I are happy with), we only managed 1 side of the 4 I had prepared. However, as that took us an hour, I was frantically gathering the papers together and Elisabeth is saying Is that all – what about the other pages? and I'm going Well, we need to get back now – lets do the other pages next week. Even without the kids, an hour is about as much as I can stand, especially at that time of day. So, now we have to find the common names in French for all of this. Also of course, whilst Elisabeth is very strict with our pronunciation, speaking to Nicole, Jean Claude, Adrienne – they aren't so particular and so you tend to copy the speech you hear most.

I haven't yet met up with Janet McNicoll – a teacher of French – a Socio-Linguist (?) by profession. Adrienne had sort of introduced me by way of a friend of hers (Anna Louise) who is a neighbour of the said teacher in Ger (about 15 km from here). Id arranged a first meeting (in order that she could evaluate my level of French) but then had to cancel it as it was the day when I awoke and found six inches of snow on the ground! I have to do it soon (but finding it easier and easier to put off) because I know Adrienne will ask me what is happening and I'm not going to be able to blame the snow forever!

Things have improved somewhat on the Goat front – for one thing, the snow kept them in their own paddock rather than straying into ours. However, since the snow disappeared, they are once again doing the Goat equivalent of a Pub crawl – they whinge around their own paddock but by about 3 o'clock in the afternoon, they are bored and, timing the electric fence to the nth degree, they are through and free ranging. Out of the 13, only 4 or 5 tend to escape – the other 8 or 9 remain in the paddock and just look longingly through the fence at the free rangers. The escapees are the same each time – Isabelle, Opaline, Ceseau and 2 others – it is becoming a battle to keep them out of any newly planted area. The Veg garden is walled/fenced and so they cannot get in there (unless someone forgets to shut the gate – not unusual!), the south and west side is now temporarily fenced (tho not properly secured as we discovered the other week when we found Isabelle hovering and hoovering (the plants that is rather than the floors which would have been more acceptable of course) on the perpendicular west slope. Apart from thinking – Any minute, this goat is going to crash down more or less directly into the Barbeque – she was also causing little landslides. So, we tightened up our defences there and also have a cunning stretch of chicken wire which we pull over the main entrance and so stop the goats getting into the courtyard. However, as we have not gated the rear entrance, the goats just potter down the common drive, along the road edging the paddock and stroll up the back way. So, strictly speaking, it is never a big surprise for us to have Goats on the terrace and peering in through the windows. The steps from the courtyard don't bother them in the least (well, being Goats, I don't suppose steps worry them). The actual paddock remains open to them as we havent yet got around to fencing it. Not a problem really so long as they just eat the grass (growing more now the Donkeys have vacated) but they also tend to nibble the tree bark – the Donkeys have already killed several trees simply by de-barking and it would be nice to avoid any more nibbling!

We dont thankfully have escaping Donkeys now as they are ensconced in a rented field opposite. Having said that tho, they have to move in a month or so – its all very complicated and feudal and family thing but it would seem Jean Claude and Nicole are Persona non grata in part of the village, mad brother, succession rights, etc. etc I can't always follow the ins and outs but there is obviously a problem with their land, what they are renting, what they are doing, et al. Its like any small community (tho here everyone seems related to everyone else so you have to be careful – insult one, insult 50 relatives) so tread carefully.

That's about it for now Pand – hope you had a good Birthday

Namonter, February 2007

Dear Pand,

I think this should be entitled Bleeding Donkeys – Again!!

You, like us, will have been lulled into a false sense of security lately in that the Donkeys have been ensconced in their new paddock for some weeks now and haven't presented a problem. No escapes, 3 pairs of ears visible every day, odd carrot, apple – everything under control.

Yesterday morning we look down the track and see the Donkey stable door wide open and, with sinking hearts note that no Ears are visible. Go down and look – no Donkeys – check our Paddock and what is their old stable and still no Donkeys. Nicole and Jean Claude, having constructed the Donkey stable have (amazingly) failed to secure the rear doors of the stable other than by 2 lengths of wood propped up against the exterior. It was very windy early in the morning and as the stable is open to the front (and to the Donkeys to access their hay), the wind must have gusted straight through and conveniently blew open the rear doors. So, at some point between 6 am (when Nicole and JC came to check them) and 8 am (when we spotted a certain Donkey deficiency), the 3 of them had pigged off on a day out!

Having only got the ansaphone up the hill, we were left with the problem of no owners and, more to the point, a worrying lack of Donkeys! To really cheer us up, it was also pouring with rain and we gave up searching after a bit – no way of knowing which way they had gone. We had just arrived back from Vic at more or less midday after more Chicken research at the market when a strange car pulled into the courtyard – Does Jean Claude still live here? – No, he lives up the hill now. – Ah, there is a slight problem! – Mmmm, could this problem just POSSIBLY have anything to do with Donkeys, by any chance? – Yes, we have seen them at Ponson Dessus (a village about 6 or 7 kms away) and you think, Oh God, how the hell are we supposed to get them back from there? This woman in the strange car said she would go up to the new house and see if anyone was at home. I nodded enthusiastically tho I knew it was useless because if Adrienne doesn't come to the Market with us (and obviously wasn't there to answer our first Donkey Emergency call), it meant that they had all poked off to the coast and the boat for the day. (I suspect the Donkeys knew this and arranged their escape accordingly!) Anwyay, about mid afternoon, we spotted a white shape in the field beyond our paddock and sure enough, 3 very damp bedraggled donkeys were standing around at the end of the track holding a conference (you know the sort of thing – should we quietly trot back into our own paddock and pretend we've never been out or shall we see if we can wind Pip and Ed up?) Quick ballot taken, unanimous vote for the latter course and so they temptingly hung around half way up the drive looking terribly docile and apologetic – even sheepish (tho to introduce yet another species is probably tempting fate – there ARE sheep round here but thankfully, we haven't yet been personally introduced!). So we rushed out with 4 or 5 rather flabby carrots plus a couple of elderly apples and a bucket (empty but it works with the Goats sometimes) and tried to persuade them further up the track so that we could get behind them and hopefully herd them into their own paddock. This was the theory. Naturally enough, they allowed us to get almost within touching distance and then, having glanced disdainfully at our admittedly rather paltry offerings, they turned tail and hoofed off down the track. Had they turned left when they got to the end, we could still possibly have stood a chance but, of course, they turned right and gaily trotted off down to Gueites and the wide open countryside. I halfheartedly traipsed down the road in their wake alternately calling to them in a wheedling sort of voice and roundly cursing them at the same time as waving a fistful of carrots at them. They would stop and have a quick browse in the hedge every so often and look enticingly over their shoulders (or should that be withers?) at me as if to say Well, isn't this FUN then? Great wheeze and how are you fixed for next weekend? By this time, I decided that they were SERIOUSLY taking the piss and with no chance of getting in front of them to turn them back, I used 2 of the carrots to make a well understood gesture at their retreating backs (or haunches? – at this point, I lost interest in correct equine terminology!) and left them hanging around at the entrance to our foremost land owner's property (the M. Gueits who lends his name to our postal address). After this little debacle, it seemed far more sensible to just sit and wait – after all, if they really HAD been as far as Ponson

Dessus (tho the various reported sightings of Elvis sitting in a pub in Reading some 30 years after his death leads one to question this?) and had found their way home from there, then as far as we were concerned, they could jolly well repeat the process.

Sure enough, an hour or so later, Morgan (with a birds eye view of the yard and front drive) suddenly started bouncing around on his perch and shouting Come on then, Come on and we thought – must be something there, looked out and – surprise, surprise, 3 Donkeys milling about in the yard, slurping out of the birds' water bowl and generally going Well, were back now – where's our scoff and nice warm stable?? Little creeps! So, abandon the aperitif and trot out into the yard armed with the old

Carrots, apples and bucket but this time, very cunningly, I stand at one exit and E at the other while we try and formulate some sort of plan which would enable us to shift the donkeys some 500 metres down an unfenced drive with open woodland on either side to the relative security of their paddock. We considered our options for about 10 minutes or so while the donkeys glared balefully at us and the carrots in turn and then worryingly took an unhealthy interest in some newly planted shrubs but with no halters, rope or (amazingly!) even any binder twine, we were about to opt for ushering them out of the yard and seeing how far we got towards their paddock and if it didn't work, we would mentally wash our hands of them and go indoors and watch TV and pretend we didn't know anything about it. Or, better still, pretend we didn't even know the donkeys!

Having reached this momentous decision, a car came hurtling up the drive and JC and N leaped out. They had arrived home only to find about a dozen messages on their ansaphone reporting Donkey sightings and so came rushing down here to see if we had seen them. Rather proudly, we said Not only have we SEEN them, we've actually CAPTURED them and here they are – all present and correct.! I realise this was perhaps stretching the truth a wee bit but what the hell – we'd been in a simmering state of panic all day whilst the donkeys had been gaily pratting around the countryside and (albeit left unsaid) their owners had been pratting around at Cap Breton without a worry in the world! Annoyingly, the miscreants were ushered without so much as a murmer into their paddock once their owners took charge – a few words in their own language and butter wouldn't melt!

I'd like to say that this latest escapade will be the final one but, realistically I don't suppose it will be. You know that really stupid guy – can't think of his name – lays in a tank of water for months or in a perspex box a mile above Hyde Park or other completely pointless feats – I wonder if he wants 3 apprentices – the 12 legs could perhaps add a bit of zest to his otherwise boring antics?

Not to be outdone, the Goats are still trying to get into the garden – in fact, they are being very, very trying! Having fenced them off from the south side, and from the main drive into the yard, they just potter along the road and come in at the other entry – until the whole place is fenced securely, it gets a bit difficult and they are so In Your Face Goats that you end up holding a conversation with them and they are going – Yeah, yeah – that's *really* interesting – can we just go and eat the Holly bush or prune the Honeysuckle (new plant – sore point!) – don't panic, we are going back into our own field in a minute and so you say, OK, exactly which minute is this? And they say, between mouthfuls, Well, yes – a minute (or two or three) – we're Free Goats, know our rights, don't Rush us! Like the Donkeys, its easier to throw up your hands and say, Sod off then. When I think of all the people who used to say – Oh, all those tortoises – arent they difficult, time consuming, etc. etc., – at least the torts actually BELONGED to us!

Birds are getting more lively and vocal now – Spring must be on its way I think. Weather has turned again now and is mild but wet. Talking to Adrienne the other day, February and March here is normally wet and in fact the last few days has been rain on and off. Most of the local streams are now running at full strength and the water in the roadside ditches is fast approaching road level. Makes it a bit of a bummer for all the chickens which stray from houses on to the road but those with free ranging ducks and Geese are on a winner – lots of flapping and diving in the roadside ditches – people emerging and going Wow, this is good.

The Hunt continues to be a bit of a problem here – there are Deer (Roe) and Wild Boar in this vicinity and rather like the Fox hunters in the UK, the hunters here have not allowed for the general antipathy or the fact that France, even though a huge country and I suppose sparsely populated in rural areas, is becoming a place of country houses and new builds and most people are not happy with the possibility of hunters too close to them. Depending on the size of your land, the Hunt is allowed to come on to your property unless you have a specific arrangement with them to forbid it. I think it is quite a big acreage before they have to obtain your permission – below a certain amount, it's like Junk mail – YOU have to make the effort to say NO, otherwise you get Junk mail and likewise, you get the hunters). Talking with Nicole and Jean Claude the other day, they said that they had written to the local Hunt President last week – apparently, the Hunters had been just yards across the valley shooting at Wild Boar and they were far too close to houses and gardens (one of which was ours of course!). Knowing how many accidents occur annually (hunters shooting innocent bystanders, other hunters, etc), its quite a big thing locally. Some English people who keep Llamas just this side of Vic have had a lot of problems with Hunters firing off within inches of the Llamas! You can imagine it can't you? Llamas pottering around their field and humming happily to themselves and suddenly, a bunch of heavily camouflaged guys pitch up on the perimeter with rifles, shot guns, etc. The bravest Llama approaches the nearest hunter – Que hacer, Senor? – and the senor replies (rather rudely) – We're hunting – Bugger off – the Llama stands there muttering rather uncertainly to itself but is eventually forced to retreat and make its report in writing and is, as we speak, waiting to be called as a witness before the Mairie!!

The satellite TV is still exciting (though its only been a week – it will soon wear off I suspect!). Anyway, Id almost forgotten what John Humphreys sounded like and how annoying it can be to hear the same old news bulletins repeated hour after hour. However, Coronation Street was a revelation – Tracy on a murder charge and new people owning the factory – its only been 8 months after all! Now, after watching the omnibus and a week of proper viewing, weve more or less got the drift of it! I'm not quite sure what that says about the programme though! Thinking back, we've had longer gaps without English language TV and when it comes to the big day, nothing seems to have changed much. This past 8 months, I'd imagined all sorts of things but, apart from the Turkey virus thing, everything seems the same – people being bombed in Iraq, some mad Mullah spouting rubbish in a London mosque, did David Cameron do drugs at Eton, the school curriculum up for a change (yet again!) and, most important of all, did Tracy REALLY murder Charlie? Same old, same old! Am already beginning to wonder how many metres of fencing I could have got for the cost of the satellite TV (and seriously wondering whether it might not have been more entertaining on the whole!)

Bulbs beginning to flower in the garden now – big clumps of Crocus – happy little faces opening up and they do look so striking in huge clumps. That is, they *did* look pretty good until Isabelle and her mates came clumping and rooting about – I could kill them – they don't actually eat them – just stomp over them – they look SO offended when I rush out and say Bog off – look, you're trampling over all the bulbs. A disdainful glance over the shoulder is about all you get. I think this year will be a case of Education or Barbeque!

Have found a good Nursery and starting to get some basic plants ready to make something of the garden. Have already begun to plant up the courtyard but limited in that there is still heavy machinery moving in and out emptying Barns and stuff and, of course, free ranging goats and donkeys. I could do with one of those TV garden makeover jobs – you know, where they transform 2 acres in a weekend. Wonder if they had Goats in the vicinity?

Have to finish now – plaster boarding the ceilings and Eds shouting for help!

Namonter, February 2007

Dear Pand,

Thought I'd give you a quick update after the latest Donkey saga and our consequent inability to work out why our neighbours don't just use proper livestock-proof fencing.

I was talking to Elisabeth (a neighbour who vaguely tries to teach us French but, more to the point, also keeps livestock – Chickens in her case) and she tells me that escaping livestock and the state of one's fences are, in fact, a topic of conversation in this community. Rather than fence livestock in properly (nasty expensive stuff!), the French method is to string up lots of Electric tape fencing and assume it will do the job. In the majority of cases, patently it doesn't work and hence neighbours get to know each other. Whether one sceaming person – Whaddya mean – my sheep came in your field – what about your Goats in mine? – is really the effective conversational starter which Elisabeth claims leaves me in some doubt. On the other hand though, the countryside hereabouts is not littered with dead bodies as a result of Goat rage so maybe she knows what she is talking about after all!

As far as I can tell, the only properly fenced fields belong to foreigners – the best example being the perfectly neat and tidy paddocks housing several Llamas just outside Vic belonging to some English people. It actually looks quite incongruous surrounded by the rough and ready fencing of their neighbours but of course, allows the Llamas to look fairly superior and wind up their less attractively fenced neighbours when they are feeling in a particularly snotty sort of mood!

A bit of a digression here but you may remember these are the self same Llamas who regularly suffer from Hunters frightening them almost to death by letting off various armaments in their close proximity. Thinking about the language difficulty (the Llamas speak only Spanish but not wanting to cast the first stone at the glass house – or Llama paddock in this particular case – this could simply be a matter of there being no French language courses locally which are specifically tailored to Llamas rather than the Llamas not wishing to integrate) it could perhaps make a difference – at least the Llamas could confidently tell the Hunters to Sod off in the language of their adopted country. On second thoughts though and working on the premise that hasty decisions are rarely the right ones, if you take this thought to its logical conclusion, I suppose the reply could well be a quick bullet in the brain (or, remembering we are in France, several bullets aimed in a vague direction and wiping out a couple of hunters as well as the unlucky Llama) so maybe its not such a good idea after all. Need to work on this integration lark – advantages, disadvantages??

This reminds me of Elisabeth recently telling me that the people here swear a lot. Naturally enough, I threw my hands up in horror! Swearing?? Elisabeth is tickled pink when I attempt to pronounce the only 2 French swear words I know – she tells me that if I swore at someone with my accent, they wouldn't understand – that's a relief then and probably explains the donkeys not quite realizing just how cross I was getting with them during their recent escapade. She is entranced by the idea that some neighbour could come along and swear bitterly at me for some reason and I would nod and smile and ask how the family was doing and have not the slightest idea that I was being cursed to death! This problem is exacerbated by the use of Bearnaise – the local dialect which people seem to drop into from proper French without a thought but leaves me gasping and going What?? Elisabeth takes a perverse pleasure in letting her 2 kids (Alina and Guillam – 5 and 3 respectively) rattle on at me and wait expectantly for my reply and when I look totally blank, she says Did you not understand what they said then? I, rather shamefacedly say Well, I got the ODD word but basically, No, havent got a clue. She then admits that they are speaking in Bearnaise – coupled with the fact that kids of that age aren't always easy to understand anyway particularly when they are excited and gabble whilst hanging round your neck and either covering you with kisses or trying to beat you to death, its hardly surprising that I find it difficult to follow!

On a more prosaic note, the weather is doing exactly what it is supposed to do here at this time of year – raining quite a lot! Yesterday, it was incredibly mild and sunny – so much so that I dug out my shorts (I admit the effect was somewhat spoiled by the necessity to wear Frogs on my feet because the ground is still wet and muddy but you can't have everything!)

We've been working on the yard and trying to brighten it up a bit by removing the very boring Box hedging and making new planting areas. After several hours of digging and sweating and cursing, E had the brilliant idea of attaching one end of a rope to each section of hedging and the other end of the rope to the 4 x 4's towbar and foot on accelerator – worked a treat – I don'know why we didn'think of it earlier in the day! It looks so different without the green wall of Box – you can see the huge clumps of Crocus and the Daffodils too. The Box hedging will go to making up the perimeter of the paddock so, fingers crossed, all pleasure and no waste. The next thing is making the pond as the Toads, Frogs and Fire Salamanders are already queuing up – there's a certain amount of disgruntled muttering going on (I caught someone saying – Tut, thought you were going to do this LAST month) and so you are almost forced to post up a daily Bulletin … Amphibians – yes, yes, ok, we ARE working on this and then the Birds – yes, yes, ok, we will go and buy yet another 50 Fat Balls despite the fact that you are consuming half a dozen a day and its getting a bit silly. What's that Pro Active cholesterol reducing stuff? Wonder if they do it for Fat Balls? (or at least for birds).

Can see this degenerating so will finish at this point.

Will write again soon

Namonter, March 2007

Dear Pand,

I think Spring has finally sprung! Not only have the Fruit trees begun to flower (well, the Pear and Peach so far but still encouraging) but its FROG time again!!

I seem to recall that I used to inform you (over excitedly at times I suspect) when the various Frogs and Toads used to creep into the house at Floriers. They used to limbo dance under the front door in the evening to spend the night in the house near the stove and then cause a big kerfuffle next morning when they were desperate to get out again – Pip, come on, wake up (this at day break when you were still blundering around trying to find the loo never mind about anything else) – Get a move on and open the door – things to do, places to go! I guess we should have been grateful that in Floriers at that time, mobile phones weren't an option. God – can you imagine? A queue of Frogs at the front door at 6 am, mobiles clutched to their ears, muttering Damn, can't get a signal – someone go and wake her up so that we can get out of here and be YUMFies!!

Having spent this afternoon looking for somewhere that sells pond liners, we arrived home early evening. Curry is now whingeing around because the Woodburner has gone out (I require Heat and Food NOW please); Morgan has completely forgotten that he was out for most of this morning causing trouble and now expects to come out again and be a pain in the bum and all we want to do is sit down quietly and have a glass of wine. So we compromise – light the stove for Curry and pick her a bunch of fresh leaves, let Morgan out again and brush him around the floor with his personal Spanish broom (which is very time consuming and just makes more mess as opposed to actually sweeping up) – then 10 minutes on the new Plant Wheelie (steering gear a bit rough at the mo as only Binder twine but working on it) – after a few scary circuits on this, Morgan retires to the Log Basket by the stove so all peaceful. Put TV on and start to prepare dinner – it's good old Anne Robinson and the Weakest Link (along with probably every other country on the planet, the French have their own version of this) and so you don't actually need to concentrate that much – just join in the general booing when someone gets voted off!!

Just as well as it happens because (and now I'm coming to the exciting part promised in the very first paragraph – thought I'd try making you read EVERTHING before the punch line – sorry!) – went into the Veranda to get the veg and … a Frog! Small, green but loud and hopping about all over the place. Quick panic – Oh My God – first Frog since we've owned the house – don't want to put it off (Pond coming soon – honestly!!) – what to do? Saucer of water, big wet plant, what? Finally, with one thing and another, settled for saucer of water, some plants and a copy of a very picturesque catalogue open at the Water Garden page – you know, Water Lilies, Rushes and stuff like that – all placed at Frog level. Which reminds me that I have to remember to move all this stuff before one or other of us trips over it in the morning and the resultant cursing gives the impression that we are not Frog Friendly!

As the weather improves, everyone is livening up. We haven't seen the deer lately but I suspect that they have simply gone deeper into the woodland to avoid the Hunters. A shame because to catch sight of half a dozen of them sneaking across the paddock in the very early morning, at times somewhat eerily wreathed in mist was a pleasure. Still, there's plenty of other stuff – the Heron which every morning settles on an old log in the little reservoir over the track now has a mate – they stand there as still as statues staring into the water – I hate disturbing them but haven't yet worked out how to creep down the drive and watch them without scaring them off (tho sometimes I think they're being a BIT silly – lets face it, at that time in the morning, I'm hardly likely to leap across a couple of hundred metres of field speedily enough to grab them by the neck). Need some camouflage gear maybe? They sell it on the market – I could even get a camouflage cap with big floppy ear things – not sure what that would allow me to get up close to – perhaps another stupid person wearing a camouflage cap with big floppy ear things? I expect if I had both the time and inclination I could find a web site dedicated to Big Camouflaged Floppy Ear People Who Watch Things and maybe learn a thing or two but – you're right – I can't be bothered and will just improve my SAS belly crawl or, thinking about it, I could just borrow Isabelle and force her to walk in front of me. The Herons don't panic at 4 legged people so that might be an idea worth exploring? Actually, I think I might be expending a lot of energy on this – after all, seen one Heron, seen 'em all!

The numerous Kites (both Red and Black) are preparing to nest up the hill behind us and the little birds (Great, Blue and Marsh Tits, Robin, Nuthatch, Chaffinch, etc.) are zipping about like no one's business. The Woodpeckers are also busy but can't really say that they are in the garden – inches away maybe (the constant drilling and drumming drives you mad at times) but not actually in the garden. The Wrens are preparing to nest either in the Barn or at the back of it whilst the Nuthatches seem to prefer the Pigeonnier. We have the occasional cloud of Goldfinches over here but the best place to see them really is at the Reservoir (Lac de Louet) – absolutely stuffed with them – you can hardly walk anywhere without tripping over a Goldfinch. The last time we went there was a couple of weeks ago – pouring with rain and so we only walked half way round (an hour or so) but still saw various Ducks, couple of Grebes, Cormorants and clouds of the aforesaid Goldfinches. Not bad considering that the rain was horizontal at times and the Binoculars kept steaming up!

Bit of a break here as we decided it was time to try and finish the new kitchen so spent most of the day at BricoDepot south of Tarbes. Its always incredibly busy there – it would seem like everyone is doing ... well ... DIY I suppose. This particular place is somewhat similar to a Quick Save (pile 'em high, sell 'em cheap) but brico rather than food. Having found it so difficult to actually get light coloured worktops in the length and quantity we need, we've decided on tiled worktops so got the bases – now another 6 month expedition to get the tiles I suppose. No easy solution! The sink units are very cleverly displayed at a height no normal person can actually see. They are numbered for ease of identification but, strangely enough, the numbers do not correlate with the boxed items below. After a couple of hours drifting around this huge warehouse, you begin to lose the will to live and so you just pluck a box off the shelf which promises its contents as being a sink unit, bung it on your already over-laden trolley (you've also got the one with a duff wheel so steering difficult) and head for the checkout – along with 50 other people who, judging by the lengthy queries at the cash desk, also have not a clue of what they have bought. So, you stand patiently and wait for your turn – when you entered the shop, it was Winter – when you finally emerge, it's Summer! Well, Ok, I may be exaggerating a little here but it almost feels that way.

The good news is NO GOATS – well, not really no Goats – simply that only the Billy goats have been let out of their house for the last few days and without Isabelle and Opaline to lead them astray, they've actually remained in their own paddock. We can see them and chat to them through the fence but don't have the aggro. Donkeys are sufficiently cowed after their last escapade (either that or they are nailed to the stable floor) to be nice happy little neighbours and are not presently giving us a problem. So that's a big improvement!

That's all for now – will write again soon

Namonter, March 2007

Dear Pand,

Not that long since I last wrote but it was a big day today.

Started as any normal day – get up, realise you have no more Fat Balls for the birds and they are getting REALLY cross – Come on – YOU said we could have at least 5 Fat balls in designated spots and look – all we've got is little empty nets – how are we supposed to raise our kids when YOU don't supply the food? And the Peanut holder is looking a bit slim and also the seed holder? Could you please go out now and get some stuff – we don't want to make a big thing about it (that's a laugh – when you get birds standing around muttering loudly and pointing at empty feeders, I think that's making a statement!).

We were working around the house – E cutting into the walls for the plumbing and electrics in the new kitchen and me raking 3 years of leaf fall from the trees down the back drive – gaily working away, and suddenly a great rush of wing beating and the unmistakable call of Cranes. They came over in waves, 50 to 100 at a time, huge V or Line formations all heading North East (I assume to Germany and Scandinavia for the summer). We were thrilled to see them – the last time we saw Cranes fly over us in these numbers was when we were in Floriers. As I stood there staring up into the sky, I imagined it must have been similar to WW2 – watching the Bombers fly overhead to wreak havoc on Germany. You read about the sky being black with planes – 60 years on, the sky was black with Cranes – far less aggressive, much prettier and that haunting call to boot. Such a sight.

A day later – well, Pand, I was SO overcome that I stopped writing – well, OK, also because Elisabeth turned up for our weekly lesson. We were looking forward to it because for once the kids weren't with her which meant it was slightly easier to concentrate. However, 5 minutes later, Eric (Elisabeth's husband) drove into the yard, skidded to a halt, disgorged 2 very excited kids and promptly drove off again without a word! Elisabeth just raised her eyebrows and said Eric is trying to do some work on the garage, the kids are obviously being *too* helpful so we have them for the lesson – AGAIN! We all gave up any serious stuff then – the kids decided to explore the Barn and were fascinated by the Block and Tackle from ground to first floor. They drove E almost round the bend as they were convinced this was a super new toy and it was to his credit (and patience) that we didn't have 2 small children hanging from the rafters! Having dragged them from the Barn (which is still 3/4 full of all sorts of dangerous and exciting stuff), their attention was caught by the roaming Goats – as usual they'd plodded thru the paddock, (the Goats that is rather than the children) along the road and in thru the back and were farting around on the steep bank at the back of the house. Once they get up there, they have a mental block and resolutely refuse to make their way back out – they pratt around at the very point we've fenced off and unless we go and lift our temporary barricade, they just stand there and whinge!

This of course provided a great deal of excitement for Alina and her brother – Oh look – the goats are here – Oh look, the goats are there – Edward – the Goats are here – what shall we do? Mummy, Mummy, look, the Goats are here – we have to get them back into their paddock – Mummy? Pippa? Look at the Goats! By this time of course, both Mummy and Pippa have removed themselves as far as possible from both children and Goats and feign severe deafness! Elisabeth says Did you hear anything? And I say No, did you? She visibly relaxes and we talk about the hoped for transformation of the garden but this lasts only minutes before Alina burst upon us full of how exciting it is here and can she possibly stay? Elisabeth can't fail to see the reaction – both E and I visibly recoil – Alina AND Goats – no way! So, we are preparing for their departure (takes ages because the children find *really* important stuff to check on before they can leave!) and I'm looking at Guillam and thinking – his feet look a bit peculiar and then realise that his shoes are on the wrong way round – I mention this to Elisabeth and she shrugs and says Yes, that's normal for Guillam. He must be going through an odd phase because as well as the reversed shoes, he has suddenly taken to being very particular about shaking hands – wrong hand and still demands a kiss but obviously getting into the Greeting bit. Rather spoilt by Alina whacking him on the head when she thinks he's not coming quite up to her standards!

Yesterday was obviously the start of the Crane migration because today the sky has been full of them. The first wave came over soon after midday and continued until 4 or 5 pm. They were much higher in the sky than they were yesterday and all told, several thousand birds must have passed over us in that time. This time, because of the height, they just reminded me of strands of Toad spawn in a clear pond – black lines strung across a blue sky. So many of them and once they got into our little valley, they circled round in a huge mass, each new wave coming from the south and joining in with the previous wave – the noise was incredible. At one point, I was standing on the south side of the house – hand held up to cover the sun whilst I watched them come over when a Jay alighted just a few feet away to drink out of a plant saucer. I was, of course, torn between the two – going Wow – look at this lot and slyly watching the Jay at the same time – in fact, the Jay was brilliant (he of course knew I didn't have the camera to hand) and did practically everything (twizzing around, posing right profile, left profile, full frontal, etc) before finally flicking his tail and saying Tough shit, that's the closest you are going to see me this year – it's not MY fault you've been watching the Cranes – I'm just as spectacular in my own way – Byeeeee! The Jay of course, was quite correct – he's here all the year, the Cranes are an annual spectacle so I slunk off duly chastened. The Cranes were exciting tho – just the sheer number of them – flight after flight for most of the afternoon and the noise. You can hear them coming long before seeing them!

Today has been mild again and the sun very warm. Good for the Lizards busily scurrying around the garden and barn. I must admit, this is the best place I've come across for Wall Lizards (no sign of any Green Lizards yet) – absolutely stuffed with them, literally all over the place – over-running the Veg garden, the Yard, performing antics on the Barn roof – tripping over them! Being used to saying Oops, sorry when you upset a bird or two, you now find yourself apologizing at almost every step – Oops, sorry Lizard – Oops, sorry Vole – and so on and so forth! There are also the numerous Beetles and Spiders which have to be carefully put to one side whenever you are working somewhere – laborious work but …

Have to think about going over to Andorre soon – for cigarettes if nothing else! Don't know what the roads are like – more often than not, we can't see the mountains but given the odd day like today when it is clear and sunny, suddenly you can see them – covered in Snow and ice – a skier's dream no doubt but a reminder of how close we are to chilly sort of stuff! A reminder also of the 10 hour round trip it takes to get thru the mountains to the first Duty Free shop … tho the last trip we saw an Egyptian Vulture circling above us (we got quite paranoid – did it think the car was about to break down?) and the Ponies were quite good too – chubby, stubby sort of jobs with thick necks and legs – they have a name (or pedigree) but I can't think of it just at the moment.

That's about it for now – just wanted to tell you about the Cranes.

See you soon

Namonter, March 2007

Dear Pand,

Well the bad news is that the Cranes seem to be finished now – this the third day and only a couple of flights came over – still, mustn't moan, it was fantastic whilst it lasted. We saw them once in Floriers but so long ago now, I can't remember whether they were coming or going. What I DO remember tho was that same thrill at seeing them – bit of envy also because they seemed to have an end in view. That's the thing about migrating birds or animals – they are SO definite – not likely to be sidetracked by the question of kitchen worktop tiles (what colour [daffodil yellow – probably not available] am I THAT fussed? – yes, daffodil yellow would be perfect) and anyway, so far, I am not a migrating bird and therefore will spend ages trying to get the right colour tiles. This will probably mean that the kitchen will not be workable for the next 20 years!

Before you think OH My God, this is a depressing letter, you can perk up now – I took my cup of coffee out this morning and crept down the back drive (I always creep down the back drive because there is invariably at least 1 Heron on the pond and he (or she?) is always wary and goes Shock, Horror and flies off at the least little disturbance. Anyway, this morning, no Heron but loadsa Ducks swimming about and making nesting noises – only Mallards so far but welcome nevertheless. The Green Woodpecker also inhabits this area – in the tree fringe along the pond but he's as wary as the Heron and so basically, it's Hello and Goodbye at the moment. Once the trees are in leaf, perhaps they won't be so shy (but also I probably won't be able to spot them either! – always a down side isn't there?) As a bonus, there was a Deer in the field – just casually munching – I wasn't sure at first that it was a deer – wondered if it was a Cat at first (as E said when I trotted in for the Binoculars – that's a bloody big cat Pip!) but my long sight is not that brilliant and it wouldn't be the first time I've mistaken stuff – like I'm never really sure, at a distance, whether I am looking at Sheep or Cows – it's bloody annoying when some Know All comes along and says – well, that's obviously a Cow – stands out a mile.

You should see it round here now – the first trees are flowering and so you can see fluffy white or pink blossom against the background of the bare trees. Where people have planted Camellias, the flowers stand out like jewels and the primroses, vinca and violets stud the undergrowth – very reminiscent of Devon years ago.

Bit of a break here – went down to look at the Donkeys – mainly just to make sure that they were still where they were supposed to be (can't afford to look a gift donkey in the mouth!) – Owners at the Seaside, don't trust the Donkeys, etc. So far, so good – check the Goats – as it is a seaside day, only the 4 Billy goats have been let out which is a relief for us. In the absence of a good woman (Isabelle and/or Opaline in this case), the Billies aren't too much of a problem – they tend not to stray too far and rarely get as far as the garden or paddock so that is a bonus.

Well, its now Friday afternoon which means Jean (the Policeman) has a free shift and so it will be Moving Stuff from the Barn time – this has been going on for the last 3 months (feels like 3 years) and only ever takes place when Jean isn't out there chasing crims! He always comes to help JC and Nicole – I suspect it must be therapeutic – you know, forget the rising crime rate – get out and shift a load of stuff here there and everywhere, a sort of mindless activity whilst helping your friends out. Actually, Jean is a really nice guy and I am forever amazed at the amount of heavy work he does here – he is, to put it politely, a BIG guy but he whacks on with stuff tho is often grateful for 5 mins chat about the garden or the birds while he sneaks a breather. Nicole's estimate of clearing the Barn in 2 months is, I think, wishful thinking – 200 square metres of Machinery, old Tractors, tools, timber, drums of questionable contents, furniture, windsurfers and God knows what else. Then of course there is the Pigeonnier – another 50 square metres or so and stuffed to the hilt with furniture, timber, packs of old tiles, endless drums of more questionable liquid (these people would scare the pants off the EC Poisons Dept) of which the majority are only a quarter full, bikes, more windsurfers, etc. The only thing NOT in the Pigeonnier is, in fact, a pigeon. In case you are wondering how I know what is in there considering none of it belongs to me (well, except for the actual building), it is simply because, having an hour or two to spare one day, I decided to root through and see if there was anything useful to borrow. After several bouts of concussion (the lower part of the

Pigeonnier was built to house Pigs and therefore doorways and ceilings are correspondingly Pig size rather than human), I discovered a Tile Cutter (which I'll need as soon as I find the right colour tiles), a tin of white paint, a drum of liquid which I translated as being applicable to killing lice, mosquitos, cows, and both wood boring and simply boring insects – we'll have some of that then!

A few days later ....

Did I tell you the Donkeys are to be evicted from their paddock? No? Well, the donkeys are currently living in a rented paddock – adjoining this is their own paddock which, as we speak, is not yet fenced, is fairly small and crowded with heaps of planked wood, 2 JCB's, a large Fork Lift, a Dumper truck and 2 or 3 tractors. The eviction order (complicated but something to do with feuds and inheritance, mad brothers, senile fathers, crap Notaires, children demanding inheritances and such like – normal sort of stuff) is due at the end of this month (March) so fencing the dreaded Goats in has taken yet another step backwards in JC's List of Things to Do! Fence the new small Donkey paddock in first which, I must admit, is a good idea, especially for us! The last couple of weeks have been very relaxed (at least on the Donkey front anyway) – get up, look out of window – 6 ears present and correct. Midday – still 6 ears wandering around – sigh of relief! Just before dark, check ears again – bit of a quandary – E claims to see 3 ears (which even after a couple of glasses of wine MUST mean there are at least one and a half donkeys there) – I say I can see a white person drifting about, but as there is a White Horse over the valley which I often mistake for a sheep, E doesn't take my word for it and so we plod down the field to check the Ears – I may have forgotten to mention here that it had been raining for 18 hours solid and so when I say Plod, I really mean skid, fall into water filled ruts, pot holes and whatever. So, we get down to the Eviction site and, taking a leaf out of Nicole's book, instead of shouting Come On then you Bastards, we've got better things to do – where the hell are you? we adopt a softer, more French approach – something like Bien, bien, bien – mes enfants – bien, bien, bien. I don't actually KNOW that that is precisely what she says but it sounds similar and is obviously an improvement on our previous efforts because, lo and behold, the fourth, fifth and sixth ear loomed up and after a careful count, we checked out 3 donkeys. Whew, that's a relief then – we can at least categorically state that at 7 pm, there were 3 Donkeys mooching around exactly where they were supposed to be.

Anyway, I digress somewhat. (I wonder how many times in the last 20 or so years that phrase has appeared in my letters – pretty often I suspect.) So anyway, back on track here but just need a few minutes to think of what I was about to write before the digression took over! Erm ... ah, yep, got it, forget the Ears – it was moving things out of the Barn again and Whoopee! The van has gone. This was an ancient Renault van which had sat in the middle of the Barn surrounded by various accoutrements (tyres, batteries, seats, couple of doors and several unidentified engine bits) – the bonnet has been open and spilling wires, pipes and important looking chunky bits ever since we came here and, I imagine for a few years before that – the Wren has been seriously eyeing it up for a nest site this last couple of weeks (and in fact, if you take a serious look in the bonnet, the Wrens been nesting there for a few years anyway). However, this afternoon, I learn that this ISN'T just a crappy old motor as I'd thought – its a Camper Van for holidays and it is going to be stored in Lise's barn across the valley for future use. The fact that it was towed out of the Barn, down the road and across to Lise's farm by means of JC's smokiest old tractor (the van itself being steered by Jean with JC at the tractor wheel shouting instructions) leads me to think that Nicole's statement about it being For Holidays was at best wishful thinking. I mean, the damn thing has been sitting there for years – one of the doors fell off as they gingerly towed it down the drive – Jean wanted to stop and retrieve it but JC was adamant – no stopping til we get to Lise's barn – come back for the bits later. Can't say I blame him – towing anything here at the moment after so much rain is risky! One of their cars is already stuck in the Donkey paddock and even Dominique (the wood cutter guy) got his lorry stuck in the mire today. Try as I might, I can't actually see this being a Camper Van – well, not a useable one anyway. Tho of course, depends what you mean by Useable – no, even from that point of view, I think it is knacked! It smacks of our Weymouth holiday – remember that freezing cold caravan we rented? The one where we warmed the plates up in the oven and stuck them in the beds (silly buggers – nylon sheets – with a melting point of ... don't know what temperature exactly but we obviously exceeded it – runny nylon beds) and all those really rare Water Voles in the stream at the back of the caravan which, on closer inspection, turned out to be Rats! The Fish and Chips were excellent tho weren't they? At least better than that Roman Villa which, if I remember correctly, turned out to be a couple of paving slabs and an ill-written sign? That's by the by tho – I still can't see this ramshackle van becoming a Motor Home. Still, whatever its ambitions, it's no longer in our Barn – instead, we can look across to Lise's Barn and wave to it every so often – you know, sort of encourage it … Pfff (this being the best I can do for a derisory snort) Pffff!!! Off to buy fence posts tomorrow and on Sunday, JC is coming to dig out our wildlife pond!

Bye for now …

In fact, bye for a good while! Yep, that's all for now. Apart from a few acknowledgments and thankyous!

Bluemoose would like to thank Andy for saving Pip's letters over the years and Pip wants to let anyone who is interested know that the Tortoise Trust's website is www.tortoisetrust.org

OTHER TITLES AVAILABLE FROM BLUEMOOSE

ANTHILLS AND STARS

KEVIN DUFFY

It's 1968, and in Paris the students are rioting but in Broughton, 20 miles East of Manchester the Permissive Society had just arrived, driving a multi couloured VW camper van …

The Rainbow corner:

Laid back, staying cool, free loving charismatic Solomon, bringing a breath of incense laden air to the grey industrial North.

In the Beige corner:

The upright, uptight, sanctimonious matriarch, minder of other people's business and upholder of moral standards as inflexible as her corsets.

And in the middle:

The man in black, the parish priest, who's questioning his own sexuality and is torn between duty and instinct. Can he help to resolve the conflict peacefully and discreetly?

Er, no.

THE BRIDGE BETWEEN

NATHAN VANEK

The Book

Born and raised in Toronto, Nathan Vanek spent much of his adult life in India. He has been an art dealer, a yogi, has written for Canadian Press/Broadcast news and taught Indian History, Eastern Philosophies and meditation

Much of his life's drama is played out in this collection of articles first printed in the 'Low down to Hull and Back News' following his return from India to Canada.

Through amusing anecdotes Vanek communicates the essence of his knowledge and gives us insights into both the dramatic contrasts between the two countries and their cultures and the essential oneness of us all.

The Author

Nathan Vanek likes in Wakefield, Quebec, Canada. He is a noted yogi and guru, running meditation courses in his native Canada.